The Complete
SHERLOCK

D0431229

LIBRARY OF

Also by Michael Hardwick:

The Revenge of the Hound
Sherlock Holmes: My Life and Crimes
The Private Life of Dr. Watson
Prisoner of the Devil

(with Mollie Hardwick)

The Private Life of Sherlock Holmes
The Sherlock Holmes Companion
Sherlock Holmes Investigates
The Man Who Was Sherlock Holmes
Four Sherlock Holmes Plays
The Game's Afoot
The Hound of the Baskervilles and Other Sherlock Holmes Plays

The Complete Guide to
SHERLOCK HOLMES

Michael Hardwick

St. Martin's Press
New York

Grateful acknowledgement to Dame Jean Conan
Doyle for permission to quote from copyrighted works
by the late Sir Arthur Conan Doyle including *The Valley
of Fear* and the stories from *His Last Bow* and *The
Case Book of Sherlock Holmes.*

THE COMPLETE GUIDE TO SHERLOCK HOLMES. Copyright © 1986 by Michael Hardwick. All rights reserved. Printed in the United States of America. No part of this book may be used or reproduced in any manner whatsoever without written permission except in the case of brief quotations embodied in critical articles or reviews. For information, address St. Martin's Press, 175 Fifth Avenue, New York, N.Y. 10010.

Library of Congress Cataloging-in-Publication Data

Hardwick, Michael.
    The complete guide to Sherlock Holmes.

    1. Doyle, Arthur Conan, Sir, 1859–1930—Characters—
Sherlock Holmes.   2. Doyle, Arthur Conan, Sir, 1859–1930—
Handbooks, manuals, etc.   3. Holmes, Sherlock
(Fictitious character)—Handbooks, manuals, etc.
4. Detective and mystery stories, English—History and
criticism—Handbooks, manuals, etc.   I. Title.
PR4624.H28   1987   823'.8   87-81
ISBN 0-312-07248-1

First U.S. Paperback Edition: April 1992
10 9 8 7 6 5 4 3 2 1

Contents

This book
is dedicated to the memory of
SIR ARTHUR CONAN DOYLE
(22 May, 1859 – 7 July, 1930)
with admiration and gratitude

Preface

This work supersedes three: *The Sherlock Holmes Companion, Sherlock Holmes Investigates,* and *The Man Who Was Sherlock Holmes.* My wife, Mollie, and I wrote them in the early 1960s, and John Murray kept them in print for a quarter of a century, alongside our four volumes of Sherlock Holmes plays, which go on still.

The aim again is to tempt new readers and entertain and prompt others who already treasure the four long and fifty-six short stories which make up the Sherlock Holmes canon. Nothing has been rehashed from those earlier works. This one has been written and compiled from scratch after a complete reappraisal of the canon.

I have tried not to give away solutions of cases or fates of characters. I have abbreviated titles, and attributed most of the quotations, at the risk of stating the obvious sometimes.

The temptation to indulge in observations and opinions was not entirely to be resisted, but what Sherlockians (American) and Holmesians (British) term 'the higher scholarship' has been determinedly eschewed.

I must say how much I have enjoyed doing this work; there is always something fresh to discover. They don't write stories like these any more. That was a remarkable coincidence in the 1890s: an under-worked doctor finding a natural ability to invent mysteries and then solve them, working backwards to show how it was done; that, and his creation of a unique and uniquely-gifted literary character, ideally fitted to top the bill of 'healthful' entertainment presented by the newly-founded *Strand Magazine* to a huge and avid audience.

Holmes (and Watson) quickly had Britain and America in thrall. It was 'Pickwick fever' all over again. John Masefield, who used to stand like so many others in bookstall queues for each latest *Strand*, told me of the 'unutterable agony' of suspense, having to wait a month for the next Holmes adventure.

My linking narrative outlines Arthur Conan Doyle's life and work, in particular his work on these stories. He was unique, too. He was the ideal man for his time in more senses than the literary. His breadth of vision and diversity of activity were astonishing. His career is a case of 'all this, and Sherlock Holmes, too'.

In the 1890s he was writing of his own time and of life as it was going on about him; that world 'where it is always 1895', which appears so deceptively desirable to us today. Later Holmes stories were retrospective, not reflecting the rapid changes to the human condition and ways of life which their author was helping to bring about. His public had changed, too. People were past marvelling at being able to read for the first time. They had become more discriminating, more demanding, wider ranging in appetite, more forward-looking, impatient, tending to dismiss the Victorians and the old ways.

Yet, the Sherlock Holmes stories never became regarded as old hat, kept in print as curiosities. Each succeeding generation has cherished them enthusiastically, bearing them along with them through the literary, as well as social, revolutions.

The short story, as a popular form, declined and almost vanished, along with the magazines. Story ideas which would once have yielded a few thousand words in a magazine got puffed up, like aerated bread, and about as nourishing, into novels. These insubstantial works are dwindling now, increasingly uneconomic to publish.

Radio drama, once a good substitute, no longer has such power to grip the imagination: social awareness and sordidness are not the desired fare of the once-faithful audience. Television drama, which held sway for a few decades, has lost much of its power to compel. New ideas are rare, recycled old ones common. Tasteless permissiveness and tawdry human values don't encourage the essential audience self-identification.

'You are the one fixed point in a changing age,' Holmes told Watson. The Sherlock Holmes canon is among world literature's most firmly rooted points; certainly the most durable and widely familiar example of the entire *genre*, the detective story. It has transcended the magazine and been adopted by each new medium that has come along. Translation has made it available everywhere. The growing tendency towards nostalgia, in an insecure world, ensures its reciprocal appeal.

Conversely, there would be no role for a real-life Sherlock Holmes today. When he was writing the earlier stories, Conan Doyle's vision reached beyond the established boundaries of forensic science. Thanks in part to his propositions, put forward through Sherlock Holmes, science quickly overtook and outstripped art. Our police are well enough educated and equipped to need no Holmes to get their results for them.

The old crimes remain, though, and the old motives: greed, lust, and man's beastliness to man. The same passions go on erupting; the age-old confidence tricks still attract gullible mugs. In essentials, people haven't changed much. Individuality is what has been swallowed up. Venturing out of his isolated retirement, Holmes would find that observation and deduction would no longer serve. The discernible differences between us are gone, even to the differences between the sexes. A man's appearance, his posture, his speech, his clothes, his skin, his callosities and trouser knees are uninformative about his occupation and habits.

Where, nowadays, is the man whose financial and marital states might be read from the condition of his hat, which would tell additionally whether he has the gas laid on at home? Where, for that matter, is the hat?

Michael Hardwick,
Barton House,
Kennington, Kent

A Study in Selection

Most of the illustrations reproduced in this volume show key scenes from the stories as published in *The Strand Magazine*. A large proportion are ones chosen by Sir Arthur Conan Doyle and the magazine's editor and art editor to illustrate a competition set in the March 1927 issue. From forty-four tales represented, readers were invited to pick the twelve best. Conan Doyle sealed his own list in an envelope, the winner to be the choice closest to it. The four long stories and those making up the *Case Book*, which had not yet appeared in volume form, were not included in the field.

The result, declared in the June number, showed a single winner, with ten out of twelve corresponding, seven tying runners-up with nine, and 'a great number' with eight. The author admitted to having daunted himself with the challenge: '"Steep, steep, weary work," as the Scottish landlady remarked.' (Could that be the confirmation we have been seeking about *the* landlady, Mrs Hudson?)

Had the *Case Book* been widely enough familiar already, he said, he would have given places to two of its stories, 'The Lion's Mane' and 'The Illustrious Client'. His other twelve, in his order of merit, were:

The Speckled Band
The Red-Headed League
The Dancing Men
The Final Problem
A Scandal in Bohemia
The Empty House
The Five Orange Pips
The Second Stain
The Devil's Foot
The Priory School
The Musgrave Ritual
The Reigate Squires

The debate continues.

1

Birth of a Detective

In March, 1886, Dr Arthur Conan Doyle began to write a detective story. He had no notion of becoming a professional writer, but he was full of ideas and replete with energy. All through his Edinburgh childhood his high-minded mother had told him tales of the romance and adventure of past ages. He wanted to write about those times, but he was conscious that he needed to learn the craft and gain the confidence which being published would bring.

He had plenty of leisure to work at it. After four years in medical practice at Southsea, a suburb of Portsmouth, he had few patients to attend. He was better known locally as a sportsman, debater, lecturer, campaigning public speaker, writer to editors, and convivial companion.

After the first frustrating months of sitting idly in his consulting-room, the only room of No 1, Bush Villas, Elm Grove, that he had been able to afford to furnish, he had resolved to go out and about, making himself known. He had an engaging presence, over six feet tall and strappingly built. He was boisterous without being unbridled, convivial, enjoying his pipe and a glass, full of stories of the voyages he had made as ship's surgeon to Greenland and South Africa. But he listened, as well as talked, and was unfailingly courteous.

He played all sorts of games, aggressively and to professional standards; but the rules and sporting spirit of cricket, football, boxing, billiards, bowls, were not for violating in order to win. He was assertive without being obnoxious; the type of committee man who would be sure to turn up at meetings, and would always have something to say. He was full of opinions about medicine, science, social matters, politics, literature, although he had to overcome intense nervousness in order to speak, trembling visibly.

Doctoring earned him no more than £300 a year. Since school magazine days at Stonyhurst he had been writing bits and pieces of prose and verse. He sold a few short stories of adventure and mystery to *All*

The Year Round, London Society, Boy's Own Paper, and other magazines. In his autobiography, *Memories and Adventures*, 1924, he recalled:

> I can hardly have earned more than ten or fifteen pounds a year from this source, so that the idea of making a living by it never occurred to me. But though I was not putting out I was taking in. I still have notebooks full of all sorts of knowledge which I acquired during that time. It is a great mistake to start putting out cargo when you have hardly stowed any on board. My own slow methods and natural limitations made me escape this danger.

It was a burgeoning time for popular journalism and fiction. Literacy was spreading rapidly in Britain. As adults and children found that reading offered them release from the tedium of Victorian home life new magazines pushed forward with promises of amusement and escapism at sixpence or a shilling a week or month. The response was eager. Informative articles, anecdotes, jokes, tales of far-off places: anything was going. Opportunities for writers, part-timers as well as professionals, abounded.

Marriage in 1885, when he was twenty-six, to gentle and amiable Louise Hawkins, a year his senior, seemed to stimulate his literary attempts. Touie, as she was known, discussed ideas with him and shared his enthusiasm for the Portsmouth Literary & Scientific Society, where their young friends included a Dr James Watson. There was no shortage of themes for what he came to look back on as 'perhaps as good, honest work as any that I have done.'

His most significant breakthrough yet had happened in 1883, when the well-regarded *Cornhill Magazine* published one of his stories, *J. Habbakuk Jephson's Statement*. It appeared anonymously and caused some speculation, from its quality, that it was the work of R.L.Stevenson. The editor, James Payn, paid Doyle ten times as much for it as the two or three guineas he was used to getting. They became friends, and it led to introductions to established literary men.

Friendship notwithstanding, Payn rejected five further submissions in a row, but accepted a sixth. So when Dr Arthur Conan Doyle sat down in the peace of his consulting-room in March, 1886, to begin his detective story, he had Payn and the *Cornhill* very much in mind.

What he really hoped to achieve was a full-length novel, which the magazine would serialize, and its publishers, Smith, Elder & Co, would bring out as a book.

> I realized that I could go on doing short stories for ever and never make headway. What is necessary is that your name should be on the back of a volume. Only so do you assert your individuality and get the full credit or discredit of your achievement.

He had completed his first novel a few weeks earlier. *The Firm of Girdlestone* had taken two years to write and had been rejected twice already. He knew it was not much good, but working at it had taught him a lot and he was ready to start again, though on a totally different tack.

Plenty of stories, from the 18th century on, had included elements of crime and its investigation, and there had been books by former policemen and detectives about their real-life cases. The detective as an intelligent, idiosyncratic central character had emerged in the 1840s in Edgar Allan Poe's Dupin stories, followed in France by Émile Gaboriau, with his professional detective Lecoq and the amateur Père Tabaret. The first full-length English detective novel was Wilkie Collins's *The Moonstone*, 1868, with its sagacious Sergeant Cuff.

Doyle had read all these. Dupin had been one of this boyhood heroes, an investigator with analytical acumen and instinctive flair, though Poe's writing style was didactic and often heavy going. Lecoq was a dogged sleuth who owed many of his results to hunches, on which he acted with cunning and often in disguise. Gaboriau's stories were neatly plotted and briskly told, with plenty of dialogue. Doyle was confident that he could do something along these lines. He had ingenuity and natural zest, and ambition was urging him on: he was approaching his thirties, but, for all his varied talents, he had made no significant mark at anything.

A Study in Scarlet – he had thought of titling it *A Tangled Skein* – was written quickly in March and April, 1886. Too quickly, in fact; the 'little novel', as his wife termed it, was only some 50,000 words. James Payn found some worthwhile things in it, but rejected it as neither long enough for a serial nor short enough for a single story.

The rebuff hurt, and there was more mortification to come. Several other publishers turned it down. After six months' to-ing and fro-ing with it, Doyle was relieved to get an offer at last, even though it was from a firm specializing in 'cheap and often sensational literature'.

Dear Sir,
We have read your story and are pleased with it. We could not publish it this year as the market is flooded at present with cheap fiction, but if you do not object to its being held over till next year, we will give you twenty-five pounds for the copyright.
Yours faithfully,
WARD, LOCK, & CO.

Oct. 30th. 1886.

'It was not a very tempting offer,' Conan Doyle recalled, 'and even I, poor as I was, hesitated to accept it. It was not merely the small sum offered, but it was the long delay, for this book might open a road for me. I was heartsick, however, at repeated disappointments, and I felt that perhaps it was true wisdom to make sure of publicity, however late. Therefore I accepted and the book became "Beeton's Xmas Annual" of 1887. I never at any time received another penny for it.'

He had asked for royalties, but had been refused. It was a case of going on hoping for a better sale elsewhere, or of accepting. Other 'large thoughts' were pressing for his attention: an historical novel 'seemed to me the one way of combining a certain amount of literary dignity with those scenes of action and adventure which were natural to my young and ardent mind.' He accepted Ward, Lock, & Co.'s offer, forgot Sherlock Holmes for the time being, and concentrated on a story of the English Civil War, *Micah Clarke*.

Nevertheless, when *Beeton's Christmas Annual* for 1887 came out in late November that year, his hope for his detective story's success returned. *Beeton's*, founded in 1860 by Sam Beeton and his wife Isabella, of *Household Management* celebrity, was well enough respected for a shilling popular annual. The title *A Study in Scarlet* dominated its front cover; the few other contents were altogether subservient. Those were days when reviewers of fiction kept an eye on magazines, as well as books. 'A. Conan Doyle', as he styled himself, believed that his 'booklet' could catch on.

So far as the reading public was concerned, it didn't. A handful of reviewers commented, briefly but kindly, on the story's ingenuity. It was from behind the scenes that positive interest was to emerge.

Ward, Lock had been recommended to buy it by their chief editor, Prof W. J. Bettany, whose wife had read it for him and liked it. His report termed Doyle 'a born novelist'. He urged the editorial board to consider republishing it as a book on its own. Having to pay nothing further for that right, the firm's only risk was the production cost. They went ahead. *A Study in Scarlet* first came out as a book in the summer of 1888. D. H. Friston's original four illustrations were replaced with six commissioned from the author's father. Charles Doyle, distinguished for his work for *Punch* and as an illustrator of Dickens, Thackeray, and other major authors, was now living in the twilight of alcoholism and epilepsy. His drawings for his son's first published book marked a rare though unimpressive reappearance.

The book sold out and went to a further edition that year, expanded with four stories by other authors. The print-runs of both these versions were small, and the few copies surviving today are highly prized by collectors. So is the 1887 *Beeton*; even a facsimile of it, published in 1960, has become expensive.

The first American publication of *A Study in Scarlet* was by Lippincott, of Philadelphia, in March, 1890. It made no stir there either, although a few discerning people appreciated its novelty. Since not long after that date the story has never been out of print, on its own or in collected editions, and it is read in all the major (and many minor) languages of the world.

A Study in Scarlet's opening chapters include so much that is basic to the entire canon of tales, and bring together so vividly the immortal double-act, in its indispensable setting, that they must follow on here without more ado.

2

A Study in Scarlet

1. Mr Sherlock Holmes

In the year 1878 I took my degree of Doctor of Medicine of the University of London, and proceeded to Netley to go through the course prescribed for surgeons in the army. Having completed my studies there, I was duly attached to the Fifth Northumberland Fusiliers as Assistant Surgeon. The regiment was stationed in India at the time, and before I could join it, the second Afghan war had broken out. On landing at Bombay, I learned that my corps had advanced through the passes, and was already deep in the enemy's country. I followed, however, with many other officers who were in the same situation as myself, and succeeded in reaching Candahar in safety, where I found my regiment, and at once entered upon my new duties.

The campaign brought honours and promotion to many, but for me it had nothing but misfortune and disaster. I was removed from my brigade and attached to the Berkshires, with whom I served at the fatal battle of Maiwand. There I was struck on the shoulder by a Jezail bullet, which shattered the bone and grazed the subclavian artery. I should have fallen into the hands of the murderous Ghazis had it not been for the devotion and courage shown by Murray, my orderly, who threw me across a packhorse, and succeeded in bringing me safely to the British lines.

Worn with pain, and weak from the prolonged hardships which I had undergone, I was removed, with a great train of wounded sufferers, to the base hospital at Peshawur. Here I rallied, and had already improved so far as to be able to walk about the wards, and even to bask a little upon the verandah, when I was struck down by enteric fever, that curse of our Indian possessions. For months my life was despaired of, and when at last I came to myself and became convalescent, I was so weak and emaciated that a medical board determined that not a day should be lost in sending me back to England. I was despatched, accordingly, in the troopship *Orontes*, and landed a month later on Portsmouth jetty, with my health irretrievably ruined, but with permission from a paternal government to spend the next nine months in attempting to improve it.

I had neither kith nor kin in England, and was therefore as free as air – or as free as an income of eleven shillings and sixpence a day will permit a man to be. Under such circumstances I naturally gravitated to London, that great cesspool into which all the loungers and idlers of the Empire are irresistibly drained. There I stayed for some time at a private hotel in the Strand, leading a comfortless, meaningless existence, and spending such money as I had, considerably more freely than I ought. So alarming did the state of my finances become, that I soon realized that I must either leave the metropolis and rusticate somewhere in the country, or that I must make a complete alteration in my style of living. Choosing the latter alternative, I began by making up my mind to leave the hotel, and to take up my quarters in some less pretentious and less expensive domicile.

On the very day that I had come to this conclusion, I was standing at the Criterion Bar, when someone tapped me on the shoulder, and turning round I recognized young Stamford, who had been a dresser under me at Barts. The sight of a friendly face in the great wilderness of London is a pleasant thing indeed to a lonely man. In old days Stamford had never been a particular crony of mine, but now I hailed him with enthusiasm, and he, in his turn, appeared to be delighted to see me. In the exuberance of my joy, I asked him to lunch with me at the Holborn, and we started off together in a hansom.

'Whatever have you been doing with yourself, Watson?' he asked in undisguised wonder, as we rattled through the crowded London streets. 'You are as thin as a lath and as brown as a nut.'

I gave him a short sketch of my adventures, and had hardly concluded it by the time that we reached our destination.

'Poor devil!' he said, commiseratingly, after he had listened to my misfortunes. 'What are you up to now?'

'Looking for lodgings,' I answered. 'Trying to solve the problem as to whether it is possible to get comfortable rooms at a reasonable price.'

'That's a strange thing,' remarked my companion, 'you are the second man to-day that has used that expression to me.'

'And who was the first?' I asked.

'A fellow who is working at the chemical laboratory up at the hospital. He was bemoaning himself this morning because he could not get someone to go halves with him in some nice rooms which he had found, and which were too much for his purse.'

'By Jove!' I cried; 'if he really wants someone to share the rooms and the expense, I am the very man for him. I should prefer having a partner to being alone.'

Young Stamford looked rather strangely at me over his wine-glass. 'You don't know Sherlock Holmes yet,' he said; 'perhaps you would not care for him as a constant companion.'

'Why, what is there against him?'

'Oh, I didn't say there was anything against him. He is a little queer in his ideas – an enthusiast in some branches of science. As far as I know he is a decent fellow enough.'

'A medical student, I suppose?' said I.

'No – I have no idea what he intends to go in for. I believe he is well up in anatomy, and he is a first-class chemist; but, as far as I know, he has never taken out any systematic medical classes. His studies are very desultory and eccentric, but he has amassed a lot of out-of-the-way knowledge which would astonish his professors.'

'Did you never ask him what he was going in for?' I asked.

'No; he is not a man that it is easy to draw out, though he can be communicative enough when the fancy seizes him.'

'I should like to meet him,' I said. 'If I am to lodge with anyone, I should prefer a man of studious and quiet habits. I am not strong enough yet to stand much noise or excitement. I had enough of both in Afghanistan to last me for the remainder of my natural existence. How could I meet this friend of yours?'

'He is sure to be at the laboratory,' returned my companion. 'He either avoids the place for weeks, or else he works there from morning till night. If you like, we will drive round together after luncheon.'

'Certainly,' I answered, and the conversation drifted away into other channels.

As we made our way to the hospital after leaving the Holborn, Stamford gave me a few more particulars about the gentleman whom I proposed to take as a fellow-lodger.

'You mustn't blame me if you don't get on with him,' he said; 'I know nothing more of him than I have learned from meeting him occasionally in the laboratory. You proposed this arrangement, so you must not hold me responsible.'

'If we don't get on it will be easy to part company,' I answered. 'It seems to me, Stamford,' I added, looking hard at my companion, 'that you have some reason for washing your hands of the matter. Is this fellow's temper so formidable, or what is it? Don't be mealy-mouthed about it.'

'It is not easy to express the inexpressible,' he answered with a laugh. 'Holmes is a little too scientific for my tastes – it approaches to coldbloodedness. I could imagine his giving a friend a little pinch of the latest vegetable alkaloid, not out of malevolence, you understand, but simply out of a spirit of inquiry in order to have an accurate idea of the effects. To do him justice, I think that he would take it himself with the same readiness. He appears to have a passion for definite and exact knowledge.'

'Very right too.'

'Yes, but it may be pushed to excess. When it comes to beating the subjects in the dissecting-rooms with a stick, it is certainly taking rather a bizarre shape.'

'Beating the subjects!'

'Yes, to verify how far bruises may be produced after death. I saw him at it with my own eyes.'

'And yet you say he is not a medical student?'

'No. Heaven knows what the objects of his studies are. But here we are, and you must form your own impressions about him.' As he spoke, we turned down a narrow lane and passed through a small side-door, which opened into a wing of the great hospital. It was familiar ground to me, and I needed no guiding as we ascended the bleak stone staircase and made our way down the long corridor with its vista of whitewashed wall and dun-coloured doors. Near the farther end a low arched passage branched away from it and led to the chemical laboratory.

This was a lofty chamber, lined and littered with countless bottles. Broad, low tables were scattered about, which bristled with retorts, test-tubes, and little Bunsen lamps, with their blue flickering flames. There was only one student in the room, who was bending over a distant table absorbed in his work. At the sound of our steps he glanced round and sprang to his feet with a cry of pleasure. 'I've found it! I've found it,' he shouted to my companion, running towards us with a test-tube in his hand. 'I have found a reagent which is precipitated by hæmoglobin, and by nothing else.' Had he discovered a gold mine, greater delight could not have shone upon his features.

'Dr Watson, Mr Sherlock Holmes,' said Stamford, introducing us.

'How are you?' he said cordially, gripping my hand with a strength for which I should hardly have given him credit. 'You have been in Afghanistan, I perceive.'

'How on earth did you know that?' I asked in astonishment.

'Never mind,' said he, chuckling to himself. 'The question now is about hæmoglobin. No doubt you see the significance of this discovery of mine?'

'It is interesting, chemically, no doubt,' I answered, 'but practically – '

'Why, man it is the most practical medico-legal discovery for years. Don't you see that it gives us an infallible test for blood stains. Come over here now!' He seized me by the coat-sleeve in his eagerness, and drew me over to the table at which he had been working. 'Let us have some fresh blood,' he said, digging a long bodkin into his finger, and drawing off the resulting drop of blood in a chemical pipette. 'Now, I add this small quantity of blood to a litre of water. You perceive that the resulting mixture has the appearance of pure water. The proportion of blood cannot be more than one in a million. I have no doubt, however, that we shall be able to obtain the characteristic reaction.' As he spoke, he threw into the vessel a few white crystals, and then added some drops of a transparent fluid. In an instant the contents assumed a dull mahogany colour, and a brownish dust was precipitated to the bottom of the glass jar.

'Ha! ha!' he cried, clapping his hands, and looking as delighted as a child with a new toy. 'What do you think of that?'

'It seems to be a very delicate test,' I remarked.

'Beautiful! beautiful! The old guaiacum test was very clumsy and uncertain. So is the microscopic examination for blood corpuscles. The latter is valueless if the stains are a few hours old. Now, this appears to act as well whether the blood is old or new. Had this test been invented, there are hundreds of men now walking the earth who would long ago have paid the penalty of their crimes.'

'Indeed!' I murmured.

'Criminal cases are continually hinging upon that one point. A man is suspected of a crime months perhaps after it has been committed. His linen or clothes are examined and brownish stains discovered upon them. Are they blood stains, or mud stains, or rust stains, or fruit stains, or what are they? That is a question which has puzzled many an expert, and why? Because there was no reliable test. Now we have the Sherlock Holmes test, and there will no longer be any difficulty.'

His eyes fairly glittered as he spoke, and he put his hand over his heart and bowed as if to some applauding crowd conjured up by his imagination.

'You are to be congratulated,' I remarked, considerably surprised at his enthusiasm.

'There was the case of Von Bischoff at Frankfort last year. He would certainly have been hung had this test been in existence. Then there was Mason of Bradford, and the notorious Muller, and Lefevre of Montpellier, and Samson of New Orleans. I could name a score of cases in which it would have been decisive.'

'You seem to be a walking calendar of crime,' said Stamford with a laugh. 'You might start a paper on those lines. Call it the "Police News of the Past."'

'Very interesting reading it might be made, too,' remarked Sherlock Holmes, sticking a small piece of plaster over the prick on his finger. 'I have to be careful,' he continued, turning to me with a smile, 'for I dabble with poisons a good deal.' He held out his hand as he spoke, and I noticed that it was all mottled over with similar pieces of plaster, and discoloured with strong acids.

'We came here on business,' said Stamford, sitting down on a high three-legged stool, and pushing another one in my direction with his foot. 'My friend here wants to take diggings; and as you were complaining that you could get no one to go halves with you, I thought that I had better bring you together.'

Sherlock Holmes seemed delighted at the idea of sharing his rooms with me. 'I have my eye on a suite in Baker Street,' he said, 'which would suit us down to the ground. You don't mind the smell of strong tobacco, I hope?'

'I always smoke "ship's" myself,' I answered.

'That's good enough. I generally have chemicals about, and occasionally do experiments. Would that annoy you?'

'By no means.'

'Let me see – what are my other shortcomings. I get in the dumps at times, and don't open my mouth for days on end. You must not think I am sulky when I do that. Just let me alone, and I'll soon be right. What have you to confess now? It's just as well for two fellows to know the worst of one another before they begin to live together.'

I laughed at this cross-examination. 'I keep a bull pup,' I said, 'and I object to row, because my nerves are shaken, and I get up at all sorts of ungodly hours, and I am extremely lazy. I have another set of vices when I'm well, but those are the principal ones at present.'

'Do you include violin playing in your category of rows?' he asked, anxiously.

'It depends on the player,' I answered. 'A well-played violin is a treat for the gods – a badly-played one – '

'Oh, that's all right,' he cried, with a merry laugh. 'I think we may consider the thing as settled – that is, if the rooms are agreeable to you.'

'When shall we see them?'

'Call for me here at noon to-morrow, and we'll go together and settle every-thing,' he answered.

'All right – noon exactly,' said I, shaking his hand.

We left him working among his chemicals, and we walked together towards my hotel.

'By the way,' I asked suddenly, stopping and turning upon Stamford, 'how the deuce did he know that I had come from Afghanistan?'

My companion smiled an enigmatical smile. 'That's just his little peculiarity,' he said. 'A good many people have wanted to know how he finds things out.'

'Oh! a mystery is it?' I cried, rubbing my hands. 'This is very piquant. I am much obliged to you for bringing us together. "The proper study of man-kind is man," you know.'

'You must study him, then,' Stamford said, as he bade me good-bye. 'You'll find him a knotty problem, though. I'll wager he learns more about you than you about him. Good-bye.'

'Good-bye,' I answered, and strolled on to my hotel, considerably interested in my new acquaintance.

2. The Science of Deduction

We met next day as he had arranged, and inspected the rooms at No. 221B, Baker Street, of which he had spoken at our meeting. They consisted of a couple of comfortable bedrooms and a single large airy sitting-room, cheer-fully furnished, and illuminated by two broad windows. So desirable in every way were the apartments, and so moderate did the terms seem when divided between us, that the bargain was concluded upon the spot, and we at once entered into possession. That very evening I moved my things round from the hotel, and on the following morning Sherlock Holmes followed me with sev-eral boxes and portmanteaus. For a day or two we were busily employed in unpacking and laying out our property to the best advantage. That done, we gradually began to settle down and to accommodate ourselves to our new sur-roundings.

Holmes was certainly not a difficult man to live with. He was quiet in his ways, and his habits were regular. It was rare for him to be up after ten at night, and he had invariably breakfasted and gone out before I rose in the morning. Sometimes he spent his day at the chemical laboratory, sometimes in the dissecting rooms, and occasionally in long walks, which appeared to take him into the lowest portions of the city. Nothing could exceed his energy when the working fit was upon him; but now and again a reaction would seize him, and for days on end he would lie upon the sofa in the sitting-room, hardly uttering a word or moving a muscle from morning to night. On these occasions I have noticed such a dreamy, vacant expression in his eyes, that I might have suspected him of being addicted to the use of some narcotic, had not the tem-perance and cleanliness of his whole life forbidden such a notion.

As the weeks went by, my interest in him and my curiosity as to his aims in life gradually deepened and increased. His very person and appearance were such as to strike the attention of the most casual observer. In height he was rather over six feet, and so excessively lean that he seemed to be considerably taller. His eyes were sharp and piercing, save during those intervals of torpor to which I have alluded; and his thin, hawk-like nose gave his whole expression an air of alertness and decision. His chin, too, had the prominence and squareness which mark the man of determination. His hands were invariably blotted with ink and stained with chemicals, yet he was possessed of extraordinary delicacy of touch, as I frequently had occasion to observe when I watched him manipulating his fragile philosophical instruments.

The reader may set me down as a hopeless busybody, when I confess how much this man stimulated my curiosity, and how often I endeavoured to break through the reticence which he showed on all that concerned himself. Before pronouncing judgment, however, be it remembered how objectless was my life, and how little there was to engage my attention. My health forbade me from venturing out unless the weather was exceptionally genial, and I had no friends who would call upon me and break the monotony of my daily existence. Under these circumstances, I eagerly hailed the little mystery which hung around my companion, and spent much of my time in endeavouring to unravel it.

He was not studying medicine. He had himself, in reply to a question, confirmed Stamford's opinion upon that point. Neither did he appear to have pursued any course of reading which might fit him for a degree in science or any other recognized portal which would give him an entrance into the learned world. Yet his zeal for certain studies was remarkable, and within eccentric limits his knowledge was so extraordinarily ample and minute that his observations have fairly astounded me. Surely no man would work so hard or attain such precise information unless he had some definite end in view. Desultory readers are seldom remarkable for the exactness of their learning. No man burdens his mind with small matters unless he has some very good reason for doing so.

His ignorance was as remarkable as his knowledge. Of contemporary literature, philosophy and politics he appeared to know next to nothing. Upon my quoting Thomas Carlyle, he inquired in the naïvest way who he might be and what he had done. My surprise reached a climax, however, when I found incidentally that he was ignorant of the Copernican Theory and of the composition of the Solar System. That any civilized human being in this nineteenth century should not be aware that the earth travelled round the sun appeared to be to me such an extraordinary fact that I could hardly realize it.

'You appear to be astonished,' he said, smiling at my expression of surprise. 'Now that I do know it I shall do my best to forget it.'

'To forget it!'

'You see,' he explained, 'I consider that a man's brain originally is like a little empty attic, and you have to stock it with such furniture as you choose. A fool takes in all the lumber of every sort that he comes across, so that the knowledge which might be useful to him gets crowded out, or at best is jumbled up with a lot of other things, so that he has a difficulty in laying his hands upon it. Now the skilled workman is very careful indeed as to what he takes into his brain-attic. He will have nothing but the tools which may help him in doing his work, but of these he has a large assortment, and all in the most perfect order. It is a mistake to think that that little room has elastic walls and can distend to any extent. Depend upon it there comes a time when for every addition of knowledge you forget something that you knew before. It is of the highest importance, therefore, not to have useless facts elbowing out the useful ones.'

'But the Solar System!' I protested.

'What the deuce is it to me?' he interrupted impatiently: 'you say that we go round the sun. If we went round the moon it would not make a pennyworth of difference to me or to my work.'

I was on the point of asking him what that work might be, but something in his manner showed me that the question would be an unwelcome one. I pondered over our short conversation, however, and endeavoured to draw my deductions from it. He said that he would acquire no knowledge which did not bear upon his object. Therefore all the knowledge which he possessed was such as would be useful to him. I enumerated in my own mind all the various points upon which he had shown me that he was exceptionally well-informed. I even took a pencil and jotted them down. I could not help smiling at the document when I had completed it. It ran in this way:

SHERLOCK HOLMES – his limits.

1. Knowledge of Literature. Nil.
2. Knowledge of Philosophy. Nil.
3. Knowledge of Astronomy. Nil.
4. Knowledge of Politics. Feeble.
5. Knowledge of Botany. Variable. Well up in belladonna, opium, and poisons generally. Knows nothing of practical gardening.
6. Knowledge of Geology. Practical, but limited. Tells at a glance different soils from each other. After walks has shown me splashes upon his trousers, and told me by their colour and consistence in what part of London he had received them.
7. Knowledge of Chemistry. Profound.
8. Knowledge of Anatomy. Accurate, but unsystematic.
9. Knowledge of Sensational Literature. Immense. He appears to know every detail of every horror perpetrated in the century.
10. Plays the violin well.
11. Is an expert singlestick player, boxer, and swordsman.
12. Has a good practical knowledge of British law.

When I had got so far in my list I threw it into the fire in despair. 'If I can only find what the fellow is driving at by reconciling all these accomplishments, and discovering a calling which needs them all,' I said to myself, 'I may as well give up the attempt at once.'

I see that I have alluded above to his powers upon the violin. These were very remarkable, but as eccentric as all his other accomplishments. That he could play pieces, and difficult pieces, I knew well, because at my request he has played me some of Mendelssohn's Lieder, and other favourites. When left to himself, however, he would seldom produce any music or attempt any recognized air. Leaning back in his arm-chair of an evening, he would close his eyes and scrape carelessly at the fiddle which was thrown across his knee. Sometimes the chords were sonorous and melancholy. Occasionally they were fantastic and cheerful. Clearly they reflected the thoughts which possessed him, but whether the music aided those thoughts, or whether the playing was simply the result of a whim or fancy, was more than I could determine. I might have rebelled against these exasperating solos had it not been that he usually terminated them by playing in quick succession a whole series of my favourite airs as a slight compensation for the trial upon my patience.

During the first week or so we had no callers, and I had begun to think that my companion was as friendless a man as I was myself. Presently, however, I found that he had many acquaintances, and those in the most different classes of society. There was one little sallow, rat-faced, dark-eyed fellow, who was introduced to me as Mr Lestrade, and who came three or four times in a single week. One morning a young girl called, fashionably dressed, and stayed for half an hour or more. The same afternoon brought a grey-headed seedy visitor, looking like a Jew pedlar, who appeared to me to be much excited, and who was closely followed by a slip-shod elderly woman. On another occasion an old white-haired gentleman had an interview with my companion ; and on another, a railway porter in his velveteen uniform. When any of these nondescript individuals put in an appearance, Sherlock Holmes used to beg for the use of the sitting-room, and I would retire to my bedroom. He always apologized to me for putting me to this inconvenience. 'I have to use this room as a place of business,' he said, 'and these people are my clients.' Again I had an opportunity of asking him a point-blank question, and again my delicacy prevented me from forcing another man to confide in me. I imagined at the time that he had some strong reason for not alluding to it, but he soon dispelled the idea by coming round to the subject of his own accord.

It was upon the 4th of March, as I have good reason to remember, that I rose somewhat earlier than usual, and found that Sherlock Holmes had not yet finished his breakfast. The landlady had become so accustomed to my late habits that my place had not been laid nor my coffee prepared. With the unreasonable petulance of mankind I rang the bell and gave a curt intimation that I was ready. Then I picked up a magazine from the table and attempted to while away the time with it, while my companion munched silently at his toast. One of the articles had a pencil mark at the heading, and I naturally began to run my eye through it.

Its somewhat ambitious title was *The Book of Life*, and it attempted to show how much an observant man might learn by an accurate and systematic examination of all that came in his way. It struck me as being a remarkable mixture of shrewdness and of absurdity. The reasoning was close and intense, but the deductions appeared to me to be far-fetched and exaggerated. The writer claimed by a momentary expression, a twitch of a muscle or a glance of an eye, to fathom a man's inmost thoughts. Deceit, according to him, was an impossibility in the case of one trained to observation and analysis. His conclusions were as infallible as so many propositions of Euclid. So startling would his results appear to the uninitiated that until they learned the processes by which he had arrived at them they might well consider him a necromancer.

'From a drop of water,' said the writer, 'a logician could infer the possibility of an Atlantic or a Niagara without having seen or heard of one or the other. So all life is a great chain, the nature of which is known whenever we are shown a single link of it. Like all other arts, the Science of Deduction and Analysis is one which can only be acquired by long and patient study, nor is life long enough to allow any mortal to attain the highest possible perfection in it. Before turning to those moral and mental aspects of the matter which present the greatest difficulties, let the inquirer begin by mastering more elementary problems. Let him on meeting a fellow-mortal, learn at a glance to distinguish the history of the man and the trade or profession to which he belongs. Puerile as such an exercise may seem, it sharpens the faculties of observation, and teaches one where to look and what to look for. By a man's finger-nails, by his coat-sleeve, by his boot, by his trouser-knees, by the callosities of his forefinger and thumb, by his expression, by his shirt-cuffs – by each of these things a man's calling is plainly revealed. That all united should fail to enlighten the competent inquirer in any case is almost inconceivable.'

'What ineffable twaddle!' I cried, slapping the magazine down on the table; 'I never read such rubbish in my life.'

'What is it?' asked Sherlock Holmes.

'Why, this article,' I said, pointing at it with my egg-spoon as I sat down to my breakfast. 'I see that you have read it since you have marked it. I don't deny that it is smartly written. It irritates me though. It is evidently the theory of some arm-chair lounger who evolves all these neat little paradoxes in the seclusion of his own study. It is not practical. I should like to see him clapped down in a third-class carriage on the Underground, and asked to give the trades of all his fellow-travellers. I would lay a thousand to one against him.'

'You would lose your money,' Holmes remarked calmly. 'As for the article, I wrote it myself.'

'You!'

'Yes; I have a turn both for observation and for deduction. The theories which I have expressed there, and which appear to you to be so chimerical, are really extremely practical – so practical that I depend upon them for my bread and cheese.'

'And how?' I asked involuntarily.

'Well, I have a trade of my own. I suppose I am the only one in the world.

I'm a consulting detective, if you can understand what that is. Here in London we have lots of Government detectives and lots of private ones. When these fellows are at fault, they come to me, and I manage to put them on the right scent. They lay all the evidence before me, and I am generally able, by the help of my knowledge of the history of crime, to set them straight. There is a strong family resemblance about misdeeds, and if you have all the details of a thousand at your finger ends, it is odd if you can't unravel the thousand and first. Lestrade is a well-known detective. He got himself into a fog recently over a forgery case, and that was what brought him here.'

'And these other people ?'

'They are mostly sent on by private inquiry agencies. They are all people who are in trouble about something, and want a little enlightening. I listen to their story, they listen to my comments, and then I pocket my fee.'

'But do you mean to say,' I said, 'that without leaving your room you can unravel some knot which other men can make nothing of, although they have seen every detail for themselves ?'

'Quite so. I have a kind of intuition that way. Now and again a case turns up which is a little more complex. Then I have to bustle about and see things with my own eyes. You see I have a lot of special knowledge which I apply to the problem, and which facilitates matters wonderfully. Those rules of deduction laid down in that article which aroused your scorn are invaluable to me in practical work. Observation with me is second nature. You appeared to be surprised when I told you, on our first meeting, that you had come from Afghanistan.'

'You were told, no doubt.'

'Nothing of the sort. I *knew* you came from Afghanistan. From long habit the train of thoughts ran so swiftly through my mind that I arrived at the conclusion without being conscious of intermediate steps. There were such steps, however. The train of reasoning ran, "Here is a gentleman of a medical type, but with the air of a military man. Clearly an army doctor, then. He has just come from the tropics, for his face is dark, and that is not the natural tint of his skin, for his wrists are fair. He has undergone hardship and sickness, as his haggard face says clearly. His left arm has been injured. He holds it in a stiff and unnatural manner. Where in the tropics could an English army doctor have seen much hardship and got his arm wounded ? Clearly in Afghanistan." The whole train of thought did not occupy a second. I then remarked that you came from Afghanistan, and you were astonished.'

'It is simple enough as you explain it,' I said, smiling. 'You remind me of Edgar Allen Poe's Dupin. I had no idea that such individuals did exist outside of stories.'

Sherlock Holmes rose and lit his pipe. 'No doubt you think that you are complimenting me in comparing me to Dupin,' he observed. 'Now, in my opinion, Dupin was a very inferior fellow. That trick of his of breaking in on his friends' thoughts with an apropos remark after a quarter of an hour's silence is really very showy and superficial. He had some analytical genius, no doubt; but he was by no means such a phenomenon as Poe appeared to imagine.'

'Have you read Gaboriau's works?' I asked. 'Does Lecoq come up to your idea of a detective?'

Sherlock Holmes sniffed sardonically. 'Lecoq was a miserable bungler,' he said, in an angry voice; 'he had only one thing to recommend him, and that was his energy. That book made me positively ill. The question was how to identify an unknown prisoner. I could have done it in twenty-four hours. Lecoq took six months or so. It might be made a text-book for detectives to teach them what to avoid.'

I felt rather indignant at having two characters whom I had admired treated in this cavalier style. I walked over to the window, and stood looking out into the busy street. 'This fellow may be very clever,' I said to myself, 'but he is certainly very conceited.'

'There are no crimes and no criminals in these days,' he said, querulously. 'What is the use of having brains in our profession. I know well that I have it in me to make my name famous. No man lives or has ever lived who has brought the same amount of study and of natural talent to the detection of crime which I have done. And what is the result? There is no crime to detect, or, at most, some bungling villainy with a motive so transparent that even a Scotland Yard official can see through it.'

I was still annoyed at his bumptious style of conversation. I thought it best to change the topic.

'I wonder what that fellow is looking for?' I asked, pointing to a stalwart, plainly-dressed individual who was walking slowly down the other side of the street, looking anxiously at the numbers. He had a large blue envelope in his hand, and was evidently the bearer of a message.

'You mean the retired sergeant of Marines,' said Sherlock Holmes.

'Brag and bounce!' thought I to myself. 'He knows that I cannot verify his guess.'

The thought had hardly passed through my mind when the man whom we were watching caught sight of the number on our door, and ran rapidly across the roadway. We heard a loud knock, a deep voice below, and heavy steps ascending the stair.

'For Mr Sherlock Holmes,' he said, stepping into the room and handing my friend the letter.

Here was an opportunity of taking the conceit out of him. He little thought of this when he made that random shot. 'May I ask, my lad,' I said, in the blandest voice, 'what your trade may be?'

'Commissionaire, sir,' he said, gruffly. 'Uniform away for repairs.'

'And you were?' I asked, with a slightly malicious glance at my companion.

'A sergeant, sir, Royal Marine Light Infantry, sir. No answer? Right, sir.'

He clicked his heels together, raised his hand in a salute, and was gone.

3. The Lauriston Gardens Mystery

I confess that I was considerably startled by this fresh proof of the practical nature of my companion's theories. My respect for his powers of analysis increased wondrously. There still remained some lurking suspicion in my mind, however, that the whole thing was a prearranged episode, intended to dazzle me, though what earthly object he could have in taking me in was past my comprehension. When I looked at him, he had finished reading the note, and his eyes had assumed the vacant, lack-lustre expression which showed mental abstraction.

'How in the world did you deduce that?' I asked.

'Deduce what?' said he, petulantly.

'Why, that he was a retired sergeant of Marines.'

'I have no time for trifles,' he answered, brusquely; then with a smile, 'Excuse my rudeness. You broke the thread of my thoughts; but perhaps it as well. So you actually were not able to see that that man was a sergeant of Marines?'

'No, indeed.'

'It was easier to know it than to explain why I know it. If you were asked to prove that two and two made four, you might find some difficulty, and yet you are quite sure of the fact. Even across the street I could see a great blue anchor tattooed on the back of the fellow's hand. That smacked of the sea. He had a military carriage, however, and regulation side whiskers. There we have the marine. He was a man with some amount of self-importance and a certain air of command. You must have observed the way in which he held his head and swung his cane. A steady, respectable, middle-aged man, too, on the face of him – all facts which led me to believe that he had been a sergeant.'

'Wonderful!' I ejaculated.

'Commonplace,' said Holmes.

The letter is from Inspector Gregson, of Scotland Yard. An American, Enoch J. Drebber, has been found dead in an empty house off the Brixton Road. There is blood, but no wound, and there has been no robbery. The affair is a 'puzzler', hence Gregson's appeal to Holmes to look into it. He takes Watson along for his first experience of his new friend's methods in earnest use.

The vital clues, to Holmes, are traces of a cab's wheels, the word RACHE printed in blood on a wall, and a woman's wedding ring. He is able to pronounce that murder, by poisoning, has been committed, and to estimate the killer's stature, the size of his feet and quality of his boots, the colour of his complexion, the length of his fingernails, and the type of cigar he had smoked. 'Rache', he is able to add, is German for 'revenge', though the man who had written it was no German.

'You have brought detection to as near an exact science as it ever will be brought in this world,' declares the awed Watson, and Holmes blushes like a woman flattered on her beauty.

A visit to off-duty Constable John Rance, who had found the body and had an unwitting encounter with the killer, confirms Holmes's postulations. Using the wedding ring as bait, through a newspaper advertisement, he attracts a claimant, though not the one hopefully anticipated.

Insp Gregson visits the deceased Drebber's landlady, Madame Charpentier, and discovers an obvious suspect in her son Arthur, who had been outraged by the lodger's suggestive manner towards his sister Alice. But Gregson's colleague and rival, Insp Lestrade, is also on the case and has gone looking for the murdered man's American secretary, Joseph Stangerson. He finds that he has just been stabbed to death.

Holmes is more interested in a little box containing two pills, brought by Lestrade from the latest victim's room. Mrs Hudson, the landlady-cum-housekeeper of 221B Baker Street, happens to have an old terrier dog which is suffering at the end of its days. Its miserable existence is ended in the pursuit of human justice; and a hansom cab driver, Jefferson Hope, fetched to 221B by Holmes's urchin helpers, the Baker Street Irregulars, finds himself in handcuffs, with a long statement to make about revenge for an old wrongdoing by Mormons in the state of Utah.

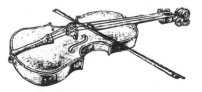

'Gregson is the smartest of the Scotland Yarders; he and Lestrade are the pick of a bad lot. They are both quick and energetic, but conventional – shockingly so. They have their knives into one another, too. They are as jealous as a pair of professional beauties.'

Holmes (Ch 3)

'I am the most incurably lazy devil that ever stood in shoe leather – that is, when the fit is on me, for I can be spry enough at times.'

Holmes (Ch 3)

'He (Gregson) knows that I am his superior, and acknowledges it to me; but he would cut his tongue out before he would own it to any third person.'

Holmes (Ch 3)

My companion was in the best of spirits, and prattled away about Cremona fiddles and the difference between a Stradivarius and an Amati.

(Ch 3)

'It is a capital mistake to theorize before you have all the evidence. It biases the judgment.'

Holmes (Ch 3)

With an air of nonchalance which, under the circumstances, seemed to me to border upon affectation, he lounged up and down the pavement, and gazed vacantly at the ground, the sky, the opposite houses and the line of railings.

(Ch 3)

'There is nothing new under the sun. It has all been done before.'

Holmes (Ch 3)

'It's all very well for you to laugh, Mr Sherlock Holmes. You may be very smart and clever, but the old hound is the best, when all is said and done.'

Lestrade (Ch 3)

(Holmes) chattered away to himself under his breath the whole time, keeping up a running fire of exclamations, groans, whistles, and little cries suggestive of encouragement and of hope. As I watched him I was irresistibly reminded of a pure-blooded, well-trained foxhound, as it dashes backward and forward through the covert, whining in its eagerness, until it comes across the lost scent.

(Ch 3)

'They say that genius is an infinite capacity for taking pains. It's a very bad definition, but it does apply to detective work.'

Holmes (Ch 3)

'The height of a man, in nine cases out of ten, can be told from the length of his stride. It is a simple calculation enough, though there is no use my boring you with figures.'

Holmes (Ch 4)

'When a man writes on a wall, his instinct leads him to write above the level of his own eyes.'

Holmes (Ch 4)

'I have made a special study of cigar ashes – in fact, I have written a monograph upon the subject. I flatter myself that I can distinguish at a glance the ash of any known brand either of cigar or of tobacco. It is just in such details that the skilled detective differs from the Gregson and Lestrade type.'

Holmes (Ch 4)

'You know a conjurer gets no credit when once he has explained his trick; and if I show you too much of my method of working, you will come to the conclusion that I am a very ordinary individual after all.'

'I shall never do that,' I answered; 'you have brought detection to as near an exact science as it ever will be brought in this world.'

My companion flushed up with pleasure at my words, and the earnest way in which I uttered them. I had already observed that he was as sensitive on the score of his art as any girl could be of her beauty.   *Holmes and Watson (Ch 4)*

'A study in scarlet, eh? Why shouldn't we use a little art jargon. There's the scarlet thread of murder running through the colourless skein of life, and our duty is to unravel it, and isolate it, and expose every inch of it. And now for lunch, and then for Norman Neruda. Her attack and her bowing are splendid. What's that little thing of Chopin's she plays so magnificently: Tra-la-la-lira-lira-lay.'   *Holmes (Ch 4)*

'Do you remember what Darwin says about music? He claims that the power of producing and appreciating it existed among the human race long before the power of speech was arrived at. Perhaps that is why we are so subtly influenced by it. There are vague memories in our souls of those misty centuries when the world was in its childhood.'   *Holmes (Ch 5)*

'One's ideas must be as broad as Nature if they are to interpret Nature.'   *Holmes (Ch 5)*

'There is a mystery about this which stimulates the imagination; where there is no imagination there is no horror.'   *Holmes (Ch 5)*

Holmes was engaged in his favourite occupation of scraping upon his violin.   *Watson (Ch 5)*

'It's the Baker Street division of the detective police force,' said my companion gravely; and as he spoke there rushed into the room half a dozen of the dirtiest and most ragged street Arabs that ever I clapped my eyes on.   *Holmes and Watson (Ch 6)*

'The tremendous exertions which I have gone through during the last day or two have worn me out. Not so much bodily exertions, you understand, as the strain upon the mind. You will appreciate that, Mr Sherlock Holmes, for we are both brain-workers.'   *Gregson (Ch 6)*

'To a great mind, nothing is little.'   *Holmes (Ch 6)*

'I ought to know by this time that when a fact appears to be opposed to a long train of deductions, it invariably proves to be capable of bearing some other interpretation.'

Holmes (Ch 7)

'It is a mistake to confound strangeness with mystery. The most commonplace crime is often the most mysterious, because it presents no new or special features from which deductions may be drawn.'

Holmes (Ch 7)

'If there's a vacant place for a chief of the police, I reckon you are the man for it.'

Hope to Holmes (Part 2, Ch 6)

'What you do in this world is a matter of no consequence. The question is, what can you make people believe that you have done?'

Holmes (Part 2, Ch 7)

'I have already explained to you that what is out of the common is usually a guide rather than a hindrance. In solving a problem of this sort, the grand thing is to be able to reason backward. That is a very useful accomplishment, and a very easy one, but people do not practise it much. In the everyday affairs of life it is more useful to reason forward, and so the other comes to be neglected. There are fifty who can reason synthetically for one who can reason analytically ... Most people, if you describe a train of events to them, will tell you what the results would be. They can put those events together in their minds, and argue from them that something will come to pass. There are few people, however, who, if you told them a result, would be able to evolve from their own inner consciousness what the steps were which led up to that result. This power is what I mean when I talk of reasoning backward, or analytically.'

Holmes (Part 2, Ch 7)

'There is no branch of detective science which is so important and so much neglected as the art of tracing footsteps. Happily, I have always laid great stress upon it, and much practice has made it second nature to me.'

Holmes (Part 2, Ch 7)

'It is wonderful!' I cried. 'Your merits should be publicly recognized. You should publish an account of the case. If you won't, I will for you.'
    'You may do what you like, Doctor,' he answered.

Watson and Holmes (Part 2, Ch 7)

'If the case has had no other effect, it, at least, brings out in the most striking manner the efficiency of our detective police force, and will serve as a lesson to all foreigners that they will do wisely to settle their feuds at home, and not to carry them on to British soil. It is an open secret that the credit of this smart capture belongs entirely to the well-known Scotland Yard officials, Messrs Lestrade and Gregson. The man was apprehended, it appears, in the rooms of a certain Mr Sherlock Holmes, who has himself, as an amateur, shown some talent in the detective line and who, with such instructors, may hope in time to attain to some degree of their skill.'

Report in The Echo *newspaper* (Part 2, Ch 7)

'*Populus me sibilat, at mihi plaudo*
Ipse domi simul ac nummos comtemplar in arca.'

Watson quoting Horace (inaccurately) (Part 2, Ch 7)

3

The Sign of the Four

Micah Clarke, the novel about Puritan England which had resulted from Arthur Conan Doyle's 'large thoughts' and a corresponding capacity for research, was finished by the end of February, 1888, between the appearance of *A Study in Scarlet* in *Beeton's* and as a book. It, too, went first to James Payn, of the *Cornhill*. He rejected it, reproving him, 'How can you, can you, waste your time and your wits writing historical novels?' So began another depressing round of publisher after publisher. After nine months, when hope for it was almost gone, Andrew Lang accepted it for Longman's.

It appeared in February 1889 and got excellent reviews. Doyle believed increasingly that his future and fame would depend on historical novels. He pressed on fervently with the reading and note-making for a novel set even further back in time, which would glorify the bowmen, the knights and the chivalry of 14th century England.

It might have spelt the end of Sherlock Holmes and John H. Watson, MD. The legend, not yet established, might never have arisen, but for a recommendation by Payn to an American, Joseph Marshall Stoddart, recently appointed managing editor of *Lippincott's Monthly Magazine*, which was published simultaneously in Philadelphia and London. Visiting London in the summer of 1889 in search of fresh material, Stoddart gave a dinner party on 30 August. His guests were Oscar Wilde, at that time nearing the end of his term as editor of *Woman's World* magazine and still searching for his way to literary fame, T.P.Gill, MP, another witty Irishman, and Arthur Conan Doyle.

A jolly time was had by all. Oscar, as always, dominated the table-talk, impressing Doyle indelibly; but it was their host who did the most significant talking. He offered Wilde a commission to write the story which, as it turned out, would make him a cynosure of literary and society London, *The Picture of Dorian Gray*. Stoddart's offer to Conan Doyle was not for anything in the historical line, but for another Sherlock Holmes story.

He couldn't afford to refuse. Medicine still brought little income.

Micah Clarke's sales were satisfactory, but not sensational. It would be months before the new historical novel would be finished, and an incalculable time before anyone might buy it. And his family had acquired an extra member, with the birth in January, 1889, of a daughter, Mary Louise.

Wrenching his concentration forward five centuries, he sent Holmes and Watson into action again, in the case of *The Sign of the Four*, as it was titled before it was abbreviated to the less effective *The Sign of Four*.

Once more he wrote quickly and impatiently, not troubling to check certain details against ones in *A Study in Scarlet*. That had been set in 1881. *The Sign of the Four* belongs in 1888. In the seven years' interval, Watson's war wound has travelled from his shoulder to his leg – unless, that is, there had been a second wound, not mentioned in his earlier narrative.

The Sign of the Four was not meant to be a sequel. It was a one-off, written to oblige a well-wishing editor and to bring in some extra cash. If Doyle had had any higher hopes than that for it they would have been dashed, anyway. It appeared in *Lippincott's* in February, 1890, and attracted no special attention.

He managed to sell it to a few English provincial newspapers as a serial. Later in the year a London book publisher, Spencer Blackett, republished it. The book drew a few notices : 'Dr Doyle's admirers will read the little volume through eagerly enough, but they will hardly care to pick it up again,' one said.

A certain following does seem to be acknowledged, however, by the phrase 'Dr Doyle's admirers'. He got one of the first literary agents, A.P.Watt, to represent him, and through him the story was serialized in George Newnes's weekly *Tit-Bits*. Holmes and Watson came to the notice of a new and different readership.

Doyle was not much interested. With the triumphant cry, 'That's done it !' he had finished the historical novel which had become his obsession and which he was convinced was going to make him famous at last. This time there was no rejection by the *Cornhill*. Payn declared *The White Company* to be the best thing of its kind since Scott's *Ivanhoe*, and bought it for serialization.

Doyle promptly gave up his unprofitable Southsea practice. In December, 1890, he went to Vienna with Louise – 'Touie', to him and everyone close to her. He had decided to study to become an eye specialist, and establish himself in London. The Portsmouth Literary and Scientific Society gave them a send-off dinner, its President, Dr Watson, in the chair.

The Sign of the Four opens by introducing another facet of Sherlock Holmes – as drug-taker. He explains to the disapproving Watson that he does it purely because he is bored from mental inactivity, an acceptable enough reason in the late Victorian context, before the regulation of narcotics and long before their misuse. Doyle gave Holmes the trait for no other reasons than to add to his idiosyncrasies and point up his habit of slipping into introspection when he had no pressing work:

'My mind rebels at stagnation. Give me problems, give me work, give me the most abstruse cryptogram, or the most intricate analysis, and I am in my own proper atmosphere. I can dispense then with artificial stimulants. That is why I have chosen my own particular profession, or rather created it...'

We are told nothing of what has been happening to him or to Watson since *A Study in Scarlet*. It is a fair assumption, from hints in later stories, that Watson had married and moved away, but had lost his wife within a year or little more and moved back to 221B. Holmes's professional life has clearly been in the doldrums of late, which makes all the more welcome to him and Watson the unexpected visit of a Miss Mary Morstan, sweet twenty-seven, blonde, dainty and refined, with an intriguing mystery to relate. Her father, Captain Arthur Morstan, of the Indian Army, had vanished ten years ago. For the past six years, on the same annual date, she has been receiving through the post the anonymous gift of a single exquisite pearl. This time round she has been invited to meet her unknown benefactor, who has pledged to do her a justice which she has been denied. She may bring with her two friends, but no police.

Holmes co-opts Watson to make up the trio. Their destination proves to be an exotically got-up suburban house, termed by its hypochondriacal, hookah-smoking owner, Thaddeus Sholto, 'an oasis of art in the howling desert of South London'. They hear his account of Capt Morstan's death, and of a treasure which he had half owned. Miss Morstan is his heiress, and the time is overdue for her part to be handed over to her.

This necessitates a journey to an even further-flung South London suburb, Upper Norwood. Thaddeus Sholto's twin brother Bartholomew lives here, at Pondicherry Lodge, which had been the home of their late father, Major John Sholto, Capt Morstan's co-commander of the military guard over the convicts on the Andaman Islands, in the Indian Ocean. On his deathbed, six years ago, Major Sholto had revealed to his sons the existence of the Agra Treasure, which he and Morstan had brought back from India. Just as he was about to tell them where it was hidden, the appearance of a hideous face, pressed against the window, had caused him to expire in a paroxysm. After many years' searching, Bartholomew Sholto has at last found the hoard and has been persuaded by Thaddeus to give Miss Morstan her share.

They arrive at Pondicherry Lodge too late: Bartholomew Sholto is dead in a chair in his locked room, grinning unnaturally. A note beside him refers to 'The sign of the four', an inscription identical to that on a building plan which had been found among the missing Capt Morstan's papers. Bartholomew Sholto has been killed by a poisoned dart; the treasure is gone.

Holmes and Watson are soon on the murderer's scent, literally, led by a persevering dog, Toby. The Baker Street Irregulars again demonstrate their value, this time as observers of shipping movements on the River Thames. The great river highway sees a desperate race between a steam launch and a police boat, culminating in a shoot-out, a good arrest for Athelney Jones, of Scotland Yard, and a confession by a wooden-legged ex-soldier and convict, Jonathan Small. Its elements include the Indian Mutiny, the Agra Treasure, a criminal alliance, blackmail and betrayal; and, credit where it is due, a testimonial to the capacity for staunch comradeship of a murderous cannibal named Tonga.

There is another outcome, concerning Watson and Miss Morstan. In what might so easily have been left as the last exchange between him and Holmes ever chronicled, Watson remarks, 'The division seems rather unfair. You have done all the work in this business. I get a wife out of it, Jones gets the credit, pray what remains for you?'

'For me,' says Sherlock Holmes, 'there still remains the cocaine-bottle,' and he stretches his long white hand up for it.

Whether it was the Beaune which I had taken with my lunch, or the additional exasperation produced by the extreme deliberation of his manner, I suddenly felt that I could hold out no longer.

'Which is it to-day,' I asked, 'morphine or cocaine?'

He raised his eyes languidly from the old black-letter volume which he had opened.

'It is cocaine,' he said, 'a seven-per-cent solution. Would you care to try it?'

Watson and Holmes (Ch 1)

'I am the last and highest court of appeal in detection. When Gregson, or

Lestrade, or Athelney Jones are out of their depths – which, by the way, is their normal state – the matter is laid before me. I examine the data, as an expert, and pronounce a specialist's opinion. I claim no credit in such cases. My name figures in no newspaper. The work itself, the pleasure of finding a field for my peculiar powers, is my highest reward.'

Holmes (Ch 1)

'Detection is, or ought to be, an exact science and should be treated in the same cold and unemotional manner. You have attempted to tinge it with romanticism, which produces much the same effect as if you worked a love-story or an elopement into the fifth proposition of Euclid.'

Holmes (Ch 1)

I made no remark, however, but sat nursing my wounded leg. I had had a Jezail bullet through it some time before, and though it did not prevent me from walking it ached wearily at every change of the weather.

Watson (Ch 1)

'I have been guilty of several monographs. They are all upon technical subjects. Here, for example, is one "Upon the Distinction between the Ashes of the Various Tobaccos." In it I enumerate a hundred and forty forms of cigar, cigarette, and pipe tobacco, with coloured plates illustrating the difference in the ash ... To the trained eye there is as much difference between the black ash of a Trichinopoly and the white fluff of bird's-eye as there is between a cabbage and a potato.'

Holmes (Ch 1)

'Here is my monograph upon the tracing of footsteps, with some remarks upon the uses of plaster of Paris as a preserver of impresses. Here, too, is a curious little work upon the influence of a trade upon the form of the hand, with lithotypes of the hands of slaters, sailors, cork-cutters, compositors, weavers, and diamond-polishers. That is a matter of great practical interest to the scientific detective – especially in the case of unclaimed bodies, or in discovering the antecedents of criminals.'

Holmes (Ch 1)

'I never guess. It is a shocking habit – destructive to the logical faculty.'

Holmes (Ch 1)

'Stand at the window here. Was ever such a dreary, dismal, unprofitable world ? See how the yellow fog swirls down the street and drifts across the dun-coloured houses. What could be more hopelessly prosaic and material ? What is the use of having powers, Doctor, when one has no field upon which to exert them ? Crime is commonplace, existence is commonplace, and no qualities save those which are commonplace have any function upon earth.'

Holmes (Ch 1)

In an experience of women which extends over many nations and three separate continents, I have never looked upon a face which gave a clearer promise of a refined and sensitive nature.

Watson (Ch 2)

'What a very attractive woman!' I exclaimed, turning to my companion.

He had lit his pipe again and was leaning back with drooping eyelids. 'Is she?' he said languidly; 'I did not observe.'

'You really are an automaton – a calculating machine,' I cried. 'There is something positively inhuman in you at times.'

He smiled gently.

'It is of the first importance,' he cried, 'not to allow your judgment to be biased by personal qualities. A client is to me a mere unit, a factor in a problem. The emotional qualities are antagonistic to clear reasoning. I assure you that the most winning woman I ever knew was hanged for poisoning three little children for their insurance-money, and the most repellent man of my acquaintance is a philanthropist who has spent nearly a quarter of a million upon the London poor.'

Watson and Holmes (Ch 2)

'Look at his long letters. They hardly rise above the common herd. That *d* might be an *a*, and that *l* an *e*. Men of character always differentiate their long letters, however illegibly they may write. There is vacillation in his *k*'s and self-esteem in his capitals.'

Holmes (Ch 2)

'Let me recommend this book – one of the most remarkable ever penned. It is Winwood Reade's *Martyrdom of Man*.'

Holmes (Ch 2)

It was a September evening and not yet seven o'clock, but the day had been a dreary one, and a dense drizzly fog lay low upon the great city. Mud-coloured clouds drooped sadly over the muddy streets. Down the Strand the lamps were but misty splotches of diffused light which threw a feeble circular glimmer upon the slimy pavement. The yellow glare from the shop-windows streamed out into the steamy, vaporous air and threw a murky, shifting radiance across the crowded thoroughfare. There was, to my mind, something eerie and ghost-like in the endless procession of faces which flitted across these narrow bars of light – sad faces and glad, haggard and merry. Like all humankind, they flitted from the gloom into the light, and so back into the gloom once more.

Watson (Ch 3)

Miss Morstan's demeanour was as resolute and collected as ever. I endeavoured to cheer and amuse her by reminiscences of my adventures in Afghanistan; but, to tell the truth, I was myself so excited at our situation and so curious as to our destination that my stories were slightly involved. To this day she declares that I told her one moving anecdote as to how a musket looked into our tent at the dead of night, and how I fired a double-barrelled tiger cub at it.

Watson (Ch 3)

'I am a man of somewhat retiring, and I might even say refined, tastes, and there is nothing more unaesthetic than a policeman. I have a natural shrinking from all forms of rough materialism.'

Thaddeus Sholto (Ch 4)

'I don't think you can have forgotten me. Don't you remember that amateur who fought three rounds with you at Alison's rooms on the night of your benefit four years back?'

'Not Mr Sherlock Holmes!' roared the prize-fighter. 'God's truth! How could I have mistook you? If instead o' standin' there so quiet you had just stepped up and given me that cross-hit of yours under the jaw, I'd ha' known you without a question. Ah, you're one that has wasted your gifts, you have! You might have aimed high, if you had joined the fancy.'

Holmes and McMurdo (Ch 5)

A wondrous subtle thing is love, for here were we two, who had never seen each other before that day, between whom no word or even look of affection had ever passed, and yet now in an hour of trouble our hands instinctively sought for each other. I have marvelled at it since, but at the time it seemed the most natural thing that I should go out to her so, and, as she has often told me, there was in her also the instinct to turn to me for comfort and protection. So we stood hand in hand like two children, and there was peace in our hearts for all the dark things that surrounded us.

Watson (Ch 5)

'How often have I said to you that when you have eliminated the impossible, whatever remains, *however improbable*, must be the truth?'

Holmes (Ch 6)

So swift, silent, and furtive were his movements, like those of a trained bloodhound picking out a scent, that I could not but think what a terrible criminal he would have made had he turned his energy and sagacity against the law instead of exerting them in its defence.

Watson (Ch 6)

'How sweet the morning air is! See how that one little cloud floats like a pink feather from some gigantic flamingo. Now the red rim of the sun pushes itself over the London cloud-bank. It shines on a good many folk, but on none, I dare bet, who are on a stranger errand than you and I. How small we feel with our petty ambitions and strivings in the presence of the great elemental forces of Nature!'

Holmes (Ch 7)

'The main thing with people of that sort is never to let them think that their information can be of the slightest importance to you. If you do they will instantly shut up like an oyster. If you listen to them under protest, as it were, you are very likely to get what you want.'

Holmes (Ch 8)

'I have a curious constitution. I never remember feeling tired by work, though idleness exhausts me completely.'

Holmes (Ch 8)

He took up his violin from the corner, and as I stretched myself out he began to play some low, dreamy, melodious air – his own, no doubt, for he had a remarkable gift for improvisation.

Watson (Ch 8)

'Women are never to be entirely trusted – not the best of them.'

Holmes (Ch 9)

I found Holmes dejected and somewhat morose. He would hardly reply to my questions and busied himself all the evening in an abstruse chemical analysis which involved much heating of retorts and distilling of vapours, ending at last in a smell which fairly drove me out of the apartment. Up to the small hours of the morning I could hear the clinking of his test-tubes which told me that he was still engaged in his malodorous experiment.

Watson (Ch 9)

'Your friend, Mr Sherlock Holmes, is a wonderful man, sir. He's a man who is not to be beat. I have known that young man go into a good many cases, but I never saw the case yet that he could not throw a light upon. He is irregular in his methods and a little quick perhaps in jumping at theories, but, on the whole, I think he would have made a most promising officer.'

Athelney Jones (Ch 9)

'Ah, you rogue! You would have made an actor and a rare one. You had the proper workhouse cough, and those weak legs of yours are worth ten pound a week.'

Jones to Holmes (Ch 9)

'I insist upon your dining with us. It will be ready in half an hour. I have oysters and a brace of grouse, with something a little choice in white wines. Watson, you have never yet recognized my merits as a housekeeper.'

Holmes to Jones (Ch 9)

Our meal was a merry one. Holmes could talk exceedingly well when he chose, and that night he did choose. He appeared to be in a state of nervous exaltation. I have never known him so brilliant. He spoke on a quick succession of subjects – on miracle plays, on mediaeval pottery, on Stradivarius violins, on the Buddhism of Ceylon, and on the warships of the future – handling each as though he had made a special study of it.

Watson (Ch 10)

'Dirty-looking rascals, but I suppose every one has some little immortal spark concealed about him. You would not think it to look at them. There is no *a priori* probability about it. A strange enigma is man !'

Holmes (of shipyard workers) (Ch 10)

'Well, and there is the end of our little drama,' I remarked, after we had sat some time smoking in silence. 'I fear that it may be the last investigation in which I shall have the chance of studying your methods. Miss Morstan has done me the honour to accept me as husband in prospective.'

He gave a most dismal groan.

'I feared as much,' said he. 'I really cannot congratulate you.'

I was a little hurt.

'Have you any reason to be dissatisfied with my choice ?' I asked.

'Not at all. I think she is one of the most charming young ladies I ever met and might have been most useful in such work as we have been doing. She had a decided genius that way ... But love is an emotional thing, and whatever is emotional is opposed to that true cold reason which I place above all things. I should never marry myself, lest I bias my judgment.'

Watson and Holmes (Ch 12)

4

The Strand Magazine

Dr and Mrs Doyle returned home from Vienna and Paris in late March, 1891, to an undefined future. *The White Company*, his deeply studied and lovingly written story of the knights and bowmen of medieval England, was established in the *Cornhill Magazine* and attracting favourable comment. It remains the best known of Doyle's historical romances, although his favourite was *Sir Nigel*, its 'sequel' set in earlier time.

While abroad, he had knocked off a novelette, *The Doings of Raffles Haw*, set in suburban London, for serialization in the Harmsworth magazine *Answers*. It brought him enough to pay for their travels. They had a few hundred pounds in savings, which he subsequently lost through following an investment tip.

> It was great to find ourselves back in London once more with the feeling that we were now on the real field of battle, where we must conquer or perish, for our boats were burned behind us. It is easy now to look back and think that the issue was clear, but it was by no means so at the time, for I had earned little, though my reputation was growing. It was only my inward conviction of the permanent merits of *The White Company*, still appearing month by month in *Cornhill*, which sustained my confidence. I had come through so much in the early days at Southsea that nothing could alarm me personally, but I had a wife and child now, and the stern simplicity of life which was possible and even pleasant in early days was now no longer to be thought of.

In fact, the only boat-burning they had done had been in leaving friendly but unlucrative Southsea. His intention now was to find some premises among the 'big men' who ruled the capital's medical empire; he would hire himself out to them as an oculist available for jobbing work of a sort which they found time-consuming.

From a two-roomed lodging at 23 Montague Place, adjoining the British Museum, Dr Doyle sought westward. He soon found a room, with part-use of a waiting-room, at 2 Devonshire Place, the continuation of Wimpole Street. Fortunately for the survival of Sherlock

Holmes, the five- or six-hour daily attendance which his creator put in there proved totally undisturbed. No ring at his bell ruffled his serenity as he wrote and wrote.

A new monthly magazine had appeared on England's bookstalls. It cost sixpence, though it was claimed to be worth a shilling. More than any other British magazine, it followed the style of such smart and lively American ones as *Harper's*, *Scribner's* and *The Century*. It was called *The Strand Magazine*.

George Newnes, a former Manchester haberdashery wholesaler and vegetarian restaurateur, had made a swift fortune with *Tit-Bits*, a weekly compilation of interesting and whimsical clippings from newspapers, periodicals and books, first published in 1881. In January 1890 he was persuaded by the journalist W.T.Stead to found a more substantial digest-type magazine, *Review of Reviews*, for Stead to edit. In its first six months this prototype *Reader's Digest* did well enough, but it proved a trying time for Newnes's nerves. Stead was a controversialist, who rejoiced in sailing his editorial judgments close to the wind. Newnes wanted only a quiet, though profitable, life, through the kind of journalism which he defined as 'content to plod on, year after year, giving wholesome and harmless entertainment to crowds of hard-working people craving for a little fun and amusement.' He had soon had enough of Stead's brand, 'which directs the affairs of nations ... makes and unmakes Cabinets ... upsets governments, builds up navies and does many other great things.' He was happy to sell his interest cheaply to his volatile editor.

It left George Newnes with one problem: it was against his principles to sack the editorial staff whom Stead could not afford to take with him. A journalist from outside offered the solution, one which coincided with a notion of Newnes's own: why not emulate those stylish American magazines, using the best available writers and illustrators? H.Greenhough Smith, in his mid-thirties and anxious to leave the dull old *Temple Bar* for a livelier publication, couldn't have timed his approach better. London and other big cities were drawing in increasing hordes of railway commuters. Most of them were office workers, people who would be willing to spend a monthly sixpence on a well-illustrated mixture of 'healthful' short fiction, feature articles, and interviews with famous men and women.

The delighted Greenhough Smith was appointed literary editor and told to get the magazine on sale by the start of 1891, only four months away. 'We had no stories, no articles, no contracts for paper or printing,' he reminisced. They had no title, either. Newnes had moved from Manchester to London in 1885, and the following year had established himself in Burleigh Street, Strand. *The Burleigh Street Magazine* was an obvious choice, but *The Strand Magazine* was a better one. The cover design by G.H.Haite, later a founder of the London Sketch Club, proved a winner. It featured the busy Strand itself, looking towards the towers of the churches of St Clement Danes and St Mary-le-Strand and cleverly incorporating a direction board to the Newnes offices.

The first issue, of 112 pages with an illustration at every page opening and a free coloured print of a Royal Academy picture, duly appeared early in January, 1891. It sold 300,000 copies, a circulation figure without precedent on either side of the Atlantic.

There was no established pool of British writers of popular short stories. Most of the fiction carried in the first few numbers was in translation from French, Russian and other foreign originals. Just a few stories were by indigenous authors, who included Grant Allen, W.Clark Russell, Stanley Weyman, and E.W.Hornung. A story in the April issue, very short but with an ingenious plot involving the new phonograph machine, had the title 'The Voice of Science'. Its writer's name was not given. This was Conan Doyle's first contribution to the magazine which, more than any other, would be identified with his work for the rest of his life.

In recent years he had been thinking in terms of book-length themes. His passion for historical detail had meant much research, after which the story had to be written speculatively, then hawked around for sale. It was a long, slow process, which so far had failed to pay off in any big way. The *Strand*, whose policy was for each issue to be complete in itself, with no continuing serials, offered an excellent opening and ready payment to a fast writer whose notebooks were full of ideas for one-off tales. However, Doyle's mind had been tuned to broader conceptions, and he came up with an innovative compromise:

> It had struck me that a single character running through a series, if it only engaged the attention of the reader, would bind that reader to that particular magazine. On the other hand, it had long seemed to me that the ordinary serial might be an impediment rather than a help to a magazine, since, sooner or later, one missed one number and afterwards it had lost all interest. Clearly the ideal compromise was a character which carried through, and yet instalments which were each complete in themselves, so that the purchaser was always sure that he could read the whole contents of the magazine. I believe that I was the first to realize this and *The Strand Magazine* the first to put it into practice.
>
> Looking round for my central character I felt that Sherlock Holmes, whom I had already handled in two little books, would easily lend himself to a succession of short stories. These I began in the long hours of waiting in my consulting-room.

On Friday, 3 April, 1891, he wrote in his diary, 'Sent "A Scandal in

Bohemia" to A.P.Watt.' A week later he recorded, 'Finished "A Case of Identity".' The agent sent the two foolscap manuscripts together to Greenhough Smith, who, forty years on, recalled his excitement on reading them : 'I at once realized that here was the greatest short story writer since Edgar Allan Poe. I remember rushing into Mr Newnes's room and thrusting the stories before his eyes.'

Greenhough Smith asked for more, and A.P.Watt asked in return for £200 for a series of six. Each got what he wanted. Four more stories were delivered before May was out. The first of them, *A Scandal in Bohemia*, appeared in the *Strand* in July, 1891, and the magazine's already increasing circulation figures began to rise perceptibly.

Doyle recognized that he had come to another of his life's crossroads. He did not arrive there in the best of shape. He had almost died that May from a severe attack of the influenza which was claiming many lives. Lying in bed in its aftermath, 'as weak as a child, and as emotional', he nevertheless found his mind clear enough to assess his future:

> I saw how foolish I was to waste my literary earnings in keeping up an oculist's room in Wimpole Street, and I determined with a wild rush of joy to cut the painter and to trust for ever to my power of writing. I remember in my delight taking the handkerchief which lay upon the coverlet in my enfeebled hand and tossing it up to the ceiling in my exultation. I should at long last be my own master. No longer would I have to conform to professional dress or to please anyone else. I would be free to live how I liked and where I liked. It was one of the great moments of exultation of my life.

He could not have been more mistaken in that notion of ceasing to have to do anyone else's bidding. Arthur Conan Doyle's career, more than almost any other writer's, was to be an example of a progenitor inescapably identified with his resented creation.

For the moment, though, Sherlock Holmes had his uses. The non-productive medical practice was abandoned. The lodgings in Montague Street were given up. With Touie, Mary Louise, and Touie's mother, Mrs Hawkins, who had lived with them since they were married, the emancipated author moved in June, 1891, to 12, Tennison Road, South Norwood, the South London suburban neighbourhood of his fictional Pondicherry Lodge. In their large, pleasant, rented house he settled immediately into a daily routine of work, punctuated with various sporting activities, during which his subconscious mind digested the rich diet of facts and thoughts that he had fed it.

His latest project – 'some literary work worthy of the name' – was a novel about the Huguenots in 17th century Europe and America, *The*

Refugees. He was not to be left in peace for long, though. The appearance of *The Boscombe Valley Mystery* in the October *Strand* meant that there were only two Sherlock Holmes stories left in stock. Greenhough Smith was asking for more. Conan Doyle replied that he would write a further six for £300. The acceptance came by return of post, with a request for speedy delivery. He had to put *The Refugees* aside and turn his imagination to Baker Street again. In the Christmas number, in which appeared the last of the first six adventures, *The Man with the Twisted Lip*, A. Conan Doyle was the subject of one of the popular 'Portraits of Celebrities at different times of their Lives'. The piece incorporated timely tidings of comfort and joy: 'It gives us great pleasure to announce that the extraordinary adventures of Sherlock Holmes, which have proved so popular with our readers during the past six months, will be continued in the new year.'

The second six stories were written at high speed, all but one finished by mid-November. Reporting this in a letter to his mother, Doyle added, 'I think of slaying Holmes in the last and winding him up for good and all. He takes my mind from better things.' Her response spoke for hundreds of thousands of people in Britain and other parts of the world: 'You won't! You can't. You *mustn't*.' He picked up his pen once more to write the last of the dozen, *The Copper Beeches*. It was completed with Holmes alive and in excellent health.

The twelve stories were superbly illustrated by Sidney Paget, an inspired, though mistaken, choice by the *Strand*'s art editor, W. H. J. Boot, R.I., who thought he remembered him as the *Illustrated London News*'s young war artist with the Gordon Relief Expedition in 1884. In fact, this had been one of Paget's two artist younger brothers, Walter. Boot wrote to Sidney in error, and he snapped up the commission. Ironically, it was the deprived Walter whose appropriately aquiline features gave Sidney his model for Holmes.

Newnes republished *The Adventures of Sherlock Holmes*, as they were titled generically, in volume form in 1892. Harper & Brothers, New York, also published them as a book that year. Both these editions used Paget illustrations. The stories had already gained popularity in America through newspaper syndication, and it was this series which implanted Sherlock Holmes firmly into the world's consciousness.

5

The Adventures of Sherlock Holmes

A Scandal in Bohemia (*Strand*, July 1891)

'To Sherlock Holmes she is always *the* woman.' She is Irene Adler, New-Jersey-born former opera singer, concerning whom Holmes is consulted at 221B Baker Street by the pompous King of Bohemia. Five years earlier, then a twenty-five-year-old Crown Prince, he had been photographed with her in an unspecified pose which is certain to outrage his bride-to-be, a Scandinavian royal princess, when the resentful Irene sends it to her on the betrothal day. Attempts to steal the photograph have failed, and only three days remain to forestall the gesture.

Holmes has recourse to disguise, first as a dissipated groom, then as a guileless clergyman, incidentally standing in as witness to Irene's extremely informal marriage to a handsomer catch than the King, Godfrey Norton, a London lawyer. Holmes sets up the photograph's recovery, but Irene has seen him coming. A more innocuous portrait of her becomes a treasured memento of the only woman ever to outwit him.

To Sherlock Holmes she is always *the* woman. I have seldom heard him mention her under any other name. In his eyes she eclipses and predominates the whole of her sex. It was not that he felt any emotion akin to love for Irene Adler. All emotions, and that one particularly, were abhorrent to his cold, precise but admirably balanced mind. He was, I take it, the most perfect reasoning and observing machine that the world has seen, but as a lover he would have placed himself in a false position. He never spoke of the softer passions, save with a gibe and a sneer. They were admirable things for the observer –

excellent for drawing the veil from men's motives and actions. But for the trained reasoner to admit such intrusions into his own delicate and finely adjusted temperament was to introduce a distracting factor which might throw a doubt upon all his mental results. Grit in a sensitive instrument, or a crack in one of his own high-power lenses, would not be more disturbing than a strong emotion in a nature such as his. And yet there was but one woman to him, and that woman was the late Irene Adler, of dubious and questionable memory.

Watson

'If a gentleman walks into my rooms smelling of iodoform, with a black mark of nitrate of silver upon his right forefinger, and a bulge on the right side of his top-hat to show where he has secreted his stethoscope, I must be dull, indeed, if I do not pronounce him to be an active member of the medical profession.'

Holmes (of Watson)

'You see, but you do not observe. The distinction is clear. For example, you have frequently seen the steps which lead up from the hall to this room.'
  'Frequently.'
  'How often?'
  'Well, some hundreds of times.'
  'Then, how many are there?'
  'How many? I don't know.'
  'Quite so! You have not observed. And yet you have seen. That is just my point. Now, I know that there are seventeen steps, because I have both seen and observed.'

Holmes and Watson

'I have no data yet. It is a capital mistake to theorize before one has data. Insensibly, one begins to twist facts to suit theories, instead of theories to suit facts.'

Holmes

For many years he had adopted a system of docketing all paragraphs concerning men and things, so that it was difficult to name a subject or a person on which he could not at once furnish information. In this case I found her biography sandwiched in between that of a Hebrew rabbi and that of a staff-commander who had written a monograph upon the deep-sea fishes.

Watson

'There is a wonderful sympathy and freemasonry among horsy men. Be one of them, and you will know all that there is to know.'

Holmes

He disappeared into his bedroom and returned in a few minutes in the character of an amiable and simple-minded Nonconformist clergyman. His broad black hat, his baggy trousers, his white tie, his sympathetic smile, and general look of peering and benevolent curiosity were such as Mr John Hare alone could have equalled. It was not merely that Holmes changed his costume. His expression, his manner, his very soul seemed to vary with every fresh part that he assumed. The stage lost a fine actor, even as science lost an acute reasoner, when he became a specialist in crime.

Watson

'Women are naturally secretive, and they like to do their own secreting.'

Holmes

'When a woman thinks that her house is on fire, her instinct is at once to rush to the thing which she values most. It is a perfectly overpowering impulse, and I have more than once taken advantage of it... A married woman grabs at her baby; an unmarried one reaches for her jewel-box.'

Holmes

'You know, I have been trained as an actress myself. Male costume is nothing new to me. I often take advantage of the freedom which it gives.'

Irene Adler (Note to Holmes)

He used to make merry over the cleverness of women, but I have not heard him do it of late. And when he speaks of Irene Adler, or when he refers to her photograph, it is always under the honourable title of *the* woman.

Watson

The Red-Headed League (*Strand*, Aug 1891)

His pawnbroking business being slack, old Jabez Wilson had been glad to find an assistant so eager to learn the trade that he would take half-wages. Vincent Spaulding had shown his initiative to be even more thoroughgoing by finding his employer a lucrative way to cash in on his red hair. To benefit from an eccentric American's bequest, Wilson need only sit in the Red-Headed League's office, four hours a day, copying out the *Encyclopaedia Britannica* for £1 an hour.

After eight weeks, and not yet up to the letter B, he has found the office shut, the League dissolved, and its administrator, Duncan Ross, vanished. The meaning of it all is a three-pipe problem for Holmes; but the location of the pawnshop, and the state of Spaulding's trouser-knees, convinces him that there is 'a considerable crime in contemplation'.

'I know, my dear Watson, that you share my love of all that is bizarre and outside the conventions and humdrum routine of everyday life. You have shown your relish for it by the enthusiasm which has prompted you to chronicle, and, if you will excuse my saying so, somewhat to embellish so many of my own little adventures.'

Holmes

'For strange effects and extraordinary combinations we must go to life itself, which is always far more daring than any effort of the imagination.'

Holmes

'You have heard me remark that the strangest and most unique things are very often connected not with the larger but with the smaller crimes, and occasionally, indeed, where there is room for doubt whether any positive crime has been committed.'

Holmes

'I have made a small study of tattoo marks and have even contributed to the literature of the subject.'

Holmes

'As a rule, the more bizarre a thing is the less mysterious it proves to be. It is your commonplace, featureless crimes which are really puzzling, just as a commonplace face is the most difficult to identify.'

Holmes

'It is quite a three pipe problem, and I beg that you won't speak to me for fifty minutes.' He curled himself up in his chair, with his thin knees drawn up to his hawk-like nose, and there he sat with his eyes closed and his black clay pipe thrusting out like the bill of some strange bird. I had come to the conclusion that he had dropped asleep, and indeed was nodding myself, when he suddenly sprang out of his chair with the gesture of a man who has made up his mind and put his pipe down upon the mantelpiece.

'Sarasate plays at the St James's Hall this afternoon,' he remarked. 'What do you think, Watson? Could your patients spare you for a few hours?'

'I have nothing to do to-day. My practice is never very absorbing.'

'Then put on your hat and come. I am going through the City first, and we can have some lunch on the way. I observe that there is a good deal of German music on the programme, which is rather more to my taste than Italian or French. It is introspective, and I want to introspect. Come along!'

Holmes and Watson

My friend was an enthusiastic musician, being himself not only a very capable performer but a composer of no ordinary merit. All the afternoon he sat in the stalls wrapped in the most perfect happiness, gently waving his long, thin fingers in time to the music, while his gently smiling face and his languid, dreamy eyes were as unlike those of Holmes, the sleuth-hound, Holmes the relentless, keen-witted, ready-handed criminal agent as it was possible to conceive. In his singular character the dual nature alternately asserted itself, and his extreme exactness and astuteness represented, as I have often thought, the reaction against the poetic and contemplative mood which occasionally predominated in him. The swing of his nature took him from extreme languor to devouring energy; and as I knew well, he was never so truly formidable as when, for days on end, he had been lounging in his armchair amid his improvisations and his black-letter editions. Then it was that the lust of the chase would suddenly come upon him, and that his brilliant reasoning power would rise to the level of intuition, until those who were unacquainted with his methods would look askance at him as on a man whose knowledge was not that of other mortals. When I saw him that afternoon so enwrapped in the music at St James's Hall I felt that an evil time might be coming upon those whom he had set himself to hunt down.

Watson

'You may place considerable confidence in Mr Holmes, sir. He has his own little methods, which are, if he won't mind my saying so, just a little too theoretical and fantastic, but he has the makings of a detective in him.'

Insp Peter Jones

'My life is spent in one long effort to escape from the commonplaces of existence. These little problems help me to do so.'

Holmes

A Case of Identity (*Strand*, Sep 1891)

The heady ambience of the gasfitters' ball, which she attended against her stepfather's command, had excited the somewhat vacuous-looking Miss Mary Sutherland to reciprocate Mr Hosmer Angel's interest in her. Although shy and retiring of disposition, and faint of voice ('He'd had the quinsy and swollen glands when he was young, he told me'), he had proceeded to court her precipitately. She never learned his address, but agreed to marry him without delay. Came the morning, she found herself left waiting at the church.

It is almost enough to Holmes to know that she has a private income from a legacy. She also takes in typewriting work, and he has observed that 'a typewriter has really quite as much individuality as a man's handwriting.' An interview with her stepfather, Mr Windibank, is all he needs to settle the whereabouts of the flown Angel.

'My dear fellow,' said Sherlock Holmes as we sat on either side of the fire in his lodgings at Baker Street, 'life is infinitely stranger than anything which the mind of man could invent. We would not dare to conceive the things which are really mere commonplaces of existence. If we could fly out of that window hand in hand, hover over this great city, gently remove the roofs, and peep in at the queer things which are going on, the strange coincidences, the plannings, the cross-purposes, the wonderful chains of events, working through generations, and leading to the most *outré* results, it would make all fiction with its conventionalities and foreseen conclusions most stale and unprofitable.'

'And yet I am not convinced of it,' I answered. 'The cases which come to light in the papers are, as a rule, bald enough, and vulgar enough. We have in our police reports realism pushed to its extreme limits, and yet the result is, it must be confessed, neither fascinating nor artistic.'

'A certain selection and discretion must be used in producing a realistic effect,' remarked Holmes. 'This is wanting in the police report, where more stress is laid, perhaps, upon the platitudes of the magistrate than upon the details, which to an observer contain the vital essence of the whole matter. Depend upon it, there is nothing so unnatural as the commonplace.'

Holmes and Watson

'I have found that it is usually in unimportant matters that there is a field for the observation, and for the quick analysis of cause and effect which gives the charm to an investigation. The larger crimes are apt to be the simpler, for the bigger the crime the more obvious, as a rule, is the motive.'

Holmes

'Oscillation upon the pavement always means an *affaire de coeur*. She would like advice, but is not sure that the matter is not too delicate for communication. And yet even here we may discriminate. When a woman has been seriously wronged by a man she no longer oscillates, and the usual symptom is a broken bell wire. Here we may take it that there is a love matter, but that the maiden is not so much angry as perplexed, or grieved.'

Holmes

'It is my business to know things. Perhaps I have trained myself to see what others overlook.'

Holmes

'It has long been an axiom of mine that the little things are infinitely the most important.'

Holmes

'I can never bring you to realize the importance of sleeves, the suggestiveness of thumb-nails, or the great issues that may hang from a boot-lace. Now, what did you gather from that woman's appearance?'

Holmes

''Pon my word, Watson, you are coming along wonderfully. You have really done very well indeed. It is true that you have missed everything of importance, but you have hit upon the method, and you have a quick eye for colour. Never trust to general impressions, my boy, but concentrate yourself upon details. My first glance is always at a woman's sleeve. In a man it is perhaps better first to take the knee of the trouser.'

Holmes

'I think of writing another little monograph some of these days on the typewriter and its relation to crime. It is a subject to which I have devoted some little attention.'

Holmes

'You may remember the old Persian saying, "There is danger for him who taketh the tiger cub, and danger also for whoso snatches a delusion from a woman." There is as much sense in Hafiz as in Horace, and as much knowledge of the world.'

Holmes

The Boscombe Valley Mystery (*Strand*, Oct 1891)

The circumstantial evidence points to young James McCarthy's having murdered his father, Charles, in a wood near their Herefordshire farmhouse. Those who believe him incapable of it have invoked the expertise of Scotland Yard, in the person of Insp Lestrade, who, 'being a little puzzled', has referred the case to Holmes.

There is a history of quarrels between father and son, some arising from James's odd reluctance to marry his close friend from childhood, Alice Turner, although to Watson she is 'one of the most lovely young women that I have ever seen in my life.' She is also the daughter of the late Charles McCarthy's neighbour and old crony from Australian days, John Turner.

A bigamous Bristol barmaid proves to be the impediment to the marriage, leaving Holmes no further problem in ascribing the murder to 'a tall man, left-handed, limps with the right leg, wears thick-soled shooting-boots and a grey cloak, smokes Indian cigars, uses a cigar-holder, and carries a blunt penknife in his pocket.'

My experience of camp life in Afghanistan had at least had the effect of making me a prompt and ready traveller. My wants were few and simple.

Watson

'Singularity is almost invariably a clue. The more featureless and common-place a crime is, the more difficult it is to bring it home.'

Holmes

'Circumstantial evidence is a very tricky thing. It may seem to point very straight to one thing, but if you shift your own point of view a little, you may find it pointing in an equally uncompromising manner to something entirely different.'

Holmes

'I have a caseful of cigarettes here which need smoking, and the sofa is very much superior to the usual country hotel abomination.'

Holmes

Sherlock Holmes was transformed when he was hot upon such a scent as this. Men who had only known the quiet thinker and logician of Baker Street would have failed to recognize him. His face flushed and darkened. His brows were drawn into two hard black lines, while his eyes shone out from beneath them with a steely glitter. His face was bent downward, his shoulders bowed, his lips compressed, and the veins stood out like whipcord in his long, sinewy neck. His nostrils seemed to dilate with a purely animal lust for the chase, and his mind was so absolutely concentrated upon the matter before him that a question or remark fell unheeded upon his ears, or, at the most, only provoked a quick, impatient snarl in reply.

Watson

'You know my method. It is founded upon the observation of trifles.'

Holmes

'God help us! Why does fate play such tricks with poor, helpless worms? I never hear of such a case as this that I do not think of Baxter's words, and say, "There, but for the grace of God, goes Sherlock Holmes."'

Holmes

The Five Orange Pips (*Strand*, Nov 1891)

Even Sherlock Holmes is fallible. He has worked out that the murders of Colonel Elias Openshaw and his brother Joseph must have been done by more than one man, but are linked; each had received before-hand an envelope containing five orange pips. The sender, identified only by the initials K.K.K., is probably, therefore, an organization; and since Col Openshaw had been involved in the politics of the Southern States of the USA, that sinister society of ex-Confederates, the Ku Klux Klan, is plainly indicated.

Now the same fearful warning has reached the Colonel's young nephew, John Openshaw. Holmes, having calculated the time element involved, should have known better than to send this anxious client home to Sussex to await developments. The outcome of his blunder is wounding to his pride and stirs him to seek personal vengeance, using orange pips as a portent.

It was in the latter days of September, and the equinoctial gales had set in with exceptional violence. All day the wind had screamed and the rain had beaten against the windows, so that even here in the heart of great, hand-made London we were forced to raise our minds for the instant from the routine of life, and to recognize the presence of those great elemental forces which shriek at mankind through the bars of his civilization, like untamed beasts in a cage. As evening drew in, the storm grew higher and louder, and the wind cried and sobbed like a child in the chimney. Sherlock Holmes sat moodily at one side of the fireplace cross-indexing his records of crime, while I at the other was deep in one of Clark Russell's fine sea-stories until the howl of the gale from without seemed to blend with the text, and the splash of the rain to lengthen out into the long swash of the sea waves.

Watson

'The ideal reasoner would, when he had once been shown a single fact in all its bearings, deduce from it not only all the chain of events which led up to it but also all the results which would follow from it. As Cuvier could correctly describe a whole animal by the contemplation of a single bone, so the observer who has thoroughly understood one link in a series of incidents should be able to accurately state all the other ones, both before and after. We have not yet grasped the results which the reason alone can attain to. Problems may be solved in the study which have baffled all those who have sought a solution by the aid of the senses. To carry the art, however, to its highest pitch, it is necessary that the reasoner should be able to utilize all the facts which have come to his knowledge ; and this in itself implies, as you will readily see, a possession of all knowledge, which, even in these days of free education and encyclopaedias, is a somewhat rare accomplishment. It is not so impossible, however, that a man should possess all knowledge which is likely to be useful to him in his work, and this I have endeavoured in my case to do . . . A man should keep his little brain-attic stocked with all the furniture that he is likely to use, and the rest he can put away in the lumber-room of his library, where he can get it if he wants it.'

Holmes

'Hand me over my violin and let us try to forget for half an hour the miserable weather and the still more miserable ways of our fellowmen.'

Holmes

It was late in the evening before I returned to Baker Street. Sherlock Holmes had not come back yet. It was nearly ten o'clock before he entered, looking pale and worn. He walked up to the sideboard, and tearing a piece from the loaf he devoured it voraciously, washing it down with a long draught of water.
'You are hungry,' I remarked.

Watson

The Man with the Twisted Lip (*Strand*, Dec 1891)

Hugh Boone is a familiar and repellent figure in the City of London, where he sells matches in Threadneedle Street. His scarred face, his limp, and his ready repartee ensure that by day's end his greasy cap on the pavement beside him is well filled with coin of the realm. He lodges above a dockland opium den, the Bar of Gold, Upper Swandam Lane; and it is in passing by there that respectable Mrs Neville St Clair fancies she glimpses her missing businessman husband at a window.

The police find traces of him, indeed. When St Clair's coat, washed up on a mud-bank, is found to be ballasted with 421 pennies and 70 halfpennies there is no hesitation about arresting Hugh Boone on suspicion of having made away with him. After taking Watson down to Lee, in Kent, to interview the dainty Mrs St Clair, Holmes sits up smoking all night, and penetrates a bizarre deception.

It was difficult to refuse any of Sherlock Holmes's requests, for they were always so exceedingly definite, and put forward with such a quiet air of mastery.

Watson

'Oh, a trusty comrade is always of use, and a chronicler still more so.'

Holmes

'You have a grand gift of silence, Watson. It makes you quite invaluable as a companion.'

Holmes

'It is, of course, a trifle, but there is nothing so important as trifles.'

Holmes

'I have seen too much not to know that the impression of a woman may be more valuable than the conclusion of an analytical reasoner.'

Holmes

A large and comfortable double-bedded room had been placed at our disposal, and I was quickly between the sheets, for I was weary after my night of adventure. Sherlock Holmes was a man, however, who, when he had an unsolved problem upon his mind, would go for days, and even for a week, without rest, turning it over, rearranging his facts, looking at it from every point of view until he had either fathomed it or convinced himself that his data were insufficient. It was soon evident to me that he was preparing for an all-night sitting. He took off his coat and waistcoat, put on a large blue dressing-gown, and then wandered about the room collecting pillows from his bed and cushions from the sofa and armchairs. With these he constructed a sort of Eastern divan, upon which he perched himself cross-legged, with an ounce of shag tobacco and a box of matches laid out in front of him. In the dim light of the lamp I saw him sitting there, an old briar pipe between his lips, his eyes fixed vacantly upon the corner of the ceiling, the blue smoke curling up from him, silent, motionless, with the light shining upon his strong-set aquiline features. So he sat as I dropped off to sleep, and so he sat when a sudden ejaculation caused me to wake up, and I found the summer sun shining into the apartment. The pipe was still between his lips, the smoke still curled upward, and the room was full of a dense tobacco haze, but nothing remained of the heap of shag which I had seen upon the previous night.

Watson

'I am sure, Mr Holmes, that we are very much indebted to you for having cleared the matter up. I wish I knew how you reach your results.'

'I reached this one,' said my friend, 'by sitting upon five pillows and consuming an ounce of shag.'

Insp Bradstreet and Holmes

The Adventure of The Blue Carbuncle *(Strand,* Jan 1892)

In seasonal high spirits, Holmes challenges Watson to deduce a man's identity from his shabby top-hat. Watson cannot, but Holmes can, and its owner is easily summoned to 221B. The Christmas goose which he had also mislaid, when jostled by Tottenham Court Road loungers, had needed prompt cooking, so Holmes had given it to its and the hat's finder, Peterson, a commissionaire acquaintance.

Peterson's wife has found inside the goose a jewel it had evidently swallowed. Holmes recognizes the Countess of Morcar's missing blue carbuncle, for whose theft from her hotel room a plumber named Horner is in custody.

By tracing the fowl's progress, through the goose club from which Baker had obtained it to the Covent Garden market stall of its retailer, Breckinridge, Holmes ascertains its supplier; but he and Watson are saved a trip to the Brixton Road by the intervention of one John Ryder, whose fancy for geese is intense but circumscribed.

'No, no. No crime,' said Sherlock Holmes, laughing. 'Only one of those whimsical little incidents which will happen when you have four million human beings all jostling each other within the space of a few square miles. Amid the action and reaction of so dense a swarm of humanity, every possible combination of events may be expected to take place, and many a little problem will be presented which may be striking and bizarre without being criminal.'

Holmes

'Here you are, Peterson, run down to the advertising agency and have this put in the evening papers.'

'In which, sir?'

'Oh, in the *Globe, Star, Pall Mall, St James's, Evening News, Standard, Echo,* and any others that occur to you.'

Holmes

'It's a bonny thing. Just see how it glints and sparkles. Of course it is a nucleus and focus of crime. Every good stone is. They are the devil's pet baits. In the larger and older jewels every facet may stand for a bloody deed.'

Holmes

'My name is Sherlock Holmes. It is my business to know what other people don't know.'

Holmes

'I am not retained by the police to supply their deficiencies.'

Holmes

'I suppose that I am commuting a felony, but it is just possible that I am saving a soul. This fellow will not go wrong again; he is too terribly frightened. Send him to jail now, and you make him a jail-bird for life. Besides, it is the season of forgiveness.'

Holmes

The Adventure of The Speckled Band (*Strand*, Feb 1892)

Watson can recall no case with more singular features than that associated with the sole survivor of the ancient Surrey family, the Roylotts of Stoke Moran. Decades of dissipation and waste have reduced the once vast estates to the ancestral house near Leatherhead, and the family to Dr Grimesby Roylott, a bully of violent temper and strength. It is his terrified stepdaughter, Helen Stoner, who comes to tell Holmes of her fear for her life, now that she has ventured to announce her engagement. Her sister Julia had died in mystery and terror on her wedding eve, two years ago. Manifestations which had preceded that death, such as an eerie whistling and a clang of metal, have lately resumed.

Undeterred by a visit and poker-bending demonstration from Dr Roylott, Holmes and Watson install themselves by night in Miss Stoner's room, which proves to incorporate some odd fittings. 'How shall I ever forget that dreadful vigil?' Watson reminisces. It would have been worse still for him if Holmes had told him in advance what he knew was going to happen.

Working as he did rather for the love of his art than for the acquirement of wealth, he refused to associate himself with any investigation which did not tend towards the unusual, and even fantastic.

Watson

'My name is Sherlock Holmes. This is my intimate friend and associate, Dr Watson, before whom you can speak as freely as before myself.'

Holmes

'You have come in by train this morning, I see.'

'You know me, then?'

'No, but I observe the second half of a return ticket in the palm of your left glove. You must have started early, and yet you had a good drive in a dog-cart, along heavy roads, before you reached the station.'

The lady gave a violent start and stared in bewilderment at my companion.

'There is no mystery, my dear madam,' said he, smiling. 'The left arm of your jacket is spattered with mud in no less than seven places. The marks are

(Above) The first meeting of Sherlock Holmes
and Dr Watson. Their introduction by
Stamford, illustrated by George Hutchinson.

A Study in Scarlet

The first illustration of Sherlock Holmes.
Frontispiece by D. H. Friston to the first
edition of *A Study in Scarlet*: 1887.

'Then he stood before the fire.'

A Scandal in Bohemia

'Goodnight, Mr Sherlock Holmes.'

A Scandal in Bohemia

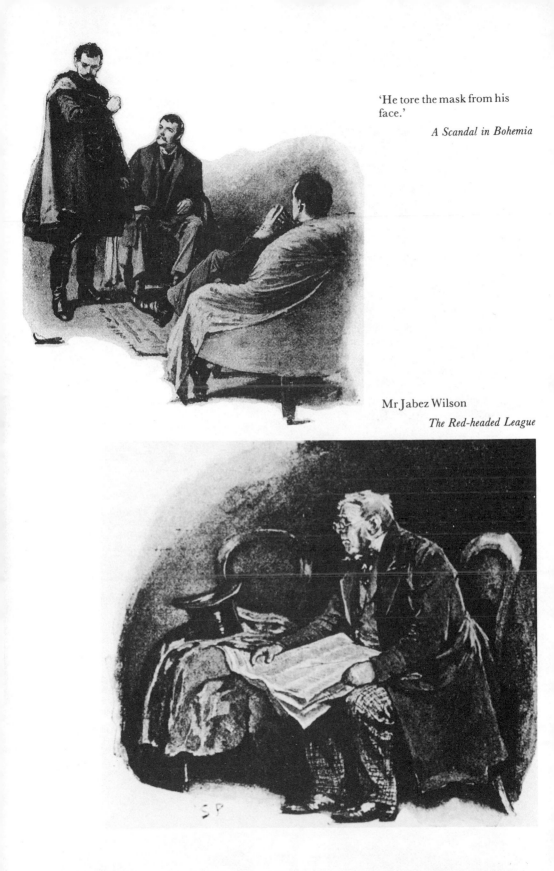

'He tore the mask from his face.'

A Scandal in Bohemia

Mr Jabez Wilson

The Red-headed League

'He is a professional beggar.'

The Man with the Twisted Lip

'The pipe was still between his lips.'

The Man with the Twisted Lip

'"Have mercy!" he shrieked.'

The Blue Carbuncle

(Above) 'Holmes lashed furiously.'

The Speckled Band

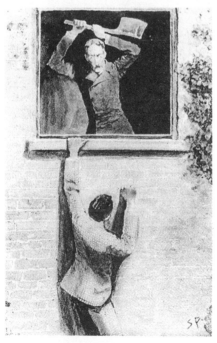

"He cut at me."'

The Engineer's Thumb

Lord Robert St Simon

The Noble Bachelor

'I clapped a pistol to his head.'

The Beryl Coronet

'"You villain!" said he. "Where's your daughter?"'

The Copper Beeches

perfectly fresh. There is no vehicle save a dog-cart which throws up mud in that way, and then only when you sit on the left-hand side of the driver.'

Holmes and Helen Stoner

'As to reward, my profession is its own reward; but you are at liberty to defray whatever expenses I may be put to, at the time which suits you best.'   *Holmes*

'I should be very much obliged if you would slip your revolver into your pocket. An Eley's No 2 is an excellent argument with gentlemen who can twist steel pokers into knots.'

Holmes

'Ah, me! it's a wicked world, and when a clever man turns his brains to crime it is the worst of all.'

Holmes

'When a doctor does go wrong he is the first of criminals. He has nerve and he has knowledge. Palmer and Pritchard were among the heads of their profession.'

Holmes

The Adventure of The Engineer's Thumb
(*Strand*, Mar 1892)

It is all very well for Holmes to laugh and tell Victor Hatherley that he can dine out on the experience for the rest of his life. The young hydraulic engineer has not only been cheated of a big consultation fee, but has been deprived of one of his thumbs, requiring Watson's standard treatment of bandages, brandy, and even, on this occasion, breakfast.

He had been engaged to repair a fuller's earth press at the premises of Colonel Lysander Stark, a few miles from Reading, Berkshire. Having noted the machine to be one quite unsuited to that purpose, Hatherley had asked incautiously the real nature of its use. The response was a demonstration of its working, with himself as the material about to be compressed. Thanks to a timely girl, named Elise, and some eccentric features of house construction, he has survived, albeit lacking a digit, to help Holmes and the police find the location of, and reason for, his ordeal.

Watson records that this is one of only two cases which he himself ever brought to Holmes's notice. (The other, concerning 'Colonel Warburton's madness', does not figure in his published chronicles.) His seemingly callous eagerness to whisk his patient round to Baker Street perhaps conceals his tardy realization that Hatherley should have been dead already from loss of blood and might not have long left in which to tell his story. That, at any rate, is the charitable view of his lackadaisical way of ministering to him.

'And now, Doctor, perhaps you would kindly attend to my thumb, or rather to the place where my thumb used to be.'

Victor Hatherley

Sherlock Holmes was, as I expected, lounging about his sitting-room in his dressing-gown, reading the agony column of *The Times* and smoking his before-breakfast pipe, which was composed of all the plugs and dottles left from his smokes of the day before, all carefully dried and collected on the corner of the mantelpiece.

Watson

'Well,' said our engineer ruefully as we took our seats to return once more to London, 'it has been a pretty business for me! I have lost my thumb and I have lost a fifty-guinea fee, and what have I gained?'

'Experience,' said Holmes, laughing. 'Indirectly it may be of value, you know; you have only to put it into words to gain the reputation of being excellent company for the remainder of your existence.'

Victor Hatherley and Holmes

The Adventure of The Noble Bachelor (*Strand*, Apr 1892)

There have been countless marriage-scandals to eclipse the Lord St Simon one, but the gossip columnist in Watson can reveal details which have never yet been made public. He himself had been approaching matrimony for the first time when it happened, in 1886, so the circumstances impressed themselves deeply on him.

It is wet autumn, and Watson's wound is throbbing 'in one of my limbs', when Lord St Simon comes to consult Holmes about untoward happenings on his wedding day. A female gate-crasher had had to be ejected from the wedding breakfast. Soon afterwards his American bride sneaked off without a word, subsequently to be spotted strolling in Hyde Park with the interloper, Flora Miller, a former danseuse of long and intimate acquaintance with his lordship. When, later still, the wedding dress and accessories were found floating in the Serpentine, with no trace of their wearer, it had been natural to Insp Lestrade to arrest the ex-mistress on suspicion of jealous murder.

Holmes has known better all along. He has deduced another man, with a stronger claim than St Simon's, and American, to boot. He persuades a Mr and Mrs Francis Hay Moulton to come and explain, then stay for a reconciliatory supper, which, however, the noble bachelor thinks it would be asking a little too much of him to share.

I had remained indoors all day, for the weather had taken a sudden turn to rain, with high autumnal winds, and the Jezail bullet which I had brought back in one of my limbs as a relic of my Afghan campaign throbbed with dull persistence. With my body in one easy-chair and my legs upon another, I had surrounded myself with a cloud of newspapers until at last, saturated with the news of the day, I tossed them all aside and lay listless.

Watson

'Yes, my correspondence has certainly the charm of variety, and the humbler are usually the more interesting. This looks like one of those unwelcome summonses which call upon a man either to be bored or to lie.'

Holmes

'I assure you, Watson, without affectation, that the status of my client is a matter of less moment to me than the interest of his case.'

Holmes

'I read nothing except the criminal news and the agony column. The latter is always instructive.'

Holmes

'American slang is very expressive sometimes.'

Holmes

'Circumstantial evidence is occasionally very convincing, as when you find a trout in the milk, to quote Thoreau's example.'

Holmes

It was after five o'clock when Sherlock Holmes left me, but I had no time to be lonely, for within an hour there arrived a confectioner's man with a very large flat box. This he unpacked with the help of a youth whom he had brought with him, and presently, to my very great astonishment, a quite epicurean little cold supper began to be laid out upon our humble lodging-house mahogany. There were a couple of brace of cold woodcock, a pheasant, a pâté-de-foie-gras pie, with a group of ancient and cobwebby bottles. Having laid out all these luxuries, my two visitors vanished away, like the genii of the Arabian nights, with no explanation save that the things had been paid for and were ordered to this address.

Watson

'Then I trust that you at least will honour me with your company,' said Sherlock Holmes. 'It is always a joy to meet an American, Mr Moulton, for I am one of those who believe that the folly of a monarch and the blundering of a minister in far-gone years will not prevent our children from being some day citizens of the same world-wide country under a flag which shall be a quartering of the Union Jack with the Stars and Stripes.'

Holmes

'Ah, Watson,' said Holmes, smiling, 'perhaps you would not be very gracious either, if after all the trouble of wooing and wedding, you found yourself deprived in an instant of wife and fortune. I think that we may judge Lord St Simon very mercifully and thank our stars that we are never likely to find ourselves in the same position. Draw your chair up and hand me my violin, for the only problem we have still to solve is how to while away these bleak autumnal evenings.'

Holmes

The Adventure of The Beryl Coronet (*Strand*, May 1892)

The unknown visitor to 221B, shortly before Christmas, 1890, has scarcely subsided into a chair before he is up again and beating his head against a wall.

'You have come to me to tell your story, have you not?' Holmes deduces.

Alexander Holder, a leading banker, has been entrusted with the safekeeping of one of the empire's most precious public possessions as security for a short-term loan of £50,000 to a customer whose name is 'a household word all over the earth'. Rather than rely on the strong-room, Holder took the bejewelled treasure home. In the night he found his son, Arthur, whom he had berated that evening for his club debts, seemingly trying to break up the coronet with his hands. He dutifully handed over his son to the police; but three of the jewels are still missing and there will be scandal if they are not found.

Holmes investigates on the spot and is sure that the boy is innocent, yet knows more than he will say. Applying his theory of elimination, Holmes turns his attention to the other member of the family, Holder's niece Mary, whose attributed 'quick insight into character' might prove less proficient than her uncle thinks.

'You owe a very humble apology to that noble lad, your son, who has carried himself in this matter as I should be proud to see my own son do, should I ever chance to have one.'

Holmes to Holder

The Adventures of the Copper Beeches (*Strand*, June 1892)

Mr Jephro Rucastle, of The Copper Beeches, near Winchester, Hampshire, could surely have been one of the greatest comedians of all time. His repertoire of funny stories is so vast, and his manner of telling them so inimitably infectious, that he can keep the respectable Miss Violet Hunter convulsed with laughter for an hour at a time, day upon day; yet the only other member of his audience, his wife (even allowing for her having heard the stories before), never smiles throughout.

These strange performances are not the sole reason for Miss Hunter's confiding in Holmes. The unconventional conditions of her well-paid engagement as governess to the Rucastles' sadistic six-year-old son include the sacrifice of her long chestnut hair and her consent to wear any dress required of her and sit precisely where she is told.

Hers is not the situation Holmes might approve for any sister of his, he remarks. As he and Watson hasten to Hampshire, where they will learn disturbing particulars of locked rooms, a drunken groom, a hunger-crazed mastiff, a missing girl, and a loiterer with intent, he observes further that the countryside's springtime face can prove to be a deceptive mask.

'To the man who loves art for its own sake,' remarked Sherlock Holmes, tossing aside the advertisement sheet of the *Daily Telegraph*, 'it is frequently in its least important and lowliest manifestations that the keenest pleasure is to be derived. It is pleasant to me to observe, Watson, that you have so far grasped this truth that in these little records of our cases which you have been good enough to draw up, and I am bound to say, occasionally to embellish, you have given prominence not so much to the many *causes célèbres* and sensational trials in which I have figured but rather to those incidents which may have been trivial in themselves, but which have given room for those faculties of deduction and of logical synthesis which I have made my special province.'

'And yet,' said I, smiling, 'I cannot quite hold myself absolved from the charge of sensationalism which has been urged against my records.'

'You have erred, perhaps,' he observed, taking up a glowing cinder with the tongs and lighting with it the long cherry-wood pipe which was wont to replace his clay when he was in a disputatious rather than a meditative mood – 'you have erred perhaps in attempting to put colour and life into each of your statements instead of confining yourself to the task of placing upon record that severe reasoning from cause to effect which is really the only notable feature about the thing.'

'It seems to me that I have done you full justice in the matter,' I remarked with some coldness, for I was repelled by the egotism which I had more than once observed to be a strong factor in my friend's singular character.

'No, it is not selfishness or conceit,' said he, answering, as was his wont, my thoughts rather than my words, 'If I claim full justice for my art, it is because it is an impersonal thing – a thing beyond myself. Crime is common. Logic is rare. Therefore it is upon the logic rather than upon the crime that you should dwell. You have degraded what should have been a course of lectures into a series of tales.'

Holmes and Watson

It was a cold morning of the early spring, and we sat after breakfast on either side of a cheery fire in the old room at Baker Street. A thick fog rolled down between the lines of dun-coloured houses, and the opposing windows loomed like dark, shapeless blurs through the heavy yellow wreaths. Our gas was lit and shone on the white cloth and glimmer of china and metal, for the table had not been cleared yet.

Watson

'At the same time,' he remarked after a pause, during which he had sat puffing at his long pipe and gazing down into the fire, 'you can hardly be open to a charge of sensationalism, for out of these cases which you have been so kind as to interest yourself in, a fair proportion do not treat of crime, in its legal sense, at all . . . But in avoiding the sensational, I fear that you may have bordered on the trivial.'

'That may have been so,' I answered, 'but the methods I hold to have been novel and of interest.'

'Pshaw, my dear fellow, what do the public, the great unobservant public, who could hardly tell a weaver by his tooth or a compositor by his left thumb, care about the finer shades of analysis and deduction! But, indeed, if you are trivial, I cannot blame you, for the days of the great cases are past. Man, or at least criminal man, has lost all enterprise and originality.'

Holmes and Watson

By eleven o'clock the next day we were well upon our way to the old English capital. Holmes had been buried in the morning papers all the way down, but after we had passed the Hampshire border he threw them down and began to admire the scenery. It was an ideal spring day, a light blue sky, flecked with little fleecy white clouds drifting across from west to east. The sun was shining very brightly, and yet there was an exhilarating nip in the air, which set an edge to a man's energy. All over the countryside, away to the rolling hills around Aldershot, the little red and gray roofs of the farm-steadings peeped out from amid the light green of the new foliage.

'Are they not fresh and beautiful?' I cried with all the enthusiasm of a man fresh from the fogs of Baker Street.

But Holmes shook his head gravely.

'Do you know, Watson,' said he, 'that it is one of the curses of a mind with a turn like mine that I must look at everything with reference to my own special subject. You look at these scattered houses, and you are impressed by their beauty. I look at them, and the only thought which comes to me is a feeling of their isolation and of the impunity with which crime may be committed there.'

'Good heavens!' I cried. 'Who would associate crime with these dear old homesteads?'

'They always fill me with a certain horror. It is my belief, Watson, founded upon my experience, that the lowest and vilest alleys in London do not present a more dreadful record of sin than does the smiling and beautiful countryside.'

'You horrify me!'

'But the reason is very obvious. The pressure of public opinion can do in the town what the law cannot accomplish. There is no lane so vile that the scream of a tortured child, or the thud of a drunkard's blow, does not beget sympathy and indignation among the neighbours, and then the whole machinery of justice is ever so close that a word of complaint can set it going, and there is but a step between the crime and the dock. But look at these lonely houses, each in its own fields, filled for the most part with poor ignorant folk who know little of the law. Think of the deeds of hellish cruelty, the hidden wickedness which may go on, year in, year out, in such places, and none the wiser. Had this lady who appeals to us for help gone to live in Winchester, I should never have had a fear for her. It is the five miles of country which makes the danger.'

Holmes and Watson

'My dear Watson, you as a medical man are continually gaining light as to the tendencies of a child by the study of the parents. Don't you see that the converse is equally valid. I have frequently gained my first real insight into the character of parents by studying their children. This child's disposition is abnormally cruel, merely for cruelty's sake, and whether he derives this from his smiling father, as I should suspect, or from his mother, it bodes evil for the poor girl who is in their power.'

Holmes

6

Mr Holmes and Dr Watson

Sherlock Holmes's place was taken over in the July 1892 *Strand* by Dick Donovan, author and first-person narrator of a short-lived series with the generic title *A Romance from a Detective's Casebook*. Readers who found these exotic tales comparatively poor stuff could take comfort from an editorial note appended to the first one. It assured them that the interval was temporary only; Holmes would be back in 'an early number. Meanwhile, there would appear in the next issue (August) an interview with Mr (*sic*) Conan Doyle, which would contain 'some particulars concerning Mr Sherlock Holmes'.

Greenhough Smith, now the editor, had begun chasing him for more stories as early as February that year. He wrote to his mother, 'Under pressure I offered to do a dozen for a thousand pounds, but I sincerely hope that they won't accept it now.' They did, of course. The best he could do to be free of Holmes for a time was to tell them they would have to wait.

These were not among the particulars which he discussed with his *Strand* interviewer, Harry How. If he let drop any hint of his impatience with Holmes it was off the record. In 'A Day with Conan Doyle', How reported instead :

> He is fearful of spoiling a character of which he is particularly fond, but he declares that already he has enough material to carry him through another series, and merrily assures me that he thought the opening story of the next series of 'Sherlock Holmes', to be published in this magazine, was of such an unsolvable character, that he had positively bet his wife a shilling that she would not guess the true solution of it until she got to the end of the chapter !

The interviewee had revealed something of his methods :

> Dr Doyle invariably conceives the end of his story first, and writes up to it. He gets the climax, and his art lies in the ingenious way in which he conceals it from his readers. A story – similar to those which have appeared in these pages – occupies about a week in writing, and the ideas have come at all manner of times – when out walking, cricketing,

tricycling, or playing tennis. He works between the hours of breakfast and lunch, and again in the evening from five to eight, writing some three thousand words a day. He receives many suggestions from the public. On the morning of my visit the particulars of a poisoning case had been sent to him from New Zealand, and the previous day a great packet of documents relating to a disputed will had been received from Bristol. But the suggestions are seldom practicable.

For Holmes's followers, the most enlightening feature of the interview was Doyle's identification of his model for the character. Many subsequent theories, persuasive, ingenious, and contrived, have been put forward in favour of other conscious and subconscious influences. They are outside this book's scope : to echo Holmes, 'The world is big enough for us. No ghosts need apply.' His creator's own account, given at the time when the subject was freshest in his memory, ought to be enough.

He showed the journalist portraits of Dr Joseph Bell, a member of the Medical Faculty of Edinburgh University when he had been a student there in the 1870s. He referred to him, unequivocally, as 'the man who suggested Sherlock Holmes to me.'

'I was clerk in Mr Bell's ward,' continued Dr Doyle. 'A clerk's duties are to note down all the patients to be seen, and muster them together. Often I would have seventy or eighty. When everything was ready, I would show them in to Mr Bell, who would have the students gathered round him. His intuitive powers were simply marvellous. Case No. 1. would step up.

'"I see," said Mr Bell, "you're suffering from drink. You even carry a flask in the inside breast pocket of your coat."

Another case would come forward.

'"Cobbler, I see." Then he would turn to the students, and point out to them that the inside of the knee of the man's trousers was worn. That was where the man had rested the lapstone – a peculiarity found only in cobblers.

'All this impressed me very much. He was continually before me – his sharp, piercing grey eyes, eagle nose, and striking features. There he would sit in his chair with fingers together – he was very dextrous with his hands – and just look at the man or woman before him. He was most kind and painstaking with the students – a real good friend – and when I took my degree and went to Africa the remarkable individuality and discriminating tact of my old master made a deep and lasting impression on me, though I had not the faintest idea that it would one day lead me to forsake medicine for story writing.'

Harry How wrote to Joseph Bell, asking for his comments, and used the reply at the end of his article.

Dear Sir, – You ask me about the kind of teaching to which Dr Conan Doyle has so kindly referred, when speaking of his ideal character, 'Sherlock Holmes'. Dr Conan Doyle has, by his imaginative genius, made a great deal out of very little, and his warm remembrance of one of his old teachers has coloured the picture. In teaching the treatment of disease and accident, all careful teachers have first to show the student how to recognise accurately the case. The recognition depends in great measure on the accurate and rapid appreciation of *small* points in which the diseased differs from the healthy state. In fact, the student must be taught to observe. To interest him in this kind of work we teachers find it useful to show the student how much a trained use of the observation can discover in ordinary matters such as the previous history, nationality, and occupation of a patient.

The patient, too, is likely to be impressed by your ability to cure him in the future if he sees you, at a glance, know much of his past. And the whole trick is much easier than it appears at first.

For instance, physiognomy helps you to nationality, accent to district, and, to an educated ear, almost to county. Nearly every handicraft writes its sign manual on the hands. The scars of the miner differ from those of the quarryman. The carpenter's callosities are not those of the mason. The shoemaker and the tailor are quite different.

The soldier and the sailor differ in gait, though last month I had to tell a man who said he was a soldier that he had been a sailor in his boyhood. The subject is endless : the tattoo marks on hand or arm will tell their own tale as to voyages ; the ornaments on the watch chain of the successful settler will tell you where he made his money. A New Zealand squatter will not wear a gold mohur, nor an engineer on an Indian railway a Maori stone. Carry the same idea of using one's senses accurately and constantly, and you will see that many a surgical case will bring his past history, national, social, and medical, into the consulting-room as he walks in. Dr Conan Doyle's genius and intense imagination has on this slender basis made his detective stories a distinctly new departure, but he owes much less than he thinks to yours truly,
JOSEPH BELL.

It sounds rather like a proud man's modest disclaimer. Joe Bell, as he was widely known, was not above boasting of the association, and sometimes sent his former pupil ideas for stories, though they were never written. The association evidently brought him some unwelcome attention, though. He told Mrs Jessie Saxby, who was preparing his biography, 'Why bother yourself about the cataract of drivel for which Conan Doyle is responsible? I am sure he never imagined that such a heap of rubbish would fall on my devoted head in consequence of his stories.'

He wrote to Doyle, 'You are yourself Sherlock Holmes.' It was true. Like most fictional characters, Holmes is a composite, but it was his creator, more than anyone, whom he reflected. They were unalike in appearance and many habits, but strikingly similar in a great many other respects, notably their highly developed ability to observe and deduce. Conan Doyle's son, Adrian, always maintained that Bell's exemplary influence on his father had been overrated. His diagnostic technique was not unique; it had been passed on to Bell by his own eminent teacher, Prof James Syme, and there were others using similar methods in medical practice. His father's gift, Adrian insisted, was a natural one, brought to light by his recollection of Bell's entertaining displays.

All the same, but for Joe Bell's example Sherlock Holmes might not have been given that flair for instant deduction which placed him at the head of his profession and has kept him there, impervious to all imitation and competition, for a century.

In *Memories and Adventures* Sir Arthur Conan Doyle answered another question of identity:

> I have often been asked whether I had myself the qualities which I depicted, or whether I was merely the Watson that I look. Of course, I am well aware that it is one thing to grapple with a practical problem and quite another thing when you are allowed to solve it under your own conditions. I have no delusions about that. At the same time a man cannot spin a character out of his own inner consciousness and make it really life-like unless he has some possibilities of that character within him – which is a dangerous admission for one who has drawn so many villains as I...
>
> (I) have several times solved problems by Holmes's methods after the police have been baffled. Yet I must admit that in ordinary life I am by no means observant, and that I have to throw myself into an artificial frame of mind before I can weigh evidence and anticipate the sequence of events.

Yet, Adrian Conan Doyle, in his little book *The True Conan Doyle*, recalled:

> In travelling through the capital cities of the world, it was one of my keenest enjoyments to accompany my father to any principal restaurant, and there to listen to his quiet speculations as to the characteristics, professions and other idiosyncracies, all quite hidden from my eyes, of our fellow diners. Sometimes we could not prove the correctness or otherwise of his findings as the particular subject might be unknown to the head-waiter; but whenever those concerned were known to the *maître d'hôtel*, the accuracy of my father's deduction was positively startling.

'Merely the Watson that I look' is unduly self-dismissive, as well as unfair to Watson. There is nothing *mere* about him that has not been suggested by screen portrayals of him as a bumbling dimwit. He is full of admirable qualities such as loyalty, courage, patriotism, imperviousness to pressure: what the psychiatrists would term mentally well adjusted, with a settled, happy viewpoint on life. Watson belongs in Hippocrates' phlegmatic category of personality, calm and imperturbable, and likely to stay so under any form of stress. Doyle tended more to the sanguine, and, when rubbed up the wrong way, choleric. His opinion of Watson is even inaccurate: he said that the poor fellow had not a gleam of humour, and never made a joke. It is a curious misjudgment.

The year 1892 saw Doyle expanding his range as a writer. He and J.M.Barrie had been at Edinburgh University at the same time, but hadn't become acquainted there (Doyle had also missed getting to know another great contemporary, R.L.Stevenson). Now they met at a literary dinner in London and became immediate friends. Barrie was in his period of transition from successful novelist – *A Window in Thrums*, 1889, *The Little Minister*, 1891 – to dramatist. He was trying to write the libretto of a light opera for Richard D'Oyly Carte to produce at the Savoy Theatre. It was giving him problems, and he invited Doyle to collaborate on it.

Doyle had tried his hand at dramatic writing with a three-act play based on the American scenes in *A Study in Scarlet*, featuring a Watson character but no Holmes. By the time he had thought of submitting it somewhere, with the title *Angels of Darkness*, the Holmes-Watson partnership had become immutable and the play was abandoned for ever.

The exercise of working with Barrie stimulated him to try again on his own account. He adapted his own short story *A Straggler of '15* into a one-act play, about a dying veteran of the Guards reliving his finest hours. He sent it to Henry Irving, who bought it willingly, as an ideal vehicle for himself. *A Story of Waterloo* (later, simply *Waterloo*), with Irving as Corporal Gregory Brewster, was presented late in 1894 at the Prince's Theatre, Bristol, and then in London at the Garrick, in a double bill with the ever-popular *The Bells*. It proved an instant success, which was more than could have been said of the light opera, *Jane Annie, or, The Good Conduct Prize*, which had failed at the Savoy in May, 1893.

For Christmas 1892 the *Strand* was able to give its readers a present which many would treasure above most others. The December issue carried the first of what had been announced as 'a new series of "The Adventures of Sherlock Holmes"', *Silver Blaze*.

The series of twelve stories ran in thirteen issues up to and including December, 1893, one of them, *The Naval Treaty*, spreading over two monthly numbers. Sidney Paget was again the illustrator.

When Newnes reissued the series in volume form, with Paget's illustrations, in 1894, it had the title *The Memoirs of Sherlock Holmes*. One story, *The Cardboard Box*, had been omitted as not 'healthful' enough for family reading: it involves sexual infidelity in marriage, leading to murder and mutilation. Its early scene in which Holmes deduces Watson's emotions from his friend's glances at his framed portrait of General Gordon, the hero of Khartoum, and his unframed one of the Rev Henry Ward Beecher, the disgraced American evangelist, seemed too good to drop, however, so it had been transferred to the opening of another tale, *The Resident Patient*.

The American volume edition of *The Memoirs of Sherlock Holmes*, with illustrations by William H. Hyde and Sidney Paget, was published in the same year, 1894, by Harper & Bros. It included *The Cardboard Box*, the only edition of the *Memoirs* to do so. The story made its subsequent reappearance in the 1917 collection, *His Last Bow*. The American omnibus edition of all the Sherlock Holmes stories bewilderingly retains the same opening scene in both *The Resident Patient* and *The Cardboard Box*.

The stories had been published individually in the United States in *Harper's Weekly*, with Hyde's illustrations, from 25 February to 21 October, 1893; but the last of them, *The Final Problem*, appeared in *McClure's Magazine*, December, 1893, illustrated by H.C.Edwards.

7

The Memoirs of Sherlock Holmes

Silver Blaze (*Strand*, Dec 1892, ill. S. Paget; *Harper's*, 25 Feb 1893, ill. W. H. Hyde

This was the case whose solution Doyle was confident his wife would not guess. Nor, it was pointed out by a critic on a sporting paper, would anyone else have done, if they judged it by the actual laws of training and racing horses, subjects about which the author later confessed he knew nothing.

> Holmes may have been at the top of his form, but my ignorance cries aloud to heaven ... He (the critic) explained the exact penalties which would have come upon anyone concerned if they had acted as I described. Half would have been in jail and the other half warned off the Turf for ever. However, I have never been nervous about details, and one must be masterful sometimes.

Silver Blaze also furnishes two instances of life imitating art. A 'murder' case in Kent in 1956, with a similar explanation, was solved by a detective who had read the story and was able to apply Holmes's principle that nothing much in life is new. Earlier, in 1920, New Zealand's celebrated 'Hoof-print' murder mystery was solved through a dog's having done very little in the night-time. The dog was found to have belonged previously to the suspect. When he approached the lonely farmstead of its present owner, intent on killing him, the dog barked only briefly before recognizing him, so raising no alarm.

By drugging the stable-boy's supper of curried mutton, the gentlemanly-looking tout who had earlier tried to bribe him to tip the winner of the Wessex Cup had managed to kidnap the favourite, Silver Blaze. John Straker, the animal's trainer, had turned out in search of it, and had gone missing, too, later to be found dead of a savage blow to his head. The Devonshire police have brought in their obvious suspect,

Fitzroy Simpson, a well-bred amateur bookmaker, who has placed heavy bets against the favourite.

Such is the story that is the one topic of conversation through the length and breadth of England. Only a few days remain before the race, and the horse has not been recovered, which is why Holmes and Watson are taking the train (at an average 53½ miles an hour) to Devonshire, on their way to the King's Pyland training stables on Dartmoor.

Holmes locates the horse, and we get a rare glimpse of him as a betting man. As to the killer, he had been as convinced as anyone about Simpson. However, he has seen this from the outset as 'one of those cases where the art of the reasoner should be used rather for the sifting of details than for the acquiring of fresh evidence.' On hearing that a dog had done nothing in the night-time he had cause to think further, which leads him to a remarkable solution.

'We are going well,' said he, looking out of the window and glancing at his watch. 'Our rate at present is fifty-three and a half miles an hour.'

'I have not observed the quarter-mile posts,' said I.

'Nor have I. But the telegraph posts upon this line are sixty yards apart, and the calculation is a simple one.'

Holmes and Watson

'At least I have got a grip of the essential facts of the case. I shall enumerate them to you, for nothing clears up a case so much as stating it to another person, and I can hardly expect your cooperation if I do not show you the position from which we start.'

Holmes

'The horse is a very gregarious creature.'

Holmes

'Is there any point to which you would wish to draw my attention?'

'To the curious incident of the dog in the night-time.'

'The dog did nothing in the night-time.'

'That was the curious incident.'

Insp Gregory and Holmes

The Yellow Face (*Strand*, Feb 1893, ill. S. Paget; *Harper's*, 11 Feb 1893, ill. W.H.Hyde)

Paraphrasing W.S.Gilbert – *Ruddigore* had had its first performance at the Savoy Theatre in 1887, the year before this case occurs – Holmes invites Watson in future to whisper 'Norbury' in his ear if he should show signs of over-confidence and carelessness. His self-deprecation is justified; his inattention and recourse to surmise without all the facts are embarrassingly apparent.

Norbury, an outer London hamlet at the time, has few dwellings. A young businessman, Grant Munro, lives in a nice little villa there, with his affectionate though highly-strung wife, Effie. She has been acting strangely of late, asking him for a hundred pounds (albeit of her own money) and sneaking off to a formerly disused nearby cottage, which seems to have acquired some odd tenants : Mr Munro has glimpsed an 'unnatural' face at one of its windows. Effie is clearly up to something, but will explain nothing.

Holmes, who, one suspects, had dozed off during his anxious client's tale, babbles out a wild theory which even Watson has to dismiss as 'all surmise' (he might have used a more forceful epithet in his military days). Events prove Holmes quite wrong, to the extent that Watson has to precede his narrative with an apology.

Sherlock Holmes was a man who seldom took exercise for exercise's sake. Few men were capable of greater muscular effort, and he was undoubtedly one of the finest boxers of his weight that I have ever seen ; but he looked upon aimless bodily exertion as a waste of energy, and he seldom bestirred himself save when there was some professional object to be served. Then he was absolutely untiring and indefatigable. That he should have kept himself in training under such circumstances is remarkable, but his diet was usually of the sparest, and his habits were simple to the verge of austerity. Save for the occasional use of cocaine, he had no vices, and he only turned to the drug as a protest against the monotony of existence when cases were scanty and the papers uninteresting.

Watson

'Pipes are occasionally of extraordinary interest. Nothing has more individuality, save perhaps watches and bootlaces. The indications here, however, are neither very marked nor very important. The owner is obviously a muscular man, left-handed, with an excellent set of teeth, careless in his habits, and with no need to practise economy.'

Holmes

'If you wish to preserve your incognito, I would suggest that you cease to write your name upon the lining of your hat, or else that you turn the crown towards the person whom you are addressing.'

Holmes to Grant Munro

The Stockbroker's Clerk (*Strand*, Mar 1893, ill. S. Paget; *Harper's*, 11 Mar 1893, ill. W.H.Hyde)

'My dear fellow, you know my methods,' Holmes reminds Watson, before explaining how a glance at his friend's slippers has been enough to tell him that Watson has been housebound with a summer cold (and, one is tempted to suggest, with his recently-married second wife, Mary Morstan). Another of those methods is to invoke precedents; in this case, that of the case of the Red-Headed League.

This time it is a perky young clerk, Hall Pycroft, who is being flattered and bribed to keep him away from the place where he would otherwise have been working, the grand offices of just about the richest stockbroking firm in the City of London. Days spent instead in a seedy Birmingham office, poring over directories of Paris in preparation for his lucrative appointment as business manager to the Franco-Midland Hardware Company, arouse sufficient unease to make him consult Holmes.

'Rather fine, Watson, is it not?' Holmes asks gleefully, having heard all the particulars. His explanation for what crooked game is afoot is astonishing enough to cause even his astute cockney client to cry, 'My God! What a blind beetle I have been!'

Shortly after my marriage I had bought a connection in the Paddington district. Old Mr Farquhar, from whom I purchased it, had at one time an excellent general practice; but his age, and an affliction of the nature of St Vitus's dance from which he suffered, had very much thinned it. The public not unnaturally goes on the principle that he who would heal others must himself be whole, and looks askance at the curative powers of the man who is beyond the reach of his drugs. Thus as my predecessor weakened his practice declined, until when I purchased it from him it had sunk from twelve hundred to little more than three hundred a year. I had confidence, however, in my own youth and energy and was convinced that in a very few years the concern would be as flourishing as ever.

Watson

'Can you come at once?'
'In an instant.' I scribbled a note to my neighbour, rushed upstairs to explain the matter to my wife, and joined Holmes upon the doorstep.
'Your neighbour is a doctor,' said he, nodding at the brass plate.
'Yes, he bought a practice as I did.'
'An old-established one?'
'Just the same as mine. Both have been ever since the houses were built.'
'Ah! then you got hold of the best of the two.'
'I think I did. But how do you know?'
'By the steps, my boy. Yours are worn three inches deeper than his.'

Holmes and Watson

Sherlock Holmes cocked his eye at me, leaning back on the cushions with a pleased and yet critical face, like a connoisseur who has just taken his first sip of a comet vintage.

Watson

'Human nature is a strange mixture, Watson. You see that even a villain and murderer can inspire such affection that his brother turns to suicide when he learns that his neck is forfeited.'

Holmes

The 'Gloria Scott' (*Strand*, Apr 1893, ill. S. Paget; *Harper's*, 15 Apr 1893, ill. W.H.Hyde)

Holmes is in the mood for winter fireside reminiscence to his friend, in the form of one of his rare disclosures from his own past. It is nothing less than an account of his very first case, in the mid-1870s, when he was still a university student in his early twenties.

He had been laid up in his rooms for ten days after a bull-terrier, tethered while its master was in college chapel, had found relief from its boredom in freezing its jaws on the passing Holmes's ankle. Its owner, Victor Trevor, like Holmes a loner, had become his friend and invited him to his father's place on the Norfolk Broads. A gratuitous observation by their visitor had a dramatic effect on Trevor Snr:
'You have done a great deal of digging, by your callosities.'
'Made all my money at the goldfields.'
'You have been in New Zealand.'
'Right again.'

'You have visited Japan.'

'Quite true.'

'And you have been most intimately associated with someone whose initials were J.A., and whom you afterwards were eager to entirely forget.'

The old gentleman stared wildly, then fainted, not in reaction to the appalling syntax of a young man of far better education than himself, but from the impact of this first manifestation of Holmes's startling gift. When he recovers he declares, 'I don't know how you manage this, Mr Holmes, but it seems to me that all the detectives of fact and fancy would be children in your hands. That's your line of life, sir ...'

The case in which Holmes finds himself marginally involved in consequence is, like many another which would come his way, one of a man's past life catching him up in the evening of his days. Holmes is not called on to act; merely to listen to a tale of mayhem aboard the bark *Gloria Scott*, transporting convicts to Australia at the time of the Crimean War.

He had picked from a drawer a little tarnished cylinder, and, undoing the tape, he handed me a short note scrawled upon a half-sheet of slate-gray paper.

> The supply of game from London is going steadily up (it ran). Head-keeper Hudson, we believe, has now been told to receive all orders for fly-paper and for preservation of your hen-pheasant's life.

As I glanced up from reading this enigmatical message, I saw Holmes chuckling at the expression upon my face.

'You look a little bewildered,' said he.

'I cannot see how such a message as this could inspire horror. It seems to me to be rather grotesque than otherwise.'

'Very likely. Yet the fact remains that the reader, who was a fine, robust old man, was knocked clean down by it as if it had been the butt end of a pistol.'

'You arouse my curiosity,' said I.

Watson and Holmes

'I was never a very sociable fellow, Watson, always rather fond of moping in my rooms and working out my own little methods of thought, so that I never mixed much with the men of my year. Bar fencing and boxing I had few athletic tastes, and then my line of study was quite distinct from that of the other fellows, so that we had no points of contact at all.'

Holmes

'Of all ghosts the ghosts of our old loves are the worst.'

James Trevor to Holmes

'The blood and the brown sherry on that table turn me sick now when I think of it.'

James Trevor (from his statement)

The Musgrave Ritual (*Strand*, May 1893, ill. S. Paget; *Harper's*, 13 May 1893, ill. W.H.Hyde)

Watson hears another winter fireside tale from Holmes about his early career, before his name was made.

Having determined to be the world's first unofficial consulting detective, he had taken rooms in London, in Montague Street, beside the British Museum, where he pursued a self-imposed regime of eccentric reading in 'all those branches of science which might make me more efficient.' A few investigations began to come his way through the Varsity old-boy network. To this particular one he attributes 'my first stride towards the position which I now hold.'

Reginald Musgrave, a slight acquaintance only, invited him to apply 'those powers with which you used to amaze us' to something inexplicable at his ancestral home, Hurlstone Manor, perhaps the oldest inhabited building in Sussex. The butler, Brunton, under notice for prying into family papers, had absented himself suspiciously prematurely.

Having seen what the butler saw, Holmes was in no doubt about what he had been up to. By solving the meaning of the arcane ritual with which all Musgrave males have been catechized since the mid-17th century, he found not only the missing man, but – and more importantly for its value in advancing his reputation – that which the butler had gone seeking.

An anomaly which often struck me in the character of my friend Sherlock Holmes was that, although in his methods of thought he was the neatest and most methodical of mankind, and although also he affected a certain quiet primness of dress, he was none the less in his personal habits one of the most untidy men that ever drove a fellow-lodger to distraction. Not that I am in the least conventional in that respect myself. The rough-and-tumble work in Afghanistan, coming on the top of natural Bohemianism of disposition, has made me rather more lax than befits a medical man. But with me there is a limit, and when I find a man who keeps his cigars in the coal-scuttle, his tobacco in the toe end of a Persian slipper, and his unanswered correspondence transfixed by a jack-knife into the very centre of his wooden mantelpiece, then I begin to give myself virtuous airs. I have always held, too, that pistol practice should be distinctly an open-air pastime ; and when Holmes, in one of his queer humours, would sit in an armchair with his hair-trigger and a hundred Boxer cartridges and proceed to adorn the opposite wall with a patriotic V.R. done in bullet-pocks, I felt strongly that neither the atmosphere nor the appearance of our room was improved by it.

Our chambers were always full of chemicals and of criminal relics which had a way of wandering into unlikely positions, and of turning up in the butter-dish or in even less desirable places. But his papers were my great crux. He had a horror of destroying documents, especially those which were connected with his past cases, and yet it was only once in every year or two that he would muster energy to docket and arrange them ; for, as I have mentioned somewhere in these incoherent memoirs, the outbursts of passionate energy when he performed the remarkable feats with which his name is associated were followed by reactions of lethargy during which he would lie about with his violin and his books, hardy moving save from the sofa to the table. Thus month after month his papers accumulated until every corner of the room was stacked with bundles of manuscrpt which were on no account to be burned, and which could not be put away save by their owner.

Watson

'You may remember how the affair of the *Gloria Scott*, and my conversation with the unhappy man whose fate I told you of, first turned my attention in the direction of the profession which has become my life's work. You see me now when my name has become known far and wide, and when I am generally recognized both by the public and by the official force as being a final court of appeal in doubtful cases. Even when you knew me first, at the time of the affair which you have commemorated in 'A Study in Scarlet,' I had already established a considerable, though not a very lucrative, connection. You can hardly realize, then, how difficult I found it at first, and how long I had to wait before I succeeded in making any headway.'

Holmes

Whose was it ?
His who is gone.
Who shall have it ?
He who will come.
Where was the sun ?
Over the oak.

Where was the shadow?
Under the elm.
How was it stepped?
North by ten and by ten, east by five and by five, south by two and by two, west by one and by one, and so under.
What shall we give for it?
All that is ours.
Why should we give it?
For the sake of the trust.

The Musgrave Ritual

'You know my methods in such cases, Watson. I put myself in the man's place, and, having first gauged his intelligence, I try to imagine how I should myself have proceeded under the same circumstances. In this case the matter was simplified by Brunton's intelligence being quite first-rate, so that it was unnecessary to make any allowance for the personal equation, as the astronomers have dubbed it.'

Holmes

The Reigate Squires (*Strand*, June 1893, ill. S. Paget; *Harper's*, 17 June 1893, ill. W.H.Hyde)

The original title, in this issue of the *Strand*, was *The Reigate Squire*; it was pluralized in the collected *Memoirs*. The American title has always been *The Reigate Puzzle*, the genus squire being largely unfamiliar.

It is a pity that Watson did not chronicle at least some of those of Holmes's cases to which he alludes merely in passing. There are almost as many of them again as there are in the published canon. Some of the titles he gives to them are tantalizing: the Singular Tragedy of the Atkinson Brothers at Trincomalee; the Singular Adventure of the Aluminium Crutch; the Sudden Death of Cardinal Tosca (investigated by personal request of the Pope); the case of Wilson, the Notorious Canary Trainer; the Repulsive Story of the Red Leech; the Strange Case of Isadora Persano, found stark staring mad with a matchbox in front of him which contained a worm said to be unknown to science; and, perhaps more so than any, the Giant Rat of Sumatra ('a story for which the world is not yet ready'), Ricoletti of the Club Foot and his Abominable Wife, the Affair of the Politician, the Lighthouse, and the Trained Cormorant, and the Incredible Mystery of Mr James Phillimore, who, stepping back into his own house to get his umbrella, was never more seen in this world. (*For a representative list see page 239.*)

As for the questions of the Netherland-Sumatra Company and the colossal schemes of Baron Maupertuis, they were too closely concerned with politics and finance to make fitting subjects, Watson explains, in opening this latest chronicle. They might have bored his readers, but they have done worse than that to Holmes during the Spring of 1887: they have strained his energies to exhaustion-point. Watson cajoles him off to recover quietly in the household of a former army associate, Colonel Hayter, a worthy of the Reigate district of Surrey. It is a bachelor establishment, therefore guaranteed undemanding.

There is no rest for the overworked, however. Burglary and murder in the neighbourhood are reported within hours. It is not the first recent outrage, though more serious than the preceding one which had merely involved the ransacking of a rich man's library and the theft of a volume of Pope's *Homer*, two plated candlesticks, an ivory letter-weight, a small oak barometer, and a ball of twine.

There is significance enough in the thieves' selection to stir Holmes's wearied mind. Nervous collapse is the price he has to pay for interviewing the Cunninghams, father and son, whose coachman has been robbed of his life. For once only we even hear Holmes scream. Investigation is its own therapy, though, and he is able to pronounce himself reinvigorated for an immediate return to Baker Street.

Even his iron constitution, however, had broken down under the strain of an investigation which had extended over two months, during which period he had never worked less than fifteen hours a day and had more than once, as he assured me, kept to his task for five days at at stretch.

Watson

'I am afraid that my explanation may disillusion you, but it has always been my habit to hide none of my methods, either from my friend Watson or from anyone who might take an intelligent interest in them.'

Holmes to Col Ross

'It is of the highest importance in the art of detection to be able to recognize, out of a number of facts, which are incidental and which vital. Otherwise your energy and attention must be dissipated instead of being concentrated.'

Holmes

'I make a point of never having any prejudices, and of following docilely wherever fact may lead me.'

Holmes

'There is something in common between these hands. They belong to men who are blood-relatives. It may be most obvious to you in the Greek *e*'s, but to me there are many small points which indicate the same thing. I have no doubt at all that a family mannerism can be traced in these two specimens of writing. I am only, of course, giving you the leading results now of my examination of the paper. There are twenty-three other deductions which would be of more interest to experts than to you.'

Holmes

The Crooked Man (*Strand*, July 1893, ill. S. Paget; *Harper's*, 8 July 1893, ill. W. H. Hyde)

What might any housemaid, cook and coachman conclude from overhearing their mistress upbraid the master, 'Give me back my life. I will never so much as breathe the same air with you again! You coward!' The man's dreadful cry, a crash, and the woman's piercing scream add to the suggestion of marital rift, uncharacteristic though it is of 'the very model of a middle-aged couple'.

Holmes bears off Watson from his Mary and his comparatively busy Paddington practice to the army town of Aldershot, to help him look into the supposed murder of Colonel (former Sergeant) James Barclay, of the Royal Mallows (Royal Munsters in American texts). He had been found clubbed to death, with his wife insensible beside him. The room had been locked from the inside, but no key has been found. There is a variety of unusual weapons, one of which seems to have been used by the hysterical woman, perhaps after her husband confessed to 'some passages' between himself and their neighbour, Miss Morrison.

Holmes discovers that there had been a third person in the room, and also some small animal. When the pious Miss Morrison tells him how the Colonel's lady had not flinched from being accosted in the street by a deformed old wretch, with a box slung over his shoulder, he knows where to find the one person in the world who can say exactly what has happened.

'Hum! You still smoke the Arcadia mixture of your bachelor days, then! There's no mistaking that fluffy ash upon your coat. It's easy to tell that you have been accustomed to wear a uniform, Watson. You'll never pass as a pure-bred civilian as long as you keep that habit of carrying your handkerchief in your sleeve.'

Holmes

'I have the advantage of knowing your habits, my dear Watson. When your round is a short one you walk, and when it is a long one you use a hansom. As I perceive that your boots, although used, are by no means dirty, I cannot doubt that you are at present busy enough to justify the hansom.'

'Excellent!' I cried.

'Elementary,' he said. 'It is one of those instances where the reasoner can produce an effect which seems remarkable to his neighbour, because the latter has missed the one little point which is the basis of the deduction. The same may be said, my dear fellow, for the effect of some of these little sketches of yours, which is entirely meretricious, depending as it does upon your retaining in your own hands some factors in the problem which are never imparted to the reader.'

Holmes and Watson

His eyes kindled and a slight flush sprang into his thin cheeks. For an instant the veil had lifted upon his keen, intense nature, but for an instant only. When I glanced again his face had resumed that red-Indian composure which had made so many regard him as a machine rather than a man.

Watson

'She has flown to tea as an agitated woman will.'

Holmes

In spite of his capacity for concealing his emotions, I could easily see that Holmes was in a state of suppressed excitement, while I was myself tingling with that half-sporting, half-intellectual pleasure which I invariably experienced when I associated myself with him in his investigations.

Watson

'There's one thing,' said I, as we walked down to the station. 'If the husband's name was James, and the other was Henry, what was this talk about David?'

'That one word, my dear Watson, should have told me the whole story had I been the ideal reasoner which you are so fond of depicting. It was evidently a term of reproach.'

'Of reproach?'

'Yes; David strayed a little occasionally, you know, and on one occasion in the same direction as Sergeant James Barclay. You remember the small affair of Uriah and Bathsheba? My Biblical knowledge is a trifle rusty, I fear, but you will find the story in the first or second of Samuel.'

Watson and Holmes

The Resident Patient (*Strand*, Aug 1893, ill. S. Paget; *Harper's*, 12 Aug 1893, ill. W. H. Hyde)

Percy Trevelyan is no advertisement for his profession (doctor), though a good exemplar of his hobby (nervous disease). He is a discontented young man, whose brilliant medical promise had been blighted by lack of funds. A fine opportunity had come out of the blue when a well-off stranger, a Mr Blessington, offered to set him up, in return for a percentage and medical care for himself as resident patient.

The arrangement has worked well for several years. Lately, though, Mr Blessington has become restless and fearful, obviously for other than health reasons. He has accused Dr Trevelyan of trespassing in his room; and when Holmes and Watson go to Brook Street, to meet him for themselves, he threatens them with a revolver.

The feature which is most significant to Holmes is the two visits paid to the nerve expert by a Russian nobleman suffering from that rare disease, catalepsy; it is a complaint which Holmes himself has 'suffered' in the line of business. There is subsequently such eloquent detail to be gained from the most cursory glance at four cigar-ends that he can wrap up – if not quite thoroughly – a case from some time in the 1880s which Watson claims to be making public in full detail for the first time.

This is the narrative which opens with the sequence originally included in *The Cardboard Box* (see p 153).

It had been a close, rainy day in October. Our blinds were half-drawn, and Holmes lay curled upon the sofa, reading and re-reading a letter which he had received by the morning post. For myself, my term of service in India had trained me to stand heat better than cold, and a thermometer of ninety was no hardship. But the paper was uninteresting. Parliament had risen. Everybody was out of town, and I yearned for the glades of the New Forest or the shingle of Southsea. A depleted bank account had caused me to postpone my holiday, and as to my companion, neither the country nor the sea presented the slightest attraction to him. He loved to lie in the very centre of five millions of people, with his filaments stretching out and running through them, responsive to every little rumour or suspicion of unsolved crime. Appreciation of nature found no place among his many gifts, and his only change was when he turned his mind from the evil-doer of the town to track down his brother of the country.

Finding that Holmes was too absorbed for conversation, I had tossed aside the barren paper, and, leaning back in my chair I fell into a brown study. Suddenly my companion's voice broke in upon my thoughts.

'You are right, Watson,' said he. 'It does seem a very preposterous way of settling a dispute.'

'Most preposterous!' I exclaimed, and then, suddenly realizing how he had echoed the inmost thought of my soul, I sat up in my chair and stared at him in blank amazement.

'What is this, Holmes?' I cried. 'This is beyond anything which I could have imagined.'

He laughed heartily at my perplexity.

'You remember,' said he, 'that some little time ago, when I read you the passage in one of Poe's sketches, in which a close reasoner follows the unspoken thoughts of his companion, you were inclined to treat the matter as a mere *tour de force* of the author. On my remarking that I was constantly in the habit of doing the same thing you expressed incredulity.'

'Oh, no!'

'Perhaps not with your tongue, my dear Watson, but certainly with your eyebrows. So when I saw you throw down your paper and enter upon a train of thought, I was very happy to have the opportunity of reading it off, and eventually of breaking into it, as a proof that I had been in rapport with you.'

But I was still far from satisfied. 'In the example which you read to me,' said I, 'the reasoner drew his conclusions from the actions of the man whom he observed. If I remember right, he stumbled over a heap of stones, looked up at the stars, and so on. But I have been seated quietly in my chair, and what clues can I have given you?'

'You do yourself an injustice. The features are given to man as the means by which he shall express his emotions, and yours are faithful servants.'

'Do you mean to say that you read my train of thoughts from my features?'

'Your features, and especially your eyes. Perhaps you cannot yourself recall how your reverie commenced?'

'No, I cannot.'

'Then I will tell you. After throwing down your paper, which was the action which drew my attention to you, you sat for half a minute with a vacant expression. Then your eyes fixed themselves upon your newly framed picture of General Gordon, and I saw by the alteration in your face that a train of thought had been started. But it did not lead very far. Your eyes turned across to the unframed portrait of Henry Ward Beecher, which stands upon the top of your books. You then glanced up at the wall, and of course your meaning was obvious. You were thinking that if the portrait were framed it would just cover that bare space and correspond with Gordon's picture over there.'

'You have followed me wonderfully!' I exclaimed.

'So far I could hardly have gone astray. But now your thoughts went back to Beecher, and you looked hard across as if you were studying the character in his features. Then your eyes ceased to pucker, but you continued to look across, and your face was thoughtful. You were recalling the incidents of Beecher's career. I was well aware that you could not do this without thinking of the mission which he undertook on behalf of the North at the time of the Civil War, for I remember you expressing your passionate indignation at the way in which he was received by the more turbulent of our people. You felt so strongly about it that I knew you could not think of Beecher without thinking of that also. When a moment later I saw your eyes wander away from the picture, I suspected that your mind had now turned to the Civil War, and when I observed that your lips set, your eyes sparkled, and your hands clinched, I was positive that you were indeed thinking of the gallantry which was shown by both sides in that desperate struggle. But then, again, your face grew sadder; you shook your head. You were dwelling upon the sadness and horror and useless waste of life. Your hand stole towards your own old wound, and a smile quivered on your lips, which showed me that the ridiculous side of this method of settling international questions had forced itself upon your mind. At this point I agreed with you that it was preposterous, and was glad to find that all my deductions had been correct.'

'Absolutely!' said I. 'And now that you have explained it, I confess that I am as amazed as before.'

'It was very superficial, my dear Watson, I assure you.'

Watson and Holmes

'This is a Havana, and these others are cigars of the peculiar sort which are imported by the Dutch from their East Indian colonies. They are usually wrapped in straw, you know, and are thinner for their length than any other brand.' He picked up the four ends and examined them with his pocket lens. 'Two of these have been smoked from a holder and two without. Two have been cut by a not very sharp knife, and two have had the ends bitten off by a set of excellent teeth.'

Holmes

The Greek Interpreter (*Strand*, Sep 1893, ill. S. Paget; *Harper's*, 16 Sep 1893, ill. W.H.Hyde)

Holmes astonishes Watson by producing his hitherto unmentioned elder brother, Mycroft, the *éminence grise* of Whitehall. At that idiosyncratic institution, the Diogenes Club, Mycroft introduces them to Melas, an official interpreter, who has a long story to tell of having been abducted temporarily and made to translate an interrogation of a

Greek who is being held captive by the abductor, Latimer, and an associate, Kemp.

There is a girl in the case, too. Her name is Sophy, and she plainly means much to the captive, Paul Kratides, who does not heed the pain of ripping off the sticking-plaster sealing his lips in order to embrace her briefly. Melas is driven homeward from the distant house where this interview had taken place, but is dumped in the wilds of Wandsworth.

Holmes, who had told Watson of his brother's comparative lack of ambition and energy, proceeds to show similar failings in himself. He locates the unidentified house in the suburbs by pure luck, through a newspaper advertisement, then goes there almost too late to be of any use.

It is a clumsy affair all round, with only one feature of interest: the introduction of Mycroft Holmes, who, like Moriarty, and with a similarly detailed descriptive build-up, is disappointingly under-used in the canon.

During my long and intimate acquaintance with Mr Sherlock Holmes I had never heard him refer to his relations, and hardly ever to his own early life. This reticence upon his part had increased the somewhat inhuman effect which he produced upon me, until sometimes I found myself regarding him as an isolated phenomenon, a brain without a heart, as deficient in human sympathy as he was preeminent in intelligence. His aversion to women and his disinclination to form new friendships were both typical of his unemotional character, but not more so than his complete suppression of every reference to his own people. I had come to believe that he was an orphan with no relatives living; but one day, to my very great surprise, he began to talk to me about his brother.

It was after tea on a summer evening, and the conversation, which had roamed in a desultory, spasmodic fashion from golf clubs to the causes of the change in the obliquity of the ecliptic, came round at last to the question of atavism and hereditary aptitudes. The point under discussion was, how far any singular gift in an individual was due to his ancestry and how far to his own early training.

'In your own case,' said I, 'from all that you have told me, it seems obvious that your faculty of observation and your peculiar facility for deduction are due to your own systematic training.'

'To some extent,' he answered thoughtfully. 'My ancestors were country squires, who appear to have led much the same life as is natural to their class. But, none the less, my turn that way is in my veins, and may have come with my grandmother, who was the sister of Vernet, the French artist. Art in the blood is liable to take the strangest forms.'

'But how do you know that it is hereditary?'

'Because my brother Mycroft possesses it in a larger degree than I do.'

This was news to me indeed. If there were another man with such singular powers in England, how was it that neither police nor public had heard of him? I put the question, with a hint that it was my companion's modesty which made him acknowledge his brother as his superior. Holmes laughed at my suggestion.

'My dear Watson,' said he, 'I cannot agree with those who rank modesty among the virtues. To the logician all things should be seen exactly as they are, and to underestimate one's self is as much a departure from truth as to exaggerate one's own powers. When I say, therefore, that Mycroft has better powers of observation than I, you may take it that I am speaking the exact and literal truth.'

'Is he your junior?'

'Seven years my senior.'

'How comes it that he is unknown?'

'Oh, he is very well known in his own circle.'

'Where, then?'

'Well, in the Diogenes Club, for example.'

I had never heard of the institution, and my face must have proclaimed as much, for Sherlock Holmes pulled out his watch.

'The Diogenes Club is the queerest club in London, and Mycroft one of the queerest men. He's always there from quarter to five to twenty to eight. It's six now, so if you care for a stroll this beautiful evening I shall be very happy to introduce you to two curiosities.'

Five minutes later we were in the street, walking towards Regent's Circus.

'You wonder,' said my companion, 'why it is that Mycroft does not use his powers for detective work. He is incapable of it.'

'But I thought you said – '

'I said that he was my superior in observation and deduction. If the art of the detective began and ended in reasoning from an armchair, my brother would be the greatest criminal agent that ever lived. But he has no ambition and no energy. He will not even go out of his way to verify his own solutions, and would rather be considered wrong than take the trouble to prove himself right. Again and again I have taken a problem to him, and have received an explanation which has afterwards proved to be the correct one. And yet he was absolutely incapable of working out the practical points which must be gone into before a case could be laid before a judge or jury.'

'It is not his profession, then?'

'By no means. What is to me a means of livelihiood is to him the merest hobby of a dilettante. He has an extraordinary faculty for figures, and audits the books in some of the government departments. Mycroft lodges in Pall Mall, and he walks round the corner into Whitehall every morning and back every evening. From year's end to year's end he takes no other exercise, and is seen nowhere else, except only in the Diogenes Club, which is just opposite his rooms.'

'I cannot recall the name.'

'Very likely not. There are many men in London, you know, who, some from shyness, some from misanthropy, have no wish for the company of their fellows. Yet they are not averse to comfortable chairs and the latest periodicals. It is for the convenience of these that the Diogenes Club was started, and it now contains the most unsociable and unclubable men in town. No member is permitted to take the least notice of any other one. Save in the Stranger's Room, no talking is, under any circumstances, allowed, and three offences, if brought to the notice of the committee, render the talker liable to expulsion. My brother was one of the founders, and I have myself found it a very soothing atmosphere.'

We had reached Pall Mall as we talked, and were walking down it from the St James's end. Sherlock Holmes stopped at a door some little distance from the Carlton, and, cautioning me not to speak, he led the way into the hall. Through the glass panelling I caught a glimpse of a large and luxurious room, in which a considerable number of men were sitting about and reading papers, each in his own little nook. Holmes showed me into a small chamber which looked out into Pall Mall, and then, leaving me for a minute, he came back with a companion whom I knew could only be his brother.

Mycroft Holmes was a much larger and stouter man than Sherlock. His body was absolutely corpulent, but his face, though massive, had preserved something of the sharpness of expression which was so remarkable in that of his brother. His eyes, which were of a peculiarly light, watery gray, seemed to always retain that far-away, introspective look which I had only observed in Sherlock's when he was exerting his full powers.

'I am glad to meet you, sir,' said he, putting out a broad, fat hand like the flipper of a seal. 'I hear of Sherlock everywhere since you became his chronicler. By the way, Sherlock, I expected to see you round last week to consult me over that Manor House case. I thought you might be a little out of your depth.'

'No, I solved it,' said my friend, smiling.

'It was Adams, of course.'

'Yes it was Adams.'

'I was sure of it from the first.' The two sat down together in the bow-window of the club. 'To anyone who wishes to study mankind this is the spot,' said Mycroft. 'Look at the magnificent types! Look at these two men who are coming towards us, for example.'

'The billiard-marker and the other?'

'Precisely. What do you make of the other?'

The two men had stopped opposite the window. Some chalk marks over the waistcoat pocket were the only signs of billiards which I could see in one of them. The other was a very small, dark fellow, with his hat pushed back and several packages under his arm.

'An old soldier, I perceive,' said Sherlock.

'And very recently discharged,' remarked the brother.

'Served in India, I see.'

'And a non-commissioned officer.'

'Royal Artillery, I fancy,' said Sherlock.

'And a widower.'

'But with a child.'

'Children, my dear boy, children.'

'Come,' said I, laughing, 'this is a little too much.'

'Surely,' answered Holmes, 'it is not hard to say that a man with that bearing, expression of authority, and sun-baked skin, is a soldier, is more than a private, and is not long from India.'

'That he has not left the service long is shown by his still wearing his ammunition boots, as they are called,' observed Mycroft.

'He had not the cavalry stride, yet he wore his hat on one side, as is shown by the lighter skin on that side of his brow. His weight is against his being a sapper. He is in the artillery.'

'Then, of course, his complete mourning shows that he has lost some-one very dear. The fact that he is doing his own shopping looks as though it were his wife. He has been buying things for children, you perceive. There is a rattle, which shows that one of them is very young. The wife probably died in childbed. The fact that he has a picture-book under his arm shows that there is another child to be thought of.'

I began to understand what my friend meant when he said that his brother possessed even keener faculties than he did himself. He glanced across at me and smiled. Mycroft took snuff from a tortoise-shell box and brushed away the wandering grains from his coat front with a large, red silk handkerchief.

'By the way, Sherlock,' said he, 'I have had something quite after your own heart – a most singular problem – submitted to my judgment. I really had not the energy to follow it up save in a very incomplete fashion, but it gave me a basis for some pleasing speculations. If you would care to hear the facts – '

'My dear Mycroft, I should be delighted.'

The Naval Treaty (*Strand*, Oct & Nov 1893, ill. S. Paget; *Harper's*, 14 & 21 Oct 1893, ill. W.H.Hyde)

'The principal difficulty in your case,' Holmes tells Percy Phelps, in what Watson terms his didactic fashion (meaning, showing off to an

'He laid his hand upon the glossy neck.'

Silver Blaze

'"Hudson it is, Sir," said the seaman.'

The 'Gloria Scott'

'It was the figure of a man.'

The Musgrave Ritual

(Below) 'He deliberately
knocked the whole thing over.'

The Reigate Squires

'It's Nancy!'

The Crooked Man

'I was thrilled with
horror.'

The Greek Interpreter

'Holmes was working hard over a chemical
investigation.'

The Naval Treaty

'Phelps raised the cover.'

The Naval Treaty

'There's our man, Watson! Come along.'

The Hound of the Baskervilles

'There in the centre lay the
unhappy maid where she had
fallen.'

The Hound of the Baskervilles

'Sir Henry suddenly drew Miss
Stapleton to his side.'

The Hound of the Baskervilles

The Empty House

'A little, wizened man darted out.'

The Norwood Builder

'Holmes clapped a pistol to his head and Martin slipped the handcuffs over his wrists.'

The Dancing Men

old school-chum of his friend?), 'lay in the fact of there being too much evidence. What was vital was overlaid and hidden by what was irrelevant. Of all the facts which were presented to us we had to pick just those which we deemed to be essential, and then piece them together in their order, so as to reconstruct this very remarkable chain of events.'

The case has certainly baffled us as we have followed this long narrative. Who *could* have got into the Whitehall office of a civil servant engaged in copying a document of vital international importance, and made off with that document without being seen or leaving a trace of himself – or herself, as it appears to the police? And why on earth did the thief ring the bell in the empty office to attract the commissionaire's attention?

The mystery is more than two months old by the time 'Tadpole' Phelps asks Watson's help. By introducing him and his troubles to Holmes, Watson is able to make some amends for having been one of the weedy swot's tormentors year ago. Holmes, in aphoristic vein, fully lives up to his reputation, and caps his success with a bravura gesture at the 221B breakfast table.

Holmes was seated at his side-table clad in his dressing-gown and working hard over a chemical investigation. A large curved retort was boiling furiously in the bluish flame of a Bunsen burner, and the distilled drops were condensing into a two-litre measure. My friend hardly glanced up as I entered, and I, seeing that this investigation must be of importance, seated myself in an armchair and waited. He dipped into this bottle or that, drawing out a few drops of each with his glass pipette, and finally brought a test-tube containing a solution over to the table. In his right hand he held a slip of litmus-paper.

'You come at a crisis, Watson,' said he. 'If this paper remains blue, all is well. If it turns red, it means a man's life.' He dipped it into the test-tube and it flushed at once into a dull, dirty crimson. 'Hum! I thought as much!' he cried. 'I will be at your service in an instant, Watson. You will find tobacco in the Persian slipper.' He turned to his desk and scribbled off several telegrams, which were handed over to the page-boy. Then he threw himself down into the chair opposite and drew up his knees until his fingers clasped round his long, thin shins.

'A very commonplace little murder,' said he. 'You've got something better, I fancy. You are the stormy petrel of crime, Watson. What is it?'

Watson and Holmes

'A scent of tobacco would have been worth a great deal to us in such an investigation.'

Holmes

'What a lovely thing a rose is!'

He walked past the couch to the open window and held up the drooping stalk of a moss-rose, looking down at the dainty blend of crimson and green. It was a new phase of his character to me, for I had never before seen him show any keen interest in natural objects.

'There is nothing in which deduction is so necessary as in religion,' said he, leaning with his back against the shutters. 'It can be built up as an exact science by the reasoner. Our highest assurance of the goodness of Providence seems to me to rest in the flowers. All other things, our powers, our desires our food, are all really necessary for our existence in the first instance. But this rose is an extra. Its smell and its colour are an embellishment of life, not a condition of it. It is only goodness which gives extras, and so I say again that we have much to hope from the flowers.'

Holmes

'It's a very cheery thing to come into London by any of these lines which run high and allow you to look down upon the houses like this.'

I thought he was joking, for the view was sordid enough, but he soon explained himself.

'Look at those big, isolated clumps of buildings rising up above the slates, like brick islands in a lead-coloured sea.'

'The board-schools.'

'Light-houses, my boy! Beacons of the future! Capsules with hundreds of bright little seeds in each, out of which will spring the wiser, better England of the future.'

Holmes and Watson

'I've heard of your methods before now, Mr Holmes,' said he tartly. 'You are ready enough to use all the information that the police can lay at your disposal, and then you try to finish the case yourself and bring discredit on them.'

'On the contrary,' said Holmes, 'out of my last fifty-three cases my name has only appeared in four, and the police have had all the credit in forty-nine. I don't blame you for not knowing this, for you are young and inexperienced, but if you wish to get on in your new duties you will work with me and not against me.'

'I'd be very glad of a hint or two,' said the detective, changing his manner.

Forbes and Holmes

He had, when he so willed it, the utter immobility of countenance of a red Indian, and I could not gather from his appearance whether he was satisfied or not with the position of the case.

Watson

'Mrs Hudson has risen to the occasion,' said Holmes, uncovering a dish of curried chicken. 'Her cuisine is a little limited, but she has as good an idea of breakfast as a Scotchwoman.'

Holmes

'I clambered over the fence into the grounds.'
'Surely the gate was open!' ejaculated Phelps.
'Yes, but I have a peculiar taste in these matters.'

Holmes and Phelps

The Final Problem (*Strand*, Dec 1893, ill. S. Paget; *McClure's*, Dec 1893, ill. H.C.Edwards)

It is the evening of 24 April, 1891. Watson, who has seen little of Holmes for a year or two, is surprised to be visited by him in the evening. Holmes has some bleeding knuckles and an uncharacteristic air of apprehension. It is not surprising, for three times that day there have been attempts to kill him.

He tells Watson for the first time of the existence of a criminal organization controlled anonymously by 'the Napoleon of crime', Prof James Moriarty, an embittered and ruthless mathematical genius. Holmes has been trying for weeks to break the gang and bring its members and their leader to justice in what will be the greatest criminal trial of the century. The police swoop which he has organized will take place in three days' time – for some inexplicable reason he has told Moriarty as much. Meanwhile, Holmes feels he would be safer out of the country. He has come seeking Watson's companionship.

They travel to France, closely pursued by Moriarty himself. They move on to Brussels and Strasbourg, where they learn that the London round-up has been successful; but Moriarty remains an ever-present danger, and as the two friends wander in Swiss Alpine regions Watson is aware of Holmes's tense watchfulness. It is as if he were aware that time is running out:

> 'I think that I may go so far as to say, Watson, that I have not lived wholly in vain. If my record were closed tonight I could still survey it with equanimity. The air of London is the sweeter for my presence. In over a thousand cases I am not aware that I have ever used my powers upon the wrong side. Of late I have been tempted to look into the problems furnished by nature rather than those more superficial ones for which our artificial state of society is responsible. Your memoirs will draw to an end, Watson, upon the day that I crown my career by the capture or extinction of the most dangerous and capable criminal in Europe.

Crossing from the village of Meiringen to the hamlet of Rosenlaui they pause to view the awesome cascade of the falls of Reichenbach. It is there that a messenger reaches them with an appeal to Watson to go back and attend a dying Englishwoman at the Englischer Hof, the hotel they have just left. He is reluctant to part company with 'him whom I shall ever regard as the best and the wisest man whom I have ever known'; but he has to go.

> My friend would stay some little time at the fall, he said, and would then walk slowly over the hill to Rosenlaui, where I was to rejoin him in the evening. As I turned away I saw Holmes, with his back against a rock and his arms folded, gazing down at the rush of the water. It was the last that I was ever destined to see of him in this world.

> It is with a heavy heart that I take up my pen to write these last words in which I shall ever record the singular gifts by which my friend Mr Sherlock Holmes was distinguished. In an incoherent and, as I deeply feel, an entirely inadequate fashion, I have endeavoured to give some account of my strange experiences in his company from the chance which first brought us together at the period of the 'Study in Scarlet,' up to the time of his interference in the matter of the 'Naval Treaty' – an interference which had the unquestionable effect of preventing a serious international complicaton. It was my intention to have stopped there, and to have said nothing of that event which has created a void in my life which the lapse of two years has done little to fill. My hand has been forced, however, by the recent letters in which Colonel James Moriarty defends the memory of his brother, and I have no choice but to lay the facts before the public exactly as they occurred.
>
> *Watson*

'You have probably never heard of Professor Moriarty?' said he.

'Never.'

'Ay, there's the genius and the wonder of the thing !' he cried. 'The man pervades London, and no one has heard of him. That's what puts him on a pinnacle in the records of crime. I tell you Watson, in all seriousness, that if I could beat that man, if I could free society of him, I should feel that my own career had reached its summit, and I should be prepared to turn to some more placid line in life. Between ourselves, the recent cases in which I have been of assistance to the royal family of Scandinavia, and to the French republic, have left me in such a position that I could continue to live in the quiet fashion which is most congenial to me, and to concentrate my attention upon my chemical researches. But I could not rest, Watson, I could not sit quiet in my chair, if I thought that such a man as Professor Moriarty were walking the streets of London unchallenged.'

'What has he done, then?'

'His career has been an extraordinary one. He is a man of good birth and excellent education, endowed by nature with a phenomenal mathematical faculty. At the age of twenty-one he wrote a treatise upon the binomial theorem, which has had a European vogue. On the strength of it he won the mathematical chair at one of our smaller universities, and had, to all appearances, a most brilliant career before him. But the man had hereditary tendencies of the most diabolical kind. A criminal strain ran in his blood, which, instead of being modified, was increased and rendered infinitely more dangerous by his extraordinary mental powers. Dark rumours gathered round him in the university town, and eventually he was compelled to resign his chair and to come down to London, where he set up as an army coach. So much is known to the world, but what I am telling you now is what I have myself discovered.

'As you are aware, Watson, there is no one who knows the higher criminal world of London so well as I do. For years past I have continually been conscious of some power behind the malefactor, some deep organizing power which forever stands in the way of the law, and throws its shield over the wrong-doer. Again and again in cases of the most varying sorts – forgery cases, robberies, murders – I have felt the presence of this force, and I have deduced its action in many of those undiscovered crimes in which I have not been personally consulted. For years I have endeavoured to break through the veil which shrouded it, and at last the time came when I seized my thread and followed it, until it led me, after a thousand cunning windings, to ex-Professor Moriarty, of mathematical celebrity.

'He is the Napoleon of crime, Watson. He is the organizer of half that is evil and of nearly all that is undetected in this great city. He is a genius, a philosopher, an abstract thinker. He has a brain of the first order. He sits motionless, like a spider in the centre of its web, but that web has a thousand radiations, and he knows well every quiver of each of them. He does little himself. He only plans. But his agents are numerous and splendidly organized. Is there a crime to be done, a paper to be abstracted, we will say, a house to be rifled, a man to be removed – the word is passed to the professor, the matter is organized and carried out. The agent may be caught. In that case money is found for his bail or his defence. But the central power which uses the agent is never caught – never so much as suspected. This was the organization which I deduced, Watson, and which I devoted my whole energy to exposing and breaking up.

'But the professor was fenced round with safeguards so cunningly devised that, do what I would, it seemed impossible to get evidence which would convict in a court of law. You know my powers, my dear Watson, and yet at the end of three months I was forced to confess that I had at last met an antagonist who was my intellectual equal. My horror at his crimes was lost in my admiration at his skill. But at last he made a trip – only a little, little trip – but it was more than he could afford, when I was so close upon him. I had my chance, and, starting from that point, I have woven my net round him until now it is all ready to close.'

Holmes and Watson

Far away, from among the Kentish woods there rose a thin spray of smoke. A minute later a carriage and engine could be seen flying along the open curve which leads to the station. We had hardly time to take our place behind a pile of luggage when it passed with a rattle and a roar, beating a blast of hot air into our faces.

'There he goes,' said Holmes.

Watson and Holmes

For a charming week we wandered up the valley of the Rhone, and then, branching off at Leuk, we made our way over the Gemmi Pass, still deep in snow, and so, by way of Interlaken, to Meiringen. It was a lovely trip, the dainty green of the spring below, the virgin white of the winter above; but it was clear to me that never for one instant did Holmes forget the shadow which lay across him. In the homely Alpine villages or in the lonely mountain passes, I could still tell by his quick glancing eyes and his sharp scrutiny of every face that passed us, that he was well convinced that, walk where we would, we could not walk ourselves clear of the danger which was dogging our footsteps.

We had strict instructions, however, on no account to pass the falls of Reichenbach, which were about halfway up the hills, without making a small detour to see them.

It is, indeed, a fearful place. The torrent, swollen by the melting snow, plunges into a tremendous abyss, from which the spray rolls up like the smoke from a burning house. The shaft into which the river hurls itself is an immense chasm, lined by glistening coal-black rock, and narrowing into a creaming, boiling pit of incalculable depth, which brims over and shoots the stream onward over its jagged lip. The long sweep of green water roaring forever down, and the thick flickering curtain of spray hissing forever upward, turn a man giddy with their constant whirl and clamour. We stood near the edge peering down at the gleam of the breaking water far below us against the black rocks, and listening to the half-human shout which came booming up with the spray out of the abyss.

Watson

My Dear Watson:

I write these few lines through the courtesy of Mr Moriarty, who awaits my convenience for the final discussion of those questions which lie between us. He has been giving me a sketch of the methods by which he avoided the English police and kept himself informed of our movements. They certainly confirm the very high opinion which I had formed of his abilities. I am pleased to think that I shall be able to free society from any further effects of his presence, though I fear that it is at a cost which will give pain to my friends, and especially, my dear Watson, to you . . .'

8

The 'Death' of
Sherlock Holmes

'It is with a heavy heart that I take up my pen to write these the last words . . .'

It was with heavier hearts that *Strand Magazine* readers stared at the page which faced the opening of *The Final Problem*. It was occupied entirely by Sidney Paget's dramatic portrayal, stark and black as a Victorian funeral, of Holmes and another man, as yet unfamiliar, wrestling on the brink of a foaming mountain chasm. The deerstalker hat was already whirling away into the depths. The caption, 'The death of Sherlock Holmes', left no doubt that its owner was doomed to follow.

Nothing had prepared the readership for this. *The Naval Treaty* had just given them Holmes at his most perceptive and triumphant; the November *Strand* had carried no announcement that the next story would be the last ever. The better part of half a million subscribers in Britain and America opened the Christmas Number, anticipating the usual treat – and discovered this!

No wonder the letters of protest poured in. No wonder that jokers in the City of London put crape mourning bands round their top hats and coatsleeves. No wonder that women wept genuinely, and one was moved to begin her letter to Conan Doyle 'You Brute!'

He had struck, in both senses of the word. He had wanted to stop, but knew that he would be begged to go on and be offered financial incentives which would be hard to refuse. To place himself beyond temptation or compassion he introduced a hitherto unknown arch-enemy of Holmes, Professor James Moriarty. After a brief build-up of the background of this criminal genius and of the enmity between him and Holmes, he sent them to Switzerland, to struggle to a mutual death in the falls of Reichenbach.

It was still the Sherlock Holmes stories for which the public clamoured, and these from time to time I endeavoured to supply. At last, after I had done two series of them, I saw that I was in danger of having my hand forced, and of being entirely identified with what I regarded as a lower stratum of literary achievement. Therefore, as a sign of resolution, I determined to end the life of my hero.

When Charles Dickens killed off Little Nell and Paul Dombey he did it with personal tears and real anguish. The innocents' deaths were artistic necessities and he could only join himself in grief with the many people who had written imploring him to spare them. Doyle's fatal deed was wholly premeditated, and unregretted. He had chosen the spot for it on a visit with Touie that August to lecture at Lucerne on 'Fiction as a Part of Literature'. They had taken a few days' holiday as well.

> We walked down the Lauterbrunnen Valley. I saw there the wonderful falls of Reichenbach, a terrible place, and one that I thought would make a worthy tomb for poor Sherlock, even if I buried my banking account along with him.

George Newnes frankly admitted to his shareholders that the dispatch of Holmes had been 'a dreadful event'. At one blow the mainstay of the *Strand's* fiction had been knocked away. The roof did not cave in, though. 'The Author of *The Medicine Lady*' (Mrs L.T. Meade and Clifford Halifax) continued to hold it up with *Stories from the Diary of a Doctor*, in Doylean episodic form. By March 1894 a strong new prop was in place in the form of the first of generations of Sherlock Holmes substitute figures, Martin Hewitt. The seven stories which comprised the series *Martin Hewitt, Investigator*, illustrated with the familiar line of Sidney Paget, were by Arthur Morrison, a socially committed depictor of low life in London's East End. His powerful stories from *Macmillan's Magazine* were collected in 1894 as *Tales of Mean Streets*, and his *A Child of the Jago*, 1896, became a classic novel of its genre. The *Strand Magazine's* circulation held up, even if monthly publication day no longer produced the bookstall queues, eager for each new Holmes adventure.

His had been the most extraordinary killing-off in all fiction: wilful, ruthless, and, to some readers' minds, callous, not only towards them, but to poor Watson who was left to grieve, though at least with a wife to console him. Doubly infuriating was the introduction in this last story, for no other purpose than to make Holmes's death plausible, of a character of such ripe potential as Moriarty. If a public which has given an author or dramatist its backing, and lifted him to fame, is justified in demanding more of what it wants in return, the people of all ages and both sexes who had made Arthur Conan Doyle the most eagerly read writer after Dickens had reasonable grievance against him.

When his blow hit his readers so devastatingly Doyle was out of the country and deaf to anguished howls. He was in Switzerland again, suffering from a personal blow: Touie had been found to have terminal tuberculosis, with only months to live. With tragic irony, he had planned Holmes's death during their recent Swiss visit; now they were back, in the hope that the Alpine air would give her life.

With their children, Mary, born 1889, and Kingsley, 1892, they spent the winter and early spring at Davos. Doyle went on writing there. He transformed some old jottings into the autobiographical novel *The Stark Munro Letters*, intended to be a serious examination of his spiritual attitudes. He was sure it would cause a religious sensation, but it became chiefly liked for its boisterous scenes based on his early days as a doctor. A short novel of suburban London, *The Parasite*, reflected his tentative approach to spiritualism at this time. He also gathered together fifteen of his other short stories about medical life for publication as a book, *Round the Red Lamp*.

Touie did benefit from the High Alpine air. As her health picked up his spirits rose. One March morning in 1894 he and two Swiss brothers, who had taught him to use the Norwegian skis which he had imported, crossed the mountains between Davos and Arosa on them. Their twelve-mile traverse, taking them as high as nine thousand feet, was a pioneering exploit which helped establish Switzerland as the world's first centre of ski sport.

Doyle's most significant new creation in this period was Brigadier Etienne Gerard, of Napoleon's army, inspired by the recent publication of the memoirs of the real-life General Baron de Marbot, and further intensive reading in Napoleonic history. Touie's continuing improvement made possible, later that year, his first visit to America, where he included the short story *The Medal of Brigadier Gerard* among public readings from his works. He visited the grave of his revered sage Oliver Wendell Holmes, who had died that year, and met many other literary celebrities and wellwishers. He castigated Americans for their isolationism and misguided anti-British sentiments, and confirmed to himself his opinion that Americans and Britons were natural blood-brothers who would eventually become reunited.

While he was on tour he was given the news of the success at home of his play, *A Story of Waterloo*. Although he had to be patient, wherever he went, with the inevitable questions about Sherlock Holmes, he could contemplate a prosperous future without him.

The interchange of their names, which had always irked him, did not cease with time. 'SHERLOCK HOLMES OFF TO THE WAR' headlined a newspaper report early in 1900 that Dr Conan Doyle had joined a privately-raised hospital going to tend fighting troops in South Africa. He had tried to enlist as a soldier, but went instead as an unpaid senior physician, paying for his butler to go with him.

It proved to be an extremely arduous experience. The hospital was established at Bloemfontein on 2 April, with the cricket ground for its site and the pavilion for its main ward. The Boers almost immediately captured the waterworks, cutting off the supply to the whole town. An epidemic of enteric fever struck down thousands of soldiers and civilians, all of whom had to be treated alike, with inadequate supplies of medical materials. The chief surgeon, a gynaecologist, left for England and the senior Army Medical Corps officer took to the bottle. Doyle was left to take over all the responsibility and a large part of the work, as many of his staff succumbed. A visiting journalist who asked him his favourite Sherlock Holmes story got short shrift.

He had been able to leave Touie because, six years after her death had been declared almost imminent, her health had stabilized. Their English home was now Undershaw, a big house which he had had built at Hindhead, Surrey, where the air was ideal for consumptives.

The Brigadier Gerard stories were established as a huge success. They and other serialized tales, *Rodney Stone* and *The Tragedy of the Korosko*, and the *Round the Fire* adventure series had kept his name in front of the *Strand*'s readers. All were republished in volume form and sold well, some hugely. The Sherlock Holmes editions kept on selling, too; and although he still refused to write new Holmes stories he had not hesitated to draw on existing ones in trying to write a full-length hit play.

Another writer, Charles Rogers, had already written a melodrama entitled *Sherlock Holmes*, which had been well established around the British provinces since 1894. Rogers was old hand enough to know that he couldn't be touched over copyright law so long as he did not use material from the original stories. Doyle of course had no such restriction on him when he sat down at Undershaw late in 1897 to write his own *Sherlock Holmes*, a play in five acts. He sent the script to Herbert Beerbohm Tree, who had recently opened his own theatre, Her Majesty's, in the Haymarket, and scored his biggest success as actor-manager with George du Maurier's *Trilby*.

The notion of playing Holmes appealed to Tree, but Doyle's play didn't. He was invited to rewrite it in a way which would make it, in effect, a play with Sherlock Holmes impersonating Beerbohm Tree. Doyle was already having misgivings anyway:

> I have grave doubts about putting Holmes on the stage at all – it is drawing attention to my weaker work which has unduly obscured my better – but, rather than re-write it on lines which would make a different Holmes from my Holmes, I would without the slightest pang put it back

in the drawer. I daresay that will be the end of it, and probably the best one.

Into the drawer it went, but that was not to prove its end. To his agent, A.P.Watt, any sign of his recountenancing Sherlock Holmes was too valuable to let pass. He persuaded Doyle to let him send the play to the American impresario Charles Frohman, a genius at promoting the right theatrical star in the ideally suited work. Frohman knew precisely whom to approach for a Holmes. The Connecticut-born William Gillette was not only his living image, but needed a new vehicle to follow his own *Secret Service*, which was nearing the end of its long run of success.

Like Tree, Gillette was interested in the proposal, but didn't like the script. He asked if he might rewrite it. Doyle had no objection. After reading the published Sherlock Holmes stories for the first time in his life, Gillette began trying to reshape the play. He soon found that the only practical course would be to write a new one from scratch. Doyle, beyond caring by now, gave his permission. Frohman persuaded Gillette to take a month out from his farewell tour in *Secret Service* and concentrate on writing.

He drew mainly on two stories: *A Scandal in Bohemia*, for female interest and the plot of a blackmail case involving, among other things, some photographs; and *The Final Problem*, so as to include Prof Moriarty. Freed to go his own way, he wrote fluently, pausing only briefly to cable Doyle, 'May I marry Holmes?' The uninterested answer was, 'You may marry or murder or do what you like with him.' Gillette did neither, but ended the piece with Holmes and the heroine, Alice Faulkner, in an embrace.

Gillette and Frohman were sure that the new four-act piece would be a success and Gillette took it to England for Doyle's approval. He had played in London, but Doyle had never seen him. Gillette wore a cape and a deerstalker to their first meeting, and Doyle was astonished to face a perfect embodiment of Holmes.

They were mutually charmed; Doyle liked the play immensely. After its New York opening, at the Garrick Theatre on 6 November, 1899, Frohman cabled him:

SPLENDID SUCCESS WITH PRESS AND PUBLIC...
'HERALD' ACCLAIMS IT AS DRAMATIC TRIUMPH.
GILLETTE SCORED SUCCESS OF HIS CAREER.

Not all the critics agreed, but *Sherlock Holmes* ran for 236 performances, and for 216 at the Lyceum Theatre when Gillette brought his company to London, to open there on 9 September, 1901. His own restrained performance was considered intelligent, though rather grim. He remained identified with the role for the rest of his life, playing it for the last time in 1932, aged 78 (he died in 1937). Both he and Doyle, who was happy to give Gillette sole credit as author, but drew a percentage for the use of his material, prospered exceedingly from it.

9

The Hound of the Baskervilles

Dr Conan Doyle came back from South Africa in July 1900. He had looked forward to the adventure as a tonic for his nerves, but he returned exhausted. He had not escaped the fever himself, and its after-effects persisted.

Nevertheless, he plunged into work. He was indignant about the British Army's outdated equipment and methods of fighting. He wanted to rebut ill-founded criticism of the personal conduct of the soldiery towards Boer prisoners and civilians. He wrote articles and letters to the press, and then a book, *The War in South Africa : its Cause and Conduct*. It sold 300,000 copies in six weeks, with all the profits used to pay for foreign translations. He advocated teaching every man and youth in the country to shoot, in case of future emergencies, and set up the first civilian rifle-range in his own grounds.

He was also troubled emotionally. Miss Jean Leckie and he had met in 1897, when she was twenty-four and he nearly thirty-eight. She was beautiful, cultured and of ancient Scottish descent. It was love at sight for them both, but they were resolved to do nothing about it while his wife lived. As year followed year he worried that Jean might be wasting her life. She insisted that she would wait for him. Their relationship in this form, intensely felt on both sides but platonic throughout, was to last ten years.

By March 1901 the accumulation of pressures forced him to seek a short break. A golfing friend, Fletcher Robinson, accompanied him to Cromer, a Regency watering place on the North Norfolk coast, where they played the notable course. The Sunday afternoon of their stay was very cold. By the fireside in their sitting-room in the Royal Links Hotel was the place to be. They smoked and talked, and Robinson told him a story about a phantom hound on Dartmoor...

The idea for a novel based on a legendary hound was roughed out between them that afternoon. Next month they were on Dartmoor together, tramping over the terrain and working further at the plot. Doyle had begun writing before he left the West Country ; and, into a narrative whose first outline had been conceived without thought of them, Sherlock Holmes and John H. Watson insinuated themselves as central characters.

In October 1930, not long after Sir Arthur Conan Doyle's death, Greenhough Smith, who retired that same year, contributed one of his own rare *Strand* articles, 'Some Letters of Conan Doyle'. He related in it how the idea for *The Hound* had been put to him.

> He (Doyle) was always ready to receive a hint from any quarter. Indeed, he once suggested that we should hold a competition with prizes for the best ideas:
>
> *I can write stories if I have good initial ideas, but have rather exhausted my own stock. No wonder! I wonder if a competition for the best mystery idea would be possible – probably you would get no fish worth taking out of the net.*
>
> The competition was never held, for his prediction of the result would have been assuredly borne out. Even as it was, he was continually receiving from his friends and from readers of the magazine all sorts of hints and notions. Yet, as far as I am aware, he found only two of these 'strike fire.' The first of these was 'The Hound of the Baskervilles,' to which the following refers:
>
> *I have the idea of a real creeper for THE STRAND. It is full of surprises, breaking naturally into good lengths for serial purposes. There is one stipulation. I must do it with my friend Fletcher Robinson, and his name must appear with mine. I can answer for the yarn being all my own in my own style without dilution, since your readers like that. But he gave me the central idea, and the local colour, and so I feel his name must appear.*
>
> As readers of the story are aware, Fletcher Robinson's name was fully acknowledged. His share in the transaction was to draw the attention of Conan Doyle to the tradition of the fiery hound in a Welsh guide-book.

Welsh hound, Devonian hound, it is of no matter. *The Hound of the Baskervilles* is the best known and regarded of all the Sherlock Holmes stories. It is the longest by far, if the non-Holmesian flashback which takes up almost half of *The Valley of Fear* is discounted. It is replete with powerful elements: a legend of the supernatural, a sombre old house in a remote fastness of bleak moorland, a gigantic hound and a murderer at large, mysterious signallings, a woman's inexplicable sobbing in the still of night, and other suggestive sounds and sightings. For once, it has a personable, manly extrovert in Sir Henry Baskerville, and a sex-symbol in Beryl Stapleton, in place of the usual inadequate or eccentric male or perplexed girl.

It is not without significance, either, that Watson has his chance to remain centre-stage when Holmes is off. Doyle used Holmes for a change, instead of Holmes using him. The reader shares the feeling of vulnerability in Holmes's absence; and when he does show up, his impact is all the stronger for it. Meanwhile, Watson copes with events with resource and courage, and takes time and space in chronicling them, to describe the natural settings in evocative detail.

Doyle gave it his best. He wanted to write this story, his first dramatic novel for four years. Holmes or no, he wasn't impatient to get it over with. His writing did full justice to the elements of what has been widely recognized as the best of all mystery thrillers.

It ran in the *Strand* from August 1901 to April 1902, enabling Sir George Newnes (a baronet since 1895) to tell his shareholders at the annual meeting that circulation had leaped by 30,000 copies. He only regretted that he couldn't announce the return of Holmes; his creator was adamant that Holmes was dead, and *The Hound of the Baskervilles* merely a case previously unchronicled.

Its first appearances in book form were in 1902, published by Newnes in London and McClure, Phillips in New York, both editions being illustrated by Sidney Paget, who had done it so notably for the *Strand*.

The Hound of the Baskervilles (*Strand*, Aug 1901–Apr 1902, ill. S. Paget; *Strand* (New York) Sep 1901–May 1902).

'Of course, I've heard of the hound ever since I was in the nursery. It's the pet story of the family.'

Sir Henry Baskerville is not wisecracking. The legend of the gigantic black hound which roams Dartmoor, ever ready to pounce on a member of the Baskerville family, is centuries old, but most people in that part of Devonshire still will not cross the moor at night. As well as the hound, there are the treacherous mires, thirsty for incautious ponies, the sudden thick mists, and, not least, the grim isolated Dartmoor (or Princetown) Prison, housing major criminals, some of whom have been known to escape.

There is an up-to-date deterrent to Sir Henry's taking up residence at Baskerville Hall, although he has come all the way from Canada to do so. His uncle, Sir Charles, from whom he has inherited estate and baronetcy, had been found dead in the grounds, his features dreadfully convulsed; and near his body were fresh traces which could only be the footprints of a gigantic hound.

Sir Henry has been urged by the local doctor, Mortimer, to take Holmes's counsel before embarking on his inheritance. Holmes soon recognizes the conjunction of rumours, death, and an anonymous warning, with certain small but puzzling incidentals as presenting one of the deepest mysteries of his career. He himself is busy, he says, so he sends Watson down with Sir Henry, as his minder and to report back any suspicious happenings.

There prove to be no shortage of these : a woman's sobs in the night, the butler waving a lamp at a window, and a light responding from out on the moor; an eery moaning which might be the hound, baying for prey; and a solitary human figure, glimpsed on the stony summit of a tor. There is even a chance for Watson to try out some of his friend's methods when he interviews a devious-sounding lady, Laura Lyons, who has been more than a little acquainted with a few of the Baskervilles' male neighbours.

The adventure is to Watson's taste, though, and his companion is an amiable man of the world. Sir Henry is young, and tough, having spent most of his life outdoors on the other side of the Atlantic. He is determined to stay on his estate and carry out his family responsibilities. Fate seems to have rewarded this worthy resolution by planting in readiness for him a beautiful brunette neighbour, Miss Beryl Stapleton, who lives with her naturalist brother in a cottage amid the treacherous Grimpen Mire.

Watson little thinks how Holmes is manipulating him, all the while. When he does find out, his recriminations about having been kept in the dark about a case of cold-blooded murder are silenced abruptly, as drama begins piling on drama; to build to a hair-raising dénouement.

'Really, Watson, you excel yourself,' said Holmes, pushing back his chair and lighting a cigarette. 'I am bound to say that in all the accounts which you have been so good as to give of my own small achievements you have habitually underrated your own abilities. It may be that you are not yourself luminous, but you are a conductor of light. Some people without possessing genius have a remarkable power of stimulating it. I confess, my dear fellow, that I am very much in your debt.'

He had never said as much before, and I must admit that his words gave me keen pleasure, for I had often been piqued by his indifference to my admiration and to the attempts which I had made to give publicity to his methods. I was proud, too, to think that I had so far mastered his system as to apply it in a way which earned his approval. He now took the stick from my hands and examined it for a few minutes with his naked eyes. Then with an expression of interest he laid down his cigarette, and, carrying the cane to the window, he looked over it again with a convex lens.

'Interesting, though elementary,' said he as he returned to his favourite corner of the settee. 'There are certainly one or two indications upon the stick. It gives us the basis for several deductions.'

'Has anything escaped me?' I asked with some self-importance. 'I trust that there is nothing of consequence which I have overlooked?'

'I am afraid, my dear Watson, that most of your conclusions were er-roneous. When I said that you stimulated me I meant, to be frank, that in noting your fallacies I was occasionally guided towards the truth.'

Holmes and Watson (Ch 1)

'It is my experience that it is only an amiable man in this world who receives testimonials, only an unambitious one who abandons a London career for the country, and only an absent-minded one who leaves his stick and not his visiting-card after waiting an hour in your room.'

Holmes (Ch 1)

'I came to you, Mr Holmes, because I recognized that I am myself an unpractical man and because I am suddenly confronted with a most serious and extraordinary problem. Recognizing, as I do, that you are the second highest expert in Europe – '

'Indeed, sir! May I inquire who has the honour to be the first?' asked Holmes with some asperity.

'To the man of precisely scientific mind the work of Monsieur Bertillon must always appeal strongly.'

'Then had you not better consult him?'

'I said, sir, to the precisely scientific mind. But as a practical man of affairs it is acknowledged that you stand alone. I trust, sir, that I have not inadver-tently – '

'Just a little,' said Holmes. 'I think, Dr Mortimer, you would do wisely if without more ado you would kindly tell me plainly what the exact nature of the problem is in which you demand my assistance.'

Dr Mortimer and Holmes (Ch 1)

'I have in my pocket a manuscript,' said Dr James Mortimer.

'I observed it as you entered the room,' said Holmes.

'It is an old manuscript.'

'Early eighteenth century, unless it is a forgery.'

'How can you say that, sir?'

'You have presented an inch or two of it to my examination all the time that you have been talking. It would be a poor expert who could not give the date of a document within a decade or so. You may possibly have read my little mono-graph upon the subject. I put that at 1730.'

'The exact date is 1742.' Dr Mortimer drew it from his breast-pocket.

Dr Mortimer and Holmes (Ch 2)

'... The company had come to a halt, more sober men, as you may guess, than when they started. The most of them would by no means advance, but three of them, the boldest, or it may be the most drunken, rode forward down the goyal. Now, it opened into a broad space in which stood two of those great stones, still to be seen there, which were set by certain forgotten peoples in the days of old. The moon was shining bright upon the clearing, and there in the centre lay the unhappy maid where she had fallen, dead of fear and fatigue. But it was not the sight of her body nor yet was it that of the body of Hugo Baskerville lying near her, which raised the hair upon the heads of these three dare-devil roysterers, but it was that, standing over Hugo, and plucking at his throat, there stood a foul thing, a great, black beast, shaped like a hound, yet larger than any hound that ever mortal eye rested upon. And even as they looked the thing tore the throat out of Hugo Baskerville, on which, as it turned its blazing eyes and dripping jaws upon them, the three shrieked with fear and rode for dear life, still screaming, across the moor. One, it is said, died that very night of what he had seen, and the other twain were but broken men for the rest of their days.

'Such is the tale, my sons, of the coming of the hound which is said to have plagued the family so sorely ever since.'

from the Legend of the Hound of the Baskervilles (Ch 2)

'Sir Charles lay on his face, his arms out, his fingers dug into the ground, and his features convulsed with some strong emotion to such an extent that I could hardly have sworn to his identity. There was certainly no physical injury of any kind. But one false statement was made by Barrymore at the inquest. He said that there were no traces upon the ground round the body. He did not observe any. But I did – some little distance off, but fresh and clear.'
'Footprints?'
'Footprints.'
'A man's or a woman's?'
Dr Mortimer looked strangely at us for an instant, and his voice sank almost to a whisper as he answered:
'Mr Holmes, they were the footprints of a gigantic hound!'

Dr Mortimer and Holmes (Ch 2)

'I have hitherto confined my investigations to this world. In a modest way I have combated evil, but to take on the Father of Evil himself would, perhaps, be too ambitious a task.'

Holmes (Ch 3)

'Going out, Watson?'
'Unless I can help you.'
'No, my dear fellow, it is at the hour of action that I turn to you for aid. But this is splendid, really unique from some points of view. When you pass Bradley's, would you ask him to send up a pound of the strongest shag tobacco? Thank you. It would be as well if you could make it convenient not to return

before evening. Then I should be very glad to compare impressions as to this most interesting problem which has been submitted to us this morning.'

I knew that seclusion and solitude were very necessary for my friend in those hours of intense mental concentration during which he weighed every particle of evidence, constructed alternative theories, balanced one against the other, and made up his mind as to which points were essential and which immaterial. I therefore spent the day at my club and did not return to Baker Street until evening. It was nearly nine o'clock when I found myself in the sitting-room once more.

My first impression as I opened the door was that a fire had broken out, for the room was so filled with smoke that the light of the lamp upon the table was blurred by it. As I entered, however, my fears were set at rest, for it was the acrid fumes of strong coarse tobacco which took me by the throat and set me coughing. Through the haze I had a vague vision of Holmes in his dressing-gown coiled up in an armchair with his black clay pipe between his lips. Several rolls of paper lay around him.

'Caught cold, Watson?' said he.

'No, it's this poisonous atmosphere.'

'I suppose that it *is* pretty thick, now that you mention it.'

'Thick! It is intolerable.'

'Open the window, then! You have been at your club all day, I perceive.'

'My dear Holmes!'

'Am I right?'

'Certainly, but how – ?'

He laughed at my bewildered expression.

'There is a delightful freshness about you, Watson, which makes it a pleasure to exercise any small powers which I possess at your expense. A gentleman goes forth on a showery and miry day. He returns immaculate in the evening with the gloss still on his hat and his boots. He has been a fixture therefore all day. He is not a man with intimate friends. Where, then, could he have been? Is it not obvious?'

'Well, it is rather obvious.'

'The world is full of obvious things which nobody by any chance ever observes. Where do you think that I have been?'

'A fixture also.'

'On the contrary, I have been to Devonshire.'

'In spirit?'

'Exactly. My body has remained in this armchair and has, I regret to observe, consumed in my absence two large pots of coffee and an incredible amount of tobacco.'

Holmes and Watson (Ch 3)

'I think we'll shut that window again, if you don't mind. It is a singular thing, but I find that a concentrated atmosphere helps a concentration of thought. I have not pushed it to the length of getting into a box to think, but that is the logical outcome of my convictions.'

Holmes (Ch 3)

'I presume, Doctor, that you could tell the skull of a negro from that of an Esquimau ?'

'Most certainly.'

'But how ?'

'Because that is my special hobby. The differences are obvious. The supra-orbital crest, the facial angle, the maxillary curve, the – '

'But this is my special hobby, and the differences are equally obvious. There is as much difference to my eyes between the leaded bourgeois type of a *Times* article and the slovenly print of an evening half-penny paper as there could be between your negro and your Esquimau. The detection of types is one of the most elementary branches of knowledge to the special expert in crime, though I confess that once when I was very young I confused the *Leeds Mercury* with the *Western Morning News*.'

Holmes and Dr Mortimer (Ch 4)

Sherlock Holmes had, in a very remarkable degree, the power of detaching his mind at will. For two hours the strange business in which he had been involved appeared to be forgotten, and he was entirely absorbed in the pictures of the modern Belgian masters. He would talk of nothing but art, of which he had the crudest ideas, from our leaving the gallery until we found ourselves at the Northumberland Hotel.

Watson (Ch 5)

Rolling pasture lands curved upward on either side of us, and the old gabled houses peeped out from amid the thick green foliage, but behind the peaceful and sunlit countryside there rose ever, dark against the evening sky, the long, gloomy curve of the moor, broken by the jagged and sinister hills.

The wagonette swung round into a side road, and we curved upward through deep lanes worn by centuries of wheels, high banks on either side, heavy with dripping moss and fleshy harts-tongue ferns. Bronzing bracken and mottled bramble gleamed in the light of the sinking sun. Still steadily rising, we passed over a narrow granite bridge and skirted a noisy stream which gushed swiftly down, foaming and roaring amid the gray boulders. Both road and stream wound up through a valley dense with scrub oak and fir. At every turn Baskerville gave an exclamation of delight, looking eagerly about him and asking countless questions. To his eyes all seemed beautiful, but to me a tinge of melancholy lay upon the countryside, which bore so clearly the mark of the waning year. Yellow leaves carpeted the lanes and fluttered down upon us as we passed. The rattle of our wheels died away as we drove through drifts of rotting vegetation – sad gifts, as it seemed to me, for Nature to throw before the carriage of the returning heir of the Baskervilles.

Watson (Ch 6)

In front of us rose the huge expanse of the moor, mottled with gnarled and craggy cairns and tors. A cold wind swept down from it and set us shivering.

Somewhere there, on that desolate plain, was lurking this fiendish man, hiding in a burrow like a wild beast, his heart full of malignancy against the whole race which had cast him out. It needed but this to complete the grim suggestiveness of the barren waste, the chill wind, and the darkling sky. Even Baskerville fell silent and pulled his overcoat more closely around him.

We had left the fertile country behind and beneath us. We looked back on it now, the slanting rays of a low sun turning the streams to threads of gold and glowing on the red earth new turned by the plough and the broad tangle of the woodlands. The road in front of us grew bleaker and wilder over huge russet and olive slopes, sprinkled with great boulders. Now and then we passed a moorland cottage, walled and roofed with stone, with no creeper to break its harsh outline. Suddenly we looked down into a cuplike depression, patched with stunted oaks and firs which had been twisted and bent by the fury of years of storm. Two high, narrow towers rose over the trees. The driver pointed with his whip.

'Baskerville Hall,' said he.

Watson and driver (Ch 6)

It was a fine apartment in which we found ourselves, large, lofty, and heavily raftered with huge baulks of age-blackened oak. In the great old-fashioned fireplace behind the high iron dogs a log-fire crackled and snapped. Sir Henry and I held out our hands to it, for we were numb from our long drive. Then we gazed round us at the high, thin window of old stained glass, the oak panelling, the stags' heads, the coats of arms upon the walls, all dim and sombre in the subdued light of the central lamp . . .

The dining-room which opened out of the hall was a place of shadow and gloom. It was a long chamber with a step separating the dais where the family sat from the lower portion reserved for their dependents. At one end a minstrel's gallery overlooked it. Black beams shot across our heads, with a smoke-darkened ceiling beyond them. With rows of flaring torches to light it up, and the colour and rude hilarity of an old-time banquet, it might have softened; but now, when two black-clothed gentlemen sat in the little circle of light thrown by a shaded lamp, one's voice became hushed and one's spirit subdued. A dim line of ancestors, in every variety of dress, from the Elizabethan knight to the buck of the Regency, stared down upon us and daunted us by their silent company.

Watson (Ch 6)

'I say, Watson,' said the baronet, 'what would Holmes say to this? How about that hour of darkness in which the power of evil is exalted?'

As if in answer to his words there rose suddenly out of the vast gloom of the moor that strange cry which I had already heard upon the borders of the great Grimpen Mire. It came with the wind through the silence of the night, a long, deep mutter, then a rising howl, and then the sad moan in which it died away. Again and again it sounded, the whole air throbbing with it, strident, wild, and menacing. The baronet caught my sleeve and his face glimmered white through the darkness.

'My God, what's that, Watson?'

'I don't know. It's a sound they have on the moor. I heard it once before.'

It died away, and an absolute silence closed in upon us. We stood straining our ears, but nothing came.

'Watson,' said the baronet, 'it was the cry of a hound.'

Sir Henry Baskerville and Watson (Ch 9)

I drew aside my curtains before I went to bed and looked out from my window. It opened upon the grassy space which lay in front of the hall door. Beyond, two copses of trees moaned and swung in a rising wind. A half moon broke through the rifts of racing clouds. In its cold light I saw beyond the trees a broken fringe of rocks, and the long, low curve of the melancholy moor. I closed the curtain, feeling that my last impression was in keeping with the rest.

Watson (Ch 6)

There, outlined as black as an ebony statue on that shining background, I saw the figure of a man upon the tor. Do not think that it was a delusion, Holmes, I have never in my life seen anything more clearly. As far as I could judge, the figure was that of a tall, thin man. He stood with his legs a little separated, his arms folded, his head bowed, as if he were brooding over that enormous wilderness of peat and granite which lay before him. He might have been the very spirit of that terrible place.

Watson (Ch 9)

He was thin and worn, but clear and alert, his keen face bronzed by the sun and roughened by the wind. In his tweed suit and cloth cap he looked like any other tourist upon the moor, and he had contrived, with that catlike love of personal cleanliness which was one of his characteristics, that his chin should be as smooth and his linen as perfect as if he were in Baker Street.

Watson (Ch 12)

'A loaf of bread and a clean collar. What does man want more?'

Holmes (Ch 12)

'My dear Watson, you were born to be a man of action. Your instinct is always to do something energetic.'

Holmes (Ch 13)

'Sufficient for to-morrow is the evil thereof.'

Holmes (Ch 13)

'Watson won't allow that I know anything of art, but that is mere jealousy because our views upon the subject differ. Now, these are a really very fine series of portraits.'

Holmes (Ch 13)

'My eyes have been trained to examine faces and not their trimmings. It is the first quality of a criminal investigator that he should see through a disguise.'

Holmes (Ch 13)

'A study of family portraits is enough to convert a man to the doctrine of re-incarnation.' ... He burst into one of his rare fits of laughter as he turned away from the picture. I have not heard him laugh often, and it has always boded ill to somebody.

Holmes (Ch 13)

One of Sherlock Holmes's defects – if, indeed, one may call it a defect – was that he was exceedingly loath to communicate his full plans to any other person until the instant of their fulfilment. Partly it came no doubt from his own masterful nature, which loved to dominate and surprise those who were around him. Partly also from his professional caution, which urged him never to take any chances. The result, however, was very trying for those who were acting as his agents and assistants. I had often suffered under it, but never more so than during that long drive in the darkness. The great ordeal was in front of us; at last we were about to make our final effort, and yet Holmes had said nothing, and I could only surmise what his course of action would be. My nerves thrilled with anticipation when at last the cold wind upon our faces and the dark, void spaces on either side of the narrow road told me that we were back upon the moor once again. Every stride of the horses and every turn of the wheels was taking us nearer to our supreme adventure.

Watson (Ch 14)

'Are you armed, Lestrade?'
The little detective smiled.
'As long as I have my trousers I have a hip-pocket, and as long as I have my hip-pocket I have something in it.'

Holmes and Lestrade (Ch 14)

Over the great Grimpen Mire there hung a dense, white fog. It was drifting slowly in our direction and banked itself up like a wall on that side of us, low but thick and well defined. The moon shone on it, and it looked like a great shimmering ice-field, with the heads of the distant tors as rocks borne upon its surface...
Every minute that white woolly plain which covered one-half of the moor was drifting closer and closer to the house. Already the first thin wisps of it were curling across the golden square of the lighted window. The farther wall of the orchard was already invisible, and the trees were standing out of a swirl of white vapour. As we watched it the fog-wreaths came crawling round both corners of the house and rolled slowly into one dense bank, on which the upper floor and the roof floated like a strange ship upon a shadowy sea.

Watson (Ch 14)

A hound it was, an enormous coal-black hound, but not such a hound as mortal eyes have ever seen. Fire burst from its open mouth, its eyes glowed with a smouldering glare, its muzzle and hackles and dewlap were outlined in flickering flame. Never in the delirious dream of a disordered brain could anything more savage, more appalling, more hellish be conceived than that dark form and savage face which broke upon us out of the wall of fog.

Watson (Ch 14)

'I cannot guarantee that I carry all the facts in my mind. Intense mental concentration has a curious way of blotting out what has passed. The barrister who has his case at his fingers' ends and is able to argue with an expert upon his own subject finds that a week or two of the courts will drive it all out of his head once more. So each of my cases displaces the last.'

Holmes (Ch 15)

'The more *outré* and grotesque an incident is the more carefully it deserves to be examined, and the very point which appears to complicate a case is, when duly considered and scientifically handled, the one which is most likely to elucidate it.'

Holmes (Ch 15)

'There are seventy-five perfumes, which it is very necessary that a criminal expert should be able to distinguish from each other, and cases have more than once within my own experience depended upon their prompt recognition.'

Holmes (Ch 15)

'And now, my dear Watson, we have had some weeks of severe work, and for one evening, I think, we may turn our thoughts into more pleasant channels. I have a box for "Les Huguenots". Have you heard the De Reszkes? Might I trouble you to be ready in half an hour, and we can stop at Marcini's for a little dinner on the way?'

Holmes (Ch 15)

10

The Return of
Sherlock Holmes

Queen Victoria died in January 1901. Edward, Prince of Wales, had met Arthur Conan Doyle and was well aware of his work for his country, which he had capped with a thoroughly detailed work, *The Great Boer War*, widely praised for being as impartial as it was colourful.

It was not as Sherlock Holmes's creator that Doyle was offered a knighthood in the new monarch's first honours list, in 1902; it was for his service to the State. Even so, he told his mother, he proposed to decline it.

> It is a silently understood thing in this world that the big men – outside diplomacy and the army, where it is a sort of professional badge – do not condescend to such things. Not that *I* am a big man, but something inside me revolts at the thought... All my work for the State would seem tainted if I took a so called 'reward'. It may be pride and it may be foolish, but I could not do it.

No one valued pride more highly than Mary Doyle, but she tore into her son as vehemently as she had done when he had told her he was going to finish off Holmes. She produced argument after argument for his accepting. He refuted each, until she hit on the indisputable one: to decline a knighthood would be to insult the King. The debate ended there and he was knighted on 9 August, 1902. He was also made Deputy-Lieutenant of Surrey, 'whatever that means', he grumbled, complaining at having to throw money away on a flamboyant uniform. He was able to take out his feelings on a hapless errand boy, sent to deliver a parcel of shirts addressed to 'Sir Sherlock Holmes'.

Being Sir Arthur made no difference to his work. He was enjoying doing a further series for the *Strand*, entitled *Adventures of Gerard*. It started appearing in the month of his knighthood with *How Brigadier Gerard lost his Ear* and ran until May, 1903. By that time, sighs of relief were resounding in Newnes's offices. The September number ended with a triumphant announcement:

'THE RETURN OF SHERLOCK HOLMES'

The readers of THE STRAND MAGAZINE have a vivid recollection of the time when Sherlock Holmes made his first appearance before the public, and of the Adventures which made his name a household word in every quarter of the world. The news of his death was received with regret as at the loss of a personal friend. Fortunately, that news, though based on circumstantial evidence which at the time seemed conclusive, turns out to be erroneous. How he escaped from his struggle with Moriarty at the Reichenbach Falls, why he remained in hiding even from his friend Watson, how he made his re-appearance, and the manner he signalized his return by one of the most remarkable of his exploits will be found narrated in the first story of the New Series, beginning

In the OCTOBER NUMBER

He never said publicly precisely why he relented. All that is recorded is that an American publisher, no doubt near-frantic at the spectacle of the immense American success of *The Hound of the Baskervilles*, cabled an unprecedented offer. If the outcome of the struggle at the Reichenbach Falls could be explained away acceptably to readers, and Holmes could be believed to have survived, he would pay five thousand dollars a short story for a minimum of six and as many more as Doyle might care to write. A. P. Watt talked to Newnes, who readily added his own offer of a little over half the American rate. It meant, in all, some eight thousand dollars for each story in a series, plus what the subsequent book rights would earn.

Arthur Conan Doyle was a man of rigid principles. He was no dissembler, which is no doubt partly why he failed to get elected to Parliament in 1900 and 1906; he was too much his own man for party expediencies. Money, once he had it, mattered little to him; his complaint at having to pay for a Deputy-Lieutenant's uniform was against wasteful extravagance. But he was also a professional, and the package deal which Watt tactfully put to him was one which none but the most ivory-tower-bound author would have turned down. Besides, after years of freedom from the tyranny of Holmes he had quite enjoyed writing *The Hound*. Its huge success was the sort of thing that writers dream about. He sent Watt a laconic postcard: 'Very well. A.C.D.'; and became the highest paid writer in history so far.

It was Jean Leckie, still patiently waiting, who suggested how Holmes could explain his survival from that dreadful abyss. Ironically, this time, Doyle's mother seems to have suggested that he would be taking a step backward and might find that he couldn't rekindle the old spark. It had the effect of a challenge. He told her indignantly that he was sure he was perfectly capable. He had completed *The Empty House*, in which Holmes returns after three years missing presumed dead, and it was a 'rare good' story: 'You will find that Holmes was never dead, and that he is now very much alive.'

Holmes's version of what had happened to him was good enough to convince Watson. It has been much questioned in recent years, as scholars of the canon have picked over its inconsistencies and errors. It is argued that either Holmes told Watson what he wanted him to believe about his escape from death and his subsequent wanderings, or Watson made a hash of recording accurately what Holmes said to him. The simple truth is that Conan Doyle wrapped up his justification in a dramatic, zestful narrative, over whose fine detail no one but a Sherlockian scholar would bother to quibble. Contributing to a *Strand Magazine* symposium of how novelists of the day worked (December 1904) he confessed:

> In short stories it has always seemed to me that so long as you produce your dramatic effect, accuracy of detail matters little. I have never striven for it and have made some bad mistakes in consequence. What matter if I can hold my readers? I claim that I may make my own conditions, and I do so. I have taken liberties in some of the Sherlock Holmes stories... That does not trouble me in the least when the story is admittedly a phantasy.

The manner of Holmes's supposed death made it possible to resurrect him without straining credence at all. If, instead of being presumed to have plunged into the cataract, without witnesses and without subsequent traces, Holmes had been shot to death, identified, buried, and memorialized, further narratives would have had to be like *The Hound*, set back in time before that fatal day in 1891. There are not the slightest grounds for suspecting that he realized this and changed the method of execution to leave himself a loophole. He wanted Holmes dead, and thought he had killed him.

Perhaps it is fanciful to suggest that he could not do it properly because, in a sense, he would have been killing something that was to a considerable extent a projection of himself. In writing to assure a fellow-author that Holmes was 'dead and damned', he had added, 'I couldn't revive him if I would (at least not for years)', he was not hinting at strategic possibilities.

Sherlock Holmes societies did not exist by the time his creator died in 1930. He was unacquainted with the recondite practices of reading hidden and wholly unintended meanings into Watson's prose and making play with his inconsistencies. If Holmes had been gunned down, slashed to ribbons, steamrollered, or even beheaded, someone would have come up with the theory that it had been a hoax to enable him to disappear for a while, or that Watson had made another of his mistakes. Doyle's explanation was enough for his readers, who only wanted Holmes back, never mind how. It worked, and the bookstall lines re-formed in even greater numbers.

The series of thirteen stories known collectively as *The Return of Sherlock Holmes* began running in *Collier's* (New York) in September 1903. The illustrator was the excellent Frederic Dorr Steele. The *Strand* series, illustrated by Sidney Paget, began in October. First publication in volume form, in 1905, was by Newnes in London and McClure, Phillips in New York. The British edition retained Paget's illustrations, while in the United States a change of illustrator for the book brought in Charles Raymond Macauley in place of Steele.

The Empty House (*Collier's*, Sep 1903, ill. F.D.Steele; *Strand*, Oct 1903, ill. S.Paget)

It is the spring of 1894. Holmes has been dead these three years, and Watson has not long since suffered a further bereavement through the shockingly premature death of his second wife, Mary. He has given up their married home at Paddington and gone back to practise in Kensington and crowd out sad thoughts by writing his chronicles of Holmes's career.

The inexplicably-managed shooting of the young Hon Ronald Adair, in his mother's Park Lane house, tempts Watson to try to apply his late friend's methods. At the scene, he blunders into an old man carrying some books, who berates him, but soon afterwards presents himself in Watson's study to apologize for his abruptness. A remark of the old man's causes Watson to turn away momentarily. When he turns back he finds Holmes smiling at him.

'I rose to my feet, stared at him for some seconds in utter amazement, and then it appears that I must have fainted for the first and the last time in my life.'

Holmes explains how he had survived the Reichenbach encounter and details his subsequent wanderings while waiting for the right moment to return and nail Moriarty's would-be avengers. The worst of them, Col Sebastian Moran, has shown his unmistakable hand at last in shooting young Adair with his unique air-gun. Now the chance has come to turn the Empire's greatest game hunter into the hunted, with Holmes himself as the bait.

The crime was of interest in itself, but that interest was as nothing to me compared to the inconceivable sequel, which afforded me the greatest shock and surprise of any event in my adventurous life. Even now, after this long interval, I find myself thrilling as I think of it, and feeling once more that sudden flood of joy, amazement, and incredulity which utterly submerged my mind.

Watson

'Holmes!' I cried. 'Is it really you? Can it indeed be that you are alive? Is it possible that you succeeded in climbing out of that awful abyss?'

Watson

'I travelled for two years in Tibet, therefore, and amused myself by visiting Lhassa, and spending some days with the head Llama (sic). You may have read of the remarkable explorations of a Norwegian named Sigerson, but I am sure that it never occurred to you that you were receiving news of your friend. I then passed through Persia, looked in at Mecca, and paid a short but interesting visit to the Khalifa at Khartoum, the results of which I have communicated to the Foreign Office. Returning to France I spent some months in a research into the coal-tar derivatives, which I conducted in a laboratory at Montpelier (sic), in the South of France.'

Holmes

Our old chambers had been left unchanged through the supervision of Mycroft Holmes and the immediate care of Mrs Hudson. As I entered I saw, it is true, an unwonted tidiness, but the old landmarks were all in their place. There were the chemical corner and the acid-stained, deal-topped table. There upon a shelf was the formidable row of scrap-books and books of reference which many of our fellow-citizens would have been so glad to burn. The diagrams, the violin-case, and the pipe-rack – even the Persian slipper which contained the tobacco – all met my eyes as I glanced round me.

Watson

'There are some trees, Watson, which grow to a certain height, and then develop some unsightly eccentricity. You will see it often in humans. I have a theory that the individual represents in his development the whole procession of his ancestors, and that such a sudden turn to good or evil stands for some strong influence which came into the line of his pedigree. The person becomes, as it were, the epitome of the history of his own family.'

Holmes

The Norwood Builder (*Collier's*, Oct 1903, ill. F.D.Steele; Strand, Nov 1903, ill. S.Paget)

The headlines read: 'Mysterious Affair at Lower Norwood. Disappearance of a Well Known Builder. Suspicion of Murder and Arson. A Clue to the Criminal.' Just as Holmes has been complaining to Watson that there are no sensational cases any more, the suspected murderer, John Hector McFarlane, comes panting to his door, with Insp Lestrade hard on his heels.

The police find the case open and shut. Having learned that Jonas Oldacre, a complete stranger, proposed to leave him his fortune, young McFarlane had seized the opportunity of killing him, after the will had been signed, and destroying the body in a blazing timber pile. McFarlane's bloodstained stick, some charred organic remains, and an identifiable set of trouser buttons, together with clear motive, add up to seemingly unassailable evidence.

An additional clue, to Holmes's eyes, makes one too many. He casts his mind back seven years to the case of *The Sign of the Four*, and the manner in which Bartholomew Sholto had calculated, from the dimensions of a house, the whereabouts of something which had gone missing.

'From the point of view of the criminal expert,' said Mr Sherlock Holmes, 'London has become a singularly uninteresting city since the death of the late lamented Professor Moriarty.'

'I can hardly think that you would find many decent citizens to agree with you,' I answered.

'Well, well, I must not be selfish,' said he, with a smile, as he pushed back his chair from the breakfast-table. 'The community is certainly the gainer, and no one the loser, save the poor out-of-work specialist, whose occupation has gone. With that man in the field, one's morning paper presented infinite possibilities. Often it was only the smallest trace, Watson, the faintest indication, and yet it was enough to tell me that the great malignant brain was there, as the gentlest tremors of the edges of the web remind one of the foul spider which lurks in the centre. Petty thefts, wanton assaults, purposeless outrage – to the man who held the clue all could be worked into one connected whole. To the scientific student of the higher criminal world, no capital in Europe offered the advantages which London then possessed. But now – ' He shrugged his shoulders in humorous deprecation of the state of things which he had himself done so much to produce.

At the time of which I speak Holmes had been back for some months, and I at his request had sold my practice and returned to share the old quarters in Baker Street. A young doctor, named Verner, had purchased my small Kensington practice, and given with astonishingly little demur the highest price that I ventured to ask – an incident which only explained itself some years later, when I found that Verner was a distant relation of Holmes, and that it was my friend who had really found the money.

Our months of partnership had not been so uneventful as he had stated, for I find, on looking over my notes, that this period includes the case of the papers of ex-President Murillo, and also the shocking affair of the Dutch steamship *Friesland*, which so nearly cost us both our lives. His cold and proud nature was always averse, however, from anything in the shape of public applause, and he bound me in the most stringent terms to say no further word of himself, his methods, or his successes.

Watson

'What do you make of that ?' said Holmes
'Well, what do *you* make of it ?'
'That it was written in a train. The good writing represents stations, the bad writing movement, and the very bad writing passing over points. A scientific expert would pronounce at once that this was drawn up on a suburban line, since nowhere save in the immediate vicinity of a great city could there be so quick a succession of points. Granting that this whole journey was occupied in drawing up the will, then the train was an express, only stopping once between Norwood and London Bridge.'

Holmes and Lestrade

My friend had no breakfast himself, for it was one of his peculiarities that in his more intense moments he would permit himself no food, and I have known him presume upon his iron strength until he has fainted from pure inanition. 'At present I cannot spare energy and nerve force for digestion,' he would say in answer to my medical remonstrances.

Watson and Holmes

The Dancing Men (*Collier's*, Dec 1903, ill. F.D.Steele; *Strand*, Dec 1903, ill. S.Paget)

'Would that I had some brighter ending to communicate to my readers,' apologizes our sensitive narrator, 'but these are the chronicles of fact, and I must follow to their dark crisis the strange chain of events which for some days made Ridling Thorpe Manor a household word through the length and breadth of England.' (A word, incidentally, which started out as Riding – a rare misreading by Holmes of a client's letter-heading.)

Hilton Cubitt, a solid Norfolk squire, has married a young American lady with some disagreeable associations in her past which she will not disclose. After a year's happiness she becomes terrified by the appearance of lines of tiny dancing men, chalked on wooden surfaces, then scrawled on paper for her to find. Her husband suspects a practical joker, but Holmes recognizes a code when he sees one, and solves it: 'What one man can invent another can discover.'

His sense of urgency is not at its keenest, however, nor does his memory refer him back nine years to the details of *The Crooked Man* case. The outcome is not so 'pretty' as he anticipates. Tragedy supervenes. All that he can do is to re-employ the tactics he had once used with orange-pips, to flush another American from cover.

Greenhough Smith, in his 1930 *Strand* article 'Some Letters of Conan Doyle', stated that the idea of the Dancing Men cryptogram came from a child's scribble. Doyle termed it 'a good bloody story', well fitted to appear between two milder ones.

For two hours I watched him as he covered sheet after sheet of paper with figures and letters, so completely absorbed in his task that he had evidently forgotten my presence. Sometimes he was making progress and whistled and sang at his work; sometimes he was puzzled, and would sit for long spells with a furrowed brow and a vacant eye. Finally he sprang from his chair with a cry of satisfaction, and walked up and down the room rubbing his hands together. Then he wrote a long telegram upon a cable form. 'If my answer to this is as I hope, you will have a very pretty case to add to your collection, Watson,' said he.

Watson and Holmes

'*Elsie prepare to meet thy God.*'

'I am fairly familiar with all forms of secret writings, and am myself the author of a trifling monograph upon the subject, in which I analyze one hundred and sixty separate cyphers.'

Holmes

'I ask nothing better,' said the American. 'I guess the very best case I can make for myself is the absolute naked truth.'

'It is my duty to warn you that it will be used against you,' cried the inspector, with the magnificent fair play of the British criminal law.

Abe Slaney and Insp Martin

The Solitary Cyclist (*Collier's*, Dec 1903, ill. F.D.Steele; Strand, Jan 1904, ill. S.Paget)

Strictly speaking, it is premature to tell a man that his wife is his widow; however, a revolver shot is a means of justifying the assertion.

Much as Holmes dislikes having his concentration disrupted, and the problem on his mind on this April day of 1895 is the abstruse and complicated one of John Vincent Harden, the well known tobacco millionaire, it would be uncharacteristically churlish of him not to listen to the story of the young and beautiful, tall, graceful, and queenly (all Watson's observations) Miss Violet Smith.

As Holmes comments afterwards, 'It is part of the settled order of Nature that such a girl should have followers, but for choice not on bicycles in lonely country roads.' Who can be the solitary cyclist who follows her each time she rides out from the Surrey house where she works as resident music teacher to the daughter of her late father's friend from South Africa, Robert Carruthers? Her employer is showing unmistakable interest in her, as is his odious friend, Woodley; and none of this is nice for a young lady engaged to be married to an electrical engineer.

Since Holmes is so busy, Watson is given a chance to shine. He gets only criticism for reward and Holmes takes over, employing his straight left to send a slogging ruffian home in a cart. The two of them intervene at a woodland wedding and witness a dramatic objection to the union.

My friend took the lady's ungloved hand, and examined it with as close an attention and as little sentiment as a scientist would show to a specimen.

'You will excuse me, I am sure. It is my business,' said he, as he dropped it. 'I nearly fell into the error of supposing that you were typewriting. Of course, it is obvious that it is music. You observe the spatulate finger-ends, Watson, which is common to both professions? There is a spirituality about the face, however' – he gently turned it towards the light – 'which the typewriter does not generate. This lady is a musician.'

'Yes, Mr Holmes, I teach music.'

'In the country, I presume, from your complexion.'

'Yes, sir, near Farnham, on the borders of Surrey.'

'A beautiful neighbourhood, and full of the most interesting associations. You remember, Watson, that it was near there that we took Archie Stamford, the forger.'

Holmes and Violet Smith

Holmes's quiet day in the country had a singular termination, for he arrived at Baker Street late in the evening, with a cut lip and a discoloured lump upon his forehead, besides a general air of dissipation which would have made his own person the fitting object of a Scotland Yard investigation. He was immensely tickled by his own adventures and laughed heartily as he recounted them.

'I get so little active exercise that it is always a treat,' said he. 'You are aware that I have some proficiency in the good old British sport of boxing. Occasionally, it is of service; to-day, for example, I should have come to very ignominious grief without it.'

Holmes and Watson

The Priory School (*Collier's*, Jan 1904, ill. F.D.Steele; *Strand*, Feb 1904, ill. S.Paget)

There has been tremendous and unnecessary argument over the nomenclature of this narrative. The simple facts are that, after writing it, Doyle changed Sir Charles Appleby's name to Appledore (there were no titled Appledores), and he preferred to substitute a fictional 'Hallamshire' and 'Mackleton, in the north of England' for the too-specific Lancashire and Castleton, in Derbyshire. The changes are there, in the manuscript.

This is another case featuring a bicycle, this time less as a means of transport than as a trailer of clues, in whose interpretation Holmes was proved, in real-life terms, to have been right for the wrong reasons. In his autobiography Doyle confessed:

Holmes remarks in his offhand way that by looking at a bicycle track on a damp moor one can say which way it was heading. I had so many remonstrances upon this point, varying from pity to anger, that I took out my bicycle and tried. I had imagined that the observations of the way in which the track of the hind wheel overlaid the track of the front one when the machine was not running dead straight would show the direction. I found that my correspondents were right and I was wrong, for this would be the same whichever way the cycle was moving. On the other hand, the real solution was much simpler, for on an undulating moor the wheels make a deeper impression uphill and a more shallow one downhill; so Holmes was justified of his wisdom after all.

Fortunately, there are other tracks than bicycle ones on the rolling moorland, inhabited only by sheep, over which the Duke of Holdernesse's son, the schoolboy Lord Saltire, has gone missing; or 'poor' Holmes might have missed out on a small fortune.

We have had some dramatic entrances and exits upon our small stage at Baker Street, but I cannot recall anything more sudden and startling than the first appearance of Thorneycroft Huxtable, M.A., Ph.D., etc. His card, which seemed too small to carry the weight of his academic distinctions, preceded him by a few seconds, and then he entered himself – so large, so pompous, and so dignified that he was the very embodiment of self-possession and solidity. And yet his first action, when the door had closed behind him, was to stagger against the table, whence he slipped down upon the floor, and there was that majestic figure prostrate and insensible upon our bearskin hearthrug.

We had sprung to our feet, and for a few moments we stared in silent amazement at this ponderous piece of wreckage, which told of some sudden and fatal storm far out on the ocean of life.

Watson

'A bicycle, certainly but not *the* bicycle. I am familiar with forty-two different impressions left by tyres. This, as you perceive, is a Dunlop, with a patch upon the outer cover. Heidegger's tyres were Palmer's, leaving longitudinal stripes.'

Holmes

'It is, of course, possible, that a cunning man might change the tyre of his bicycle in order to leave unfamiliar tracks. A criminal who was capable of such a thought is a man whom I should be proud to do business with.'

Holmes

Holmes folded up his cheque and placed it carefully in his notebook. 'I am a poor man,' said he, as he patted it affectionately, and thrust it into the depths of his inner pocket.

Holmes

Black Peter (*Collier's*, Feb 1904, ill. F.D.Steele; *Strand*, Mar 1904, ill. S.Paget)

Some game is clearly afoot in the July of this vintage year, 1895. Several rough-looking men have called at Baker Street in Holmes's absence, inquiring for a Captain Basil. Now, Holmes himself has walked in from a pre-breakfast excursion, bearing a huge barbed-headed spear under his arm. He has, he tells Watson, been trying without success to impale a dead pig, hanging from a butcher's hook, at a single blow.

If a man of his superhuman strength cannot do it, how can the puny John Hopley Neligan have transfixed the burly 'Black Peter' Carey to the wall of his wooden cabin in the garden of his Sussex retirement home with a steel harpoon? Yet Neligan had the motive to kill the former sealer and whaler. His initials are on the notebook found in Carey's gore; and when Holmes and Watson join Insp Stanley Hopkins in staking out the cabin by night it is Neligan whom they catch trying to re-enter it.

Yet, Holmes reiterates, strength and practice are needed to drive a harpoon home. He resorts to the old device of a newspaper advertisement, and is rewarded by the double coincidence of its being spotted by the very man whose initials have also been found at the scene of the killing.

I have never known my friend to be in better form, both mental and physical, than in the year '95. His increasing fame had brought with it an immense practice, and I should be guilty of an indiscretion if I were even to hint at the identity of some of the illustrious clients who crossed our humble threshold in Baker Street. Holmes, however, like all great artists, lived for his art's sake, and, save in the case of the Duke of Holdernesse, I have seldom known him claim any large reward for his inestimable services. So unworldly was he – or so capricious – that he frequently refused his help to the powerful and wealthy where the problem made no appeal to his sympathies, while he would devote weeks of most intense application to the affairs of some humble client whose case presented those strange and dramatic qualities which appealed to his imagination and challenged his ingenuity.

In this memorable year '95, a curious and incongruous succession of cases had engaged his attention, ranging from his famous investigation of the sudden death of Cardinal Tosca – an inquiry which was carried out by him at the express desire of His Holiness the Pope – down to his arrest of Wilson, the notorious canary-trainer, which removed a plague-spot from the East End of London. Close on the heels of these two famous cases came the tragedy of Woodman's Lee, and the very obscure circumstances which surrounded the death of Captain Peter Carey.

Watson

'I know your methods, sir, and I applied them. Before I permitted anything to be moved, I examined most carefully the ground outside, and also the floor of the room. There were no footprints.'

'Meaning that you saw none?'

'I assure you, sir, that there were none.'

'My good Hopkins, I have investigated many crimes, but I have never yet seen one which was committed by a flying creature. As long as the criminal remains upon two legs so must there be some indentation, some abrasion, some trifling displacement which can be detected by the scientific searcher.'

Charles Augustus Milverton (*Collier's*, Mar 1904, ill. F.D.Steele; *Strand*, Apr 1904, ill. S.Paget)

In the days when ostracism from Society followed surely after any real, or even associated, offence against its rigid and artificial codes, the blackmailer flourished as never since. As the 'king of all the blackmailers', in Holmes's estimation, Charles Augustus Milverton qualifies as 'the worst man in London'.

The beautiful Lady Eva Brackwell, about to marry an earl, has asked Holmes to act for her in the matter of some imprudent letters which she had once written to a young squire. Milverton is demanding seven thousand pounds for them, and, as he assures a seething but powerless Holmes, 'if the money is not paid on the 14th, there certainly will be no marriage on the 18th'.

Burglary is the only solution. We see Holmes in the criminal role which in other circumstances of life he might have played so formidably, and, even more rarely, as an accomplished wooer. Watson frowns on the latter activity, but is a willing accomplice in the former. They had not reckoned with revolver play, though, and if Insp Lestrade had been less easily amused grave charges could have been preferred.

'Do you feel a creeping, shrinking sensation, Watson, when you stand before the serpents in the Zoo, and see the slithery, gliding, venomous creatures, with their deadly eyes and wicked, flattened faces? Well, that's how Milverton impresses me. I've had to do with fifty murderers in my career, but the worst of them never gave me the repulsion which I have for this fellow.'

Holmes

'Heaven help the man, and still more the woman, whose secret and reputation come into the power of Milverton! With a smiling face and a heart of marble, he will squeeze and squeeze, until he has drained them dry. The fellow is a genius in his way, and would have made his mark in some more savoury trade. His method is as follows: He allows it to be known that he is prepared to pay very high sums for letters which compromise people of wealth and position... He deals with no niggard hand. I happen to know that he paid seven hundred pounds to a footman for a note two lines in length, and that the ruin of a noble family was the result. Everything which is in the market goes to Milverton, and there are hundreds in this great city who turn white at his name. No one knows where his grip may fall, for he is far too rich and far too cunning to work from hand to mouth. He will hold a card back for years in order to play it at the moment when the stake is best worth winning. I have said that he is the worst man in London, and I would ask you how could one compare the ruffian, who in hot blood bludgeons his mate, with this man, who methodically and at his leisure tortures the soul and wrings the nerves in order to add to his already swollen money-bags?'

Holmes

'You would not call me a marrying man, Watson?'
'No, indeed!'
'You'll be interested to know that I'm engaged.'
'My dear fellow! I congrat – '
'To Milverton's housemaid.'
'Good heavens, Holmes!'

Holmes and Watson

'We have shared this same room for some years, and it would be amusing if we ended by sharing the same cell. You know, Watson, I don't mind confessing to you that I have always had an idea that I would have made a highly efficient criminal. This is the chance of my lifetime in that direction. See here!' He took a neat little leather case out of a drawer, and opening it he exhibited a number of shining instruments. 'This is a first-class, up-to-date burgling kit, with a nickel-plated jemmy, diamond-tipped glass-cutter, adaptable keys, and every modern improvement which the march of civilization demands. Here, too, is my dark lantern. Everything is in order. Have you a pair of silent shoes?'
'I have my rubber-soled tennis shoes.'
'Excellent! And a mask?'
'I can make a couple out of black silk.'

'I can see that you have a strong, natural turn for this sort of thing.'

Holmes and Watson

The Six Napoleons (*Collier's*, Apr 1904, ill. F.D.Steele; *Strand*, May 1904, ill. S.Paget)

Insp Lestrade is in deferential mood. He needs to be, for he is puzzled by a matter which seems to him to be more Watson's province than Holmes's. Given his opportunity, Watson delivers one of his longest recorded pronouncements:

'There are no limits to the possibilities of monomania. There is the condition which the French psychologists have called the "*idée fixe*", which may be trifling in character, and accompanied by complete sanity in every other way: a man who had read deeply about Napoleon, or who had possibly received some hereditary family injury through the great war, might conceivably form such an *idée fixe* and under its influence be capable of any fantastic outrage.'

Holmes would not be Holmes if he did not shake his head and comment, 'That won't do, my dear Watson.'

Another explanation needs to be found for someone going about South London smashing busts of Napoleon. We might take the example of the *Blue Carbuncle* case. Holmes need only have alluded to it and sent Lestrade happily on his way; but, no, he must make his dramatic gesture. It is received as a *coup de théâtre* should be:

> Lestrade and I sat silent for a moment, and then, with a spontaneous impulse, we both broke out clapping, as at the well-wrought crisis of a play. A flush of colour sprang to Holmes's pale cheeks, and he bowed to us like the master dramatist who receives the homage of his audience. It was at such moments that for an instant he ceased to be a reasoning machine, and betrayed his human love for admiration and applause. The same singularly proud and reserved nature which turned away with disdain from popular notoriety was capable of being moved to its depths by spontaneous wonder and praise from a friend.

As we drove up, we found the railings in front of the house lined by a curious crowd. Holmes whistled.

'By George! it's attempted murder at the least. Nothing less will hold the London message-boy. There's a deed of violence indicated in that fellow's round shoulders and outstretched neck.'

Holmes

'The Press, Watson, is a most valuable institution, if you only know how to use it.'

Holmes

I was not surprised when Holmes suggested that I should take my revolver with me. He had himself picked up the loaded hunting-crop, which was his favourite weapon.

Watson

'Well,' said Lestrade, 'I've seen you handle a good many cases, Mr Holmes, but I don't know that I ever knew a more workmanlike one than that. We're not jealous of you at Scotland Yard. No, sir, we are very proud of you, and if you come down to-morrow, there's not a man, from the oldest inspector to the youngest constable, who wouldn't be glad to shake you by the hand.'

'Thank you!' said Holmes. 'Thank you!' and as he turned away, it seemed to me that he was more nearly moved by the softer human emotions than I had ever seen him.

The Three Students (*Strand*, June 1904, ill. S. Paget; *Collier's*, Sep 1904, ill. F. D. Steele)

Mention of the 'great university towns' of England fetches the Holmesian scholars out in droves, and Watson's avowed reticence about stating which of them was the scene of this case has attracted more attention to it than perhaps it merits.

Holmes has gone there to pursue laborious researches into early English charters. He is not pleased to be interrupted by Hilton Soames, tutor and lecturer in Greek at the 'College of St Luke's', asking him to ascertain which student has taken an advance look at the question papers for an important examination. 'Not one of your cases,' he jibes at the attendant Watson; 'mental, not physical.'

There are three suspects: Gilchrist, who merits the adjective 'fine' in any reference to him, scholastical or athletical; the studious, wary Indian, Daulat Ras; and the brilliant slacker, Miles McLaren. It is 'quite a little parlour game – sort of three-card trick', with a few clues to help play it, chiefly comprising some pencil shavings and three little pyramids of black, doughy clay.

'Off the wall' is an expression used by American fiction editors in criticism of chance details which present themselves to help characters out of difficulties. Holmes's solution of this rather pallid puzzle recalls that expression to mind.

My friend's temper had not improved since he had been deprived of the congenial surroundings of Baker Street. Without his scrapbooks, his chemicals, and his homely untidiness, he was an uncomfortable man.

Watson

'By Jove! my dear Watson, it is nearly nine, and the landlady babbled of green peas at seven-thirty. What with your eternal tobacco, Watson, and your irregularity at meals, I expect that you will get notice to quit, and that I shall share your downfall.'

Holmes

The Golden Pince-Nez (*Strand*, July 1904, ill. S.Paget; *Collier's*, Oct 1904, ill. F.D. Steele)

Watson tantalizes us with references to some of the unchronicled cases of 1894: the repulsive story of the red leech and the terrible death of Crosby, the banker; the Addleton tragedy, and the singular contents of the ancient British barrow; the 'famous' Smith-Mortimer succession case; and, most notably, the tracking and arrest of Huret, the Boulevard assassin, the exploit which won for Holmes an autograph letter of thanks from the French President, and the Order of the Legion of Honour. It is hard to believe that 'none of them unites so many singular points of interest as the episode of Yoxley Old Place', which Watson goes on to narrate instead.

The promising young Insp Stanley Hopkins, in whose career, Watson tells us, Holmes has several times shown practical interest, is the baffled Scotland Yarder this time. He had been summoned to the old house in Kent after Willoughby Smith, the young secretary to an invalid professor, had been found dying of a throat wound. His last words had been 'The professor – it was she.' But Prof Coram is male.

Without stirring from his armchair Holmes is able to describe the killer, largely from a pair of pince-nez, taken from the dead man's hand. He and Watson do accompany Hopkins back to the scene, however, where Holmes untidily chain-smokes Alexandrian cigarettes in order to locate the spectacles' owner.

It was a wild, tempestuous night, towards the close of November. Holmes and I sat together in silence all the evening, he engaged with a powerful lens deciphering the remains of the original inscription upon a palimpsest, I deep in a recent treatise upon surgery. Outside the wind howled down Baker Street, while the rain beat fiercely against the windows. It was strange there, in the very depths of the town, with ten miles of man's handiwork on every side of us, to feel the iron grip of Nature, and to be conscious that to the huge elemental forces all London was no more than the molehills that dot the fields. I walked to the window, and looked out on the deserted street. The occasional lamps gleamed on the expanse of muddy road and shining pavement. A single cab was splashing its way from the Oxford Street end.

Watson

'Now, my dear Hopkins, draw up and warm your toes. Here's a cigar, and the doctor has a prescription containing hot water and a lemon, which is good medicine on a night like this.'

Holmes

I may have remarked before that Holmes had, when he liked, a peculiarly ingratiating way with women, and that he very readily established terms of confidence with them. In half the time which he had named, he had captured the housekeeper's goodwill and was chatting with her as if he had known her for years.

Watson

The Missing Three-Quarter (*Strand*, Aug 1904, ill. S. Paget; *Collier's*, Nov 1904, ill. F. D. Steele)

Proficient – even outstanding – though he is at a number of sporting skills, Sherlock Holmes is too much the loner ever to have interested himself in team games. The name Staunton figures in his commonplace book under 'Arthur H.', a rising young forger, and 'Henry', whom Holmes had helped to hang; but not in reference to Godfrey Staunton, crack rugby three-quarter (Cambridge University, Blackheath, and England).

This indispensable player has gone missing on the eve of the Oxford-Cambridge match, in a year which has been most persuasively deduced as 1896. Staunton had been behaving nervously before hurriedly leaving the Cambridge team's London hotel with a rough-looking man who had brought him a distressing note. His rich but misanthropic uncle, Lord Mount-James, will not help Holmes's inquiries after the missing man, nor will the dour Dr Leslie Armstrong, of Cambridge, who appears to have been giving Staunton medical attention.

Holmes makes a strangely circuitous tour of villages in the Cambridge neighbourhood, without result. He and Watson do better with the help of a sagacious dog, Pompey, 'pride of the local draghounds', no very great flier, but staunch on a scent. They are not in time to enable Cambridge to win the match, but at least the vital player's absence is explained and condoned.

Holmes's success depends primarily on his getting a post office clerk to let him read a telegram which Staunton had sent. He tells Watson afterwards that he had had seven different schemes for achieving this next-to-impossible feat, and had simply been first-time lucky. We can only presume that he owed it to the clerk's being a young woman, and that his ingratiating charm prevailed even over stringent regulations.

Things had indeed been very slow with us, and I had learned to dread such periods of inaction, for I knew by experience that my companion's brain was so abnormally active that it was dangerous to leave it without material upon which to work. For years I had gradually weaned him from that drug mania which had threatened once to check his remarkable career. Now I knew that under ordinary conditions he no longer craved for this artificial stimulus, but I was well aware that the fiend was not dead but sleeping, and I have known that the sleep was a light one and the waking near when in periods of idleness I have seen the drawn look upon Holmes's ascetic face, and the brooding of his deep-set and inscrutable eyes. Therefore I blessed this Mr Overton, whoever he might be, since he had come with his enigmatic message to break that dangerous calm which brought more peril to my friend than all the storms of his tempestuous life.

Watson

'You live in a different world to me, Mr Overton – a sweeter and healthier one. My ramifications stretch out into many sections of society, but never, I am happy to say, into amateur sport, which is the best and soundest thing in England. However, your unexpected visit this morning shows me that even in that world of fresh air and fair play, there may be work for me to do.'

Holmes

Holmes rose. Taking the forms, he carried them over to the window and carefully examined that which was uppermost.

'It is a pity he did not write in pencil,' said he, throwing them down again with a shrug of disappointment. 'As you have no doubt frequently observed, Watson, the impression usually goes through – a fact which has dissolved many a happy marriage.'

'I daresay it may have come to your notice that, if you walk into a post office and demand to see the counterfoil of another man's message, there may be some disinclination on the part of the officials to oblige you. There is so much red tape in these matters.'

Holmes

'I have heard your name, Mr Sherlock Holmes, and I am aware of your profession – one of which I by no means approve.'

'In that, Doctor, you will find yourself in agreement with every criminal in the country,' said my friend, quietly.

'So far as your efforts are directed towards the suppression of crime, sir, they must have the support of every reasonable member of the community, though I cannot doubt that the official machinery is amply sufficient for the purpose. Where your calling is more open to criticism is when you pry into the secrets of private individuals, when you rake up family matters which are better hidden, and when you incidentally waste the time of men who are more busy than yourself. At the present moment, for example, I should be writing a treatise instead of conversing with you.'

'No doubt, Doctor; and yet the conversation may prove more important than the treatise. Incidentally, I may tell you that we are doing the reverse of what you very justly blame, and that we are endeavouring to prevent anything like public exposure of private matters which must necessarily follow when once the case is fairly in the hands of the official police. You may look upon me simply as an irregular pioneer, who goes in front of the regular forces of the country.'

Dr Armstrong and Holmes

These few inquiries proved, however, to be a more lengthy proceeding than Holmes had imagined, for he did not return to the inn until nearly nine o'clock. He was pale and dejected, stained with dust, and exhausted with hunger and fatigue. A cold supper was ready upon the table, and when his needs were satisfied and his pipe alight he was ready to take that half comic and wholly philosophic view which was natural to him when his affairs were going awry.

Watson

The Abbey Grange (*Strand*, Sep 1904, ill. S. Paget; *Collier's* Dec 1904, ill. F. D. Steele)

'Come, Watson, come! The game is afoot!'

Apart from 'Elementary, my dear Watson,' which, by now, everyone must know was never actually said, it is the most quoted line in the entire canon. With Sidney Paget's illustration, it conveys that absorbed intensity which could cause Holmes to dress himself fully before remembering to shake Watson awake, to hurry with him, in the chill of a winter's dawn, to Charing Cross and Kent.

Sir Eustace Brackenstall, one of the richest, and drunkest, men in the county, has been murdered – hit over the head so hard with a poker that it is bent – after challenging burglars at his home, Abbey Grange, near Chislehurst. His beautiful Australian wife of only one year had been already punched over the eye and trussed to a dining-chair with the torn-down bell-rope. Her maid, Theresa, had seen three men hanging round earlier, which confirms Lady Brackenstall's impression of an elderly man and two younger ones, perhaps his sons, the wanted Randall gang.

The villains had helped themselves to glasses of a vintage red wine before leaving with the sideboard silver. What could be more natural? Yet, good wine has certain characteristics, and bell-ropes do have a function. Holmes is moved to remark: 'We have not yet met our Waterloo, Watson, but this is our Marengo, for it begins in defeat and ends in victory.'

'Hopkins has called me in seven times, and on each occasion his summons has been fully justified,' said Holmes. 'I fancy that every one of his cases has found its way into your collection, and I must admit, Watson, that you have some power of selection, which atones for much which I deplore in your narratives. Your fatal habit of looking at everything from the point of view of a story instead of as a scientific exercise has ruined what might have been an instructive and even classical series of demonstrations. You slur over work of the utmost finesse and delicacy, in order to dwell upon sensational details which may excite, but cannot possibly instruct, the reader.'

'Why do you not write them yourself?' I said, with some bitterness.

'I will, my dear Watson, I will. At present I am, as you know, fairly busy, but I propose to devote my declining years to the composition of a textbook, which shall focus the whole art of detection into one volume.'

Holmes and Watson

The keen interest had passed out of Holmes's expressive face, and I knew that with the mystery all the charm of the case had departed. There still remained an arrest to be effected, but what were these commonplace rogues that he should soil his hands with them? An abstruse and learned specialist who learns that he has been called in for a case of measles would experience something of the annoyance which I read in my friend's eyes.

Watson

'Perhaps when a man has special knowledge and special powers like my own, it rather encourages him to seek a complex explanation when a simpler one is at hand.'

Holmes

'Once or twice in my career I feel that I have done more real harm by my discovery of the criminal than ever he had done by his crime. I have learned caution now, and I had rather play tricks with the law of England than with my own conscience.'

Holmes

The Second Stain (*Strand*, Dec 1904, ill. S. Paget; *Collier's*, Jan 1905, ill. F. D. Steele)

In recounting the case of the Naval Treaty, Watson had mentioned that an 'Adventure of the Second Stain', belonging to the same month following his second marriage, could not be related for many years to come. When we now find the Prime Minister of Great Britain and the Secretary for European Affairs seated on the paper-littered settee of 221B Baker Street, at the outset of a chronicle under the heading 'The Second Stain', we might be forgiven for believing this to be it at last. Not so. It turns out to be another second stain, in another place and time. Yet it is an equally sensitive matter; Watson will not even tell us in which decade it happened.

There are similarities with the Naval Treaty affair, however. A document has been stolen, whose publication could provoke international ferment, even war. The European Secretary had charge of it, in his office safe by day, in a locked dispatch-box in his bedroom by night. It is from his home that it has gone missing, yet both he and his wife, who does not know the document's nature, are certain that no one could have taken it.

There are three secret agents in London who warrant suspicion, and one of them, Eduardo Lucas, well known for his charm and his fine tenor voice, has just been murdered, which seems more than coincidence. There is also a mad Frenchwoman, who has been behaving wildly at Charing Cross Station. But Holmes is not going to let mere murder sidetrack him from finding the document. Should he succeed, 'it will certainly represent the crowing glory of my career.' Unfortunately, discretion must ultimately inhibit acclaim.

I had intended 'The Adventure of the Abbey Grange' to be the last of those exploits of my friend, Mr Sherlock Holmes, which I should ever communicate to the public. This resolution of mine was not due to any lack of material, since I have notes of many hundreds of cases to which I have never alluded, nor was it caused by any waning of interest on the part of my readers in the singular personality and unique methods of this remarkable man. The real reason lay in the reluctance which Mr Holmes has shown to the continued publication of his experiences. So long as he was in actual professional practice the records of his successes were of some practical value to him, but since he has definitely retired from London and betaken himself to study and bee-farming on the Sussex Downs, notoriety has become hateful to him, and he has peremptorily requested that his wishes in this matter should be strictly observed. It was only upon my representing to him that I had given a promise that 'The Adventure of the Second Stain' should be published when the times were ripe, and pointing out to him that it is only appropriate that this long series of episodes should culminate in the most important international case which he has ever been called upon to handle, that I at last succeeded in obtaining his consent that a carefully guarded account of the incident should at last be laid before the public. If in telling the story I seem to be somewhat vague in certain details, the public will readily understand that there is an excellent reason for my reticence.

Watson

'Now, Watson, the fair sex is your department,' said Holmes, with a smile, when the dwindling frou-frou of skirts had ended in the slam of the front door. 'What was the fair lady's game? What did she really want?'

'Surely her own statement is very clear and her anxiety very natural.'

'Hum! Think of her appearance, Watson – her manner, her suppressed excitement, her restlessness, her tenacity in asking questions. Remember that she comes of a caste who do not lightly show emotion.'

'She was certainly much moved.'

'Remember also the curious earnestness with which she assured us that it was best for her husband that she should know all. What did she mean by that? And you must have observed, Watson, how she manoeuvred to have the light at her back. She did not wish us to read her expression.'

'Yes, she chose the one chair in the room.'

'And yet the motives of women are so inscrutable. You remember the woman at Margate whom I suspected for the same reason. No powder on her nose – that proved to be the correct solution. How can you build on such a quicksand? Their most trivial action may mean volumes, or their most extraordinary conduct may depend upon a hairpin or a curling tongs.'

Holmes and Watson

All that day and the next and the next Holmes was in a mood which his friends would call taciturn, and others morose. He ran out and ran in, smoked incessantly, played snatches on his violin, sank into reveries, devoured sandwiches at irregular hours, and hardly answered the casual questions which I put to him. It was evident to me that things were not going well with him or his quest. He would say nothing of the case.

Watson

His Last Bow

Doyle had written the thirteen stories comprising *The Return of Sherlock Holmes* in one batch, keen to be finished with them. The series had provoked a flow of correspondence from many parts of the world. The letters and cards were as often as not addressed to 'Sir Sherlock Holmes' or 'Sherlock Holmes, Esq, care of Sir Arthur Conan Doyle'. 'Sherlock Holmes, London' or 'Conan Doyle, England' were enough address to reach him. As well as requests for autographs and signed photographs there were gifts, including tobacco and smoking accessories, and even the occasional set of violin strings. Some people wanted advice and help with domestic problems, missing persons and other perplexities. Alfred Wood, Conan Doyle's Watsonian-looking secretary, some six years his junior and an associate since Southsea days, sorted out the saner ones for him to deal with.

Enthusiasm for Holmes was spreading. *Le avventure di Sherlock Holmes* had been published in Italy in 1895. *Das Zeichen der Vier* (The Sign of the Four) came out in Germany in 1903, followed next year by *Der Hund von Baskerville*. *Les Aventures de Sherlock Holmes* were introduced to French readers in 1902; but it was *La Resurrection de Sherlock Holmes* (The Return), and, that same year, 1905, *Nouveaux exploits de Sherlock Holmes* (a selection from *Memoirs* and *Return*) which really sparked off French enthusiasm: those and, in December 1907, the opening at the Théâtre Antoine, Paris, of Pierre Decourcelle's French version of Gillette's play. It became all the rage, running for 335 performances.

The new medium of film suited Holmes well. The first representation on celluloid seems to have been in the very short (forty-nine feet) silent, *Sherlock Holmes Baffled*, made in America in 1900 by the Mutoscope & Biograph Company. A more substantial effort by Vitagraph in 1903 was *The Adventures of Sherlock Holmes*. It was seen in Britain in 1906 with the title *Sherlock Holmes*, but retaining the American alternative title, *Held for a Ransom*. Maurice Costello, the screen's first matinée idol, played Holmes.

A series of screen adaptations from the stories was made in Britain by the French Eclair Company, in 1912. The first substantial British-made Holmes film was *A Study in Scarlet*, by the Samuelson Film Company, shot at their Isleworth studios in 1914, with James Bragington as Holmes. The pre-war years were a boom period for the early British film industry, with more than a dozen companies at work along the south coast, where the light and air were suitably clear. Doyle himself was concerned in a number of Holmes films made at Bexhill-on-Sea, Sussex.

William Gillette co-directed and played Holmes in a 1916 American film version of his stage play. That same year, H.A.Saintsbury was Holmes in Samuelson's British-made version of *The Valley of Fear*. He, too, had first played Holmes on the stage. That had been in a new piece of Doyle's own, *The Speckled Band*. Late in 1909, Doyle had taken a six-months' lease on the Adelphi Theatre, Strand, to put on his elaborate Regency prize-fighting drama, *The House of Temperley*, written in 1894, two years before his novel *Rodney Stone*, which used some of the same incidents. No commercial manager would accept it, because it had many sets and a huge cast, but no love story, and the theme of pugilism would prove unattractive to women.

In spite of warnings that it would fail, he decided in 1909 to back it himself. The success of the first night, on 27 December, seemed to justify his risk; but audiences dwindled during the four-months' run. Edward VII died in May, and *Temperley* had to come off. Doyle had missed an opportunity, through stubbornness, to sub-let the theatre with several months of the lease remaining. Now he had over two months of it to pay for; he decided to play what he termed later 'a bold and energetic game'.

> I shut myself up and devoted my whole mind to making a sensational Sherlock Holmes drama. I wrote it in a week and called it 'The Speckled Band', after the short story of that name. I do not think that I exaggerate if I say that within a fortnight of the one play shutting down I had a company working upon the rehearsals of a second one, which had been written in the interval. It was a considerable success. Lyn Harding, as the half epileptic and wholly formidable Dr Grimesby Roylott, was most masterful, while Saintsbury as Sherlock Homes was also very good. Before the end of the run I had cleared off all that I had lost upon the boxing play, and I had created a permanent property of some value.

It ran on at the Adelphi, then transferred to the Globe on 8 August, 1910. It completed 169 West End performances, then toured widely. Holmes had proved his value again. So had Watson, played in London by Claude King; and so had that curiosity of nature, the milk-drinking, music-fancying snake, one of the original elements retained in a version which differed from it in many other ways.

We had a fine rock boa to play the title-*role*, a snake which was the pride of my heart, so one can imagine my disgust when I saw that one critic ended his disparaging review by the words, 'The crisis of the play was produced by the appearance of a palpably artificial serpent.' I was inclined to offer him a goodly sum if he would undertake to go to bed with it. We had several snakes at different times, but they were none of them born actors and they were all inclined either to hang down from the hole in the wall like inanimate bell-pulls, or else to turn back through the hole and get even with the stage carpenter, who pinched their tails to make them more lively. Finally we used artificial snakes, and everyone, including the stage carpenter, agreed that it was more satisfactory.

Off the stage and screen, Sherlock Holmes had not been much in evidence since publication of *The Return*. There were people who said that he wasn't the man he had been before his 'death'. Certainly, some readers had taken to heart Watson's announcement, in *The Second Stain*, of Holmes's retirement. Several respectable ladies wrote in, offering to be his housekeeper; one, more enterprising, added that she knew all about bee-keeping and could 'segregate the queen'. There seemed a finality to his career this time which had never been acceptable through the Reichenbach Falls incident. He had been resurrected, had given a satisfactory number of encores, but had come to seem rather less than indispensable. Kipling, Wodehouse, Hornung, and others had become well accepted as writers of the *Strand's* contemporary short stories. Doyle was more familiar of late as the author of the long-running historical serial *Sir Nigel* (December 1905–December 1906), his 'sequel', although set earlier, to *The White Company*.

Sidney Paget, whose illustrations had been associated by *Strand* readers with the Sherlock Holmes stories from their start, died, aged forty-seven, in January 1908; and although Arthur Twidle, who replaced him for a few stories in the magazine that year, drew well and powerfully, his Holmes and his world were not the same as before. Also, the two-part 'reminiscence' of Sherlock Holmes, *Wisteria Lodge*, which reintroduced him in September and October 1908, was a long-winded, less than riveting tale, which Holmes himself summed-up as 'A chaotic case, my dear Watson. It will not be possible for you to present it in that compact form which is dear to your heart.'

Seven of the eight stories which comprise the collection entitled *His Last Bow* appeared at sporadic intervals during the years 1908–17. British publication was invariably in *The Strand Magazine*: Conan Doyle remained faithful to it for the rest of his life. His American magazine publishers, as well as his illustrators, had begun to vary. The story which made up the eight was *The Cardboard Box*, considered unclean for book readers in 1894, but now cleared for the very different readership of *His Last Bow*, published in 1917 by John Murray, London, and George H. Doran, New York.

Arthur Conan Doyle's own world had changed much by then. His wife, Louise, had died, aged forty-nine, on 4 July, 1906. She had lived more than twelve years longer than at first expected. Those years of concern and care, emotional and physical restraint and frustration, and continuous literary and public work, had built up their effect on him. He became seriously ill, unable to sleep properly, devoid of creative energy.

Another man's crueller misfortune proved to be his antidote. Alfred Wood drew his attention to a letter and some press cuttings from an Anglo-Indian living in a rural district in Staffordshire. He was appealing for help in trying to clear his name of criminal guilt. George Edalji explained that he had been released suddenly, without explanation or offer of redress, after serving three years of a seven-year sentence for a crime which he had not committed.

Smelling miscarriage of justice, police falsification of evidence, and racial prejudice, Doyle was roused to action. He interviewed Edalji and investigated the sequence of events, uncovering a sordid vendetta which in many respects paralleled the recent Dreyfus Affair in France, which had disgusted the world. His 18,000-word denunciation of the prosecution appeared in the *Daily Telegraph* in January 1907. An editorial next day pointed to the inescapable similarity with his fictional defender of the unjustly accused, the self-proclaimed 'last and highest court of appeal in detection':

SHERLOCK HOLMES AT WORK

So, Sherlock Holmes is having one more 'Last Adventure', and this time in real life! These are the two remarks which will instantly occur to every reader of Sir Conan Doyle's arresting article in yesterday's 'Daily Telegraph'. One has often wondered, in reading the Sherlock Holmes stories, whether the skill which unfolds the process of detection from data invented by the author, would have any success if set to work upon data provided by others. Well, here, in this 'special investigation' of 'the case of Mr Edalji', Sir Conan Doyle is putting himself to the test. It is a tribute to the force with which he has impressed the personality of his hero upon the reader's mind that one instinctively merges the creator in his creation and thinks of this special investigation as the work of the great Sherlock. So far as the story goes at present, nobody who makes the identification will be disappointed.

He did not fight alone for Edalji, and his zeal led him to flaw his case by adducing evidence against an alternative culprit. He failed to heed Holmes's maxim that it is a mistake to construct a theory without being able to prove all the facts. Edalji's name was cleared and he was reinstated as a lawyer, though not compensated. The experience went a long way to increasing Doyle's contempt for obdurate officialdom, with which he would battle on further fronts in coming years. Almost as a proclamation of challenge to it, he invited George Edalji to the reception which followed his wedding with Jean Leckie on 18 September, 1907. 'SHERLOCK HOLMES QUIETLY MARRIED' was the headline of one newspaper's report.

The long-awaited marriage proved idyllic; the love which had endured unconsummated for a decade lasted for the rest of their lives, Jean outliving him by ten years, until 1940. They had three children: Denis (1909), Adrian (1910), and Jean (1912). Their home was an enlarged country house, Windlesham, high up on Crowborough Beacon, in Sussex. He nicknamed it 'Swindlesham' for the amount it had cost to extend and refurbish, but it was their cherished home for the rest of his life.

It had been in 1902 that he had found himself obliged to accept a knighthood. In one of the first Sherlock Holmes stories written at Windlesham, *The Bruce-Partington Plans*, he let Holmes declare that he had no interest in seeing his name in the Honours List. It was many years later, in *The Three Garridebs*, before Watson revealed that in that same year of 1902 Holmes had actually turned down a knighthood. It would not have done to let himself become Sir Sherlock Holmes: that would have been to surrender some part of himself to the Establishment.

Sir Arthur Conan Doyle did not let his title inhibit him. In issues of what he conceived to be public concern there was no greater patriot, but the rights of the voiceless underdog made him fight equally hard. He stood for Parliament twice, for the Unionist cause, because he was urged to, but his heart was not wholly in it. He stood up before audiences as what he was, and said what he thought and believed, which was not always what they wanted to hear from their candidate. He was not elected. He would have made an alert, noisy Parliamentarian, but not a successful one. He would not have been able to dissemble to suit party policy.

He fought his public campaigns chiefly through newspapers, pamphlets, and correspondence. Often, when his name was in the news, the 'Sherlock Holmes' allusions were introduced – by others, never by himself. It is a measure of his integrity, rather than of any contempt for Holmes, that he never invoked him as a campaign ally. Without doubt, though, the creator of Sherlock Holmes, whose following never stopped growing, was noticed and listened to more readily for it. Holmes never ceased to have his uses, even if they went unthanked by his author. The public causes were many and varied. Some were urged on him, others were his own finding. He was more opinionated and impatient nowadays. Years of nerve-strain had changed his personality. He had always been able to write in any surroundings, oblivious to people or their noise. Now, he sometimes needed absolute peace and quiet. The vicinity of his study became at times a no-go area. The children knew that to irritate him with an ill-judged remark or slip of manners would be to set off an explosion of wrath, which was terrible while it was short-lived.

Civil servants and others in authority could expect a fight to the finish when he took them on. He had his opinions, and they had to be the truth. Sometimes they were. 'Sir Arthur, there is no use your arguing here,' he was told at the Ministry of Munitions when he was campaigning for bullet-proof clothing for soldiers; 'there is no one in the building who does not know that you are right.' He went away to prove his point practically by firing test shots at sheets of different metals in the Windlesham garden. He got his way, and British soldiers got steel helmets. He noticed that French soldiers who had been wounded wore a badge; he got wound badges instituted as the British Army's forerunner of the wound stripe. He argued for the replacement of the cavalry with bicycle corps, because bicycles were easier, and cheaper, to maintain and repair than horses. The war soon proved his point.

He had seen the First World War coming, and feared that the submarine and airship would give Germany victory by blockade. His solution was as simplistic and direct as all his notions: build a Channel tunnel. It would nullify the U-boat menace and give the army speedy access to France, which he was sure Germany would invade. A closely reasoned article in the *Fortnightly Review* stirred Parliament into setting up a commission to consider it. His estimate of the time it would take to build the tunnel was three years. A commission would be likely to waste most of that time simply grinding out its report. Some more dramatic means of alerting the nation was needed. He was its most widely read storyteller, so he would make his appeal with dramatic fiction.

Danger!, published in *The Strand* in July 1914, though written in 1913, showed a small power possessing a mere eight submarines frustrating the might of the Royal Navy by attacking all merchant shipping trading with Britain. Famine ensues, financial stability ends, and little 'Norland' accepts a surrender.

To get his parable taken seriously, he asked Greenhough Smith to invite the reactions of a dozen naval experts. The consensus was politely dismissive of the submarine blockade as a weapon of attrition. One admiral likened the story to a Jules Verne improbability. Another declared, 'No nation would permit it, and the officer who did it would be shot.' Two years later the German Naval Secretary was able to say in the Reichstag, 'The German people can thank the British Admiralty for disregarding the warning on U-boat warfare given by Sir Arthur Conan Doyle.'

When the unarmed cargo vessels and packed liners began to go down in the way he had foreseen, Doyle directed his efforts towards helping those who would find themselves struggling in the sea. He organized the manufacture of an inflatable 'swimming collar', to be supplied to every man in the Royal Navy. He called for all ships to carry ample safety waistcoats and collapsible boats, the precursors of inflatable dinghies. Winston Churchill supported him this time, so he got his way.

In 1914 he offered the War Office his more active service:

> I have been told that there may be some difficulty in finding Officers for the New Army. I think I may say that my name is well known to the younger men of this country and that if I were to take a commission at my age it would set an example which might be of help. I can drill a company – I do so every evening. I have seen something of campaigning, having served as a surgeon in South Africa. I am fifty-five but I am very strong and hardy, and can make my voice audible at great distances, which is useful at drill . . .

The company he was drilling every evening was the Crowborough Civilian Reserve, another of his innovations. It was the forefather of 'Dad's Army'.

> On August 4th, 1914, when war seemed assured, I had a note from Mr Goldsmith, a plumber in the village : 'There is a feeling in Crowborough that something should be done.' This made me laugh at first, but presently I thought more seriously of it. After all Crowborough was one of a thousand villages, and we might be planning and acting for all. Therefore I had notices rapidly printed. I distributed them and put them at road corners, and the same evening (August 4th) we held a village meeting and established the Volunteers, a force which soon grew to two hundred thousand men.

Not in Crowborough alone, of course ; there were 120 of them there, all too old or unfit for the army proper. They assembled at the drill hall, elected their non-commissioned officers (needless to say who took command), and got down to weaponless drilling. He described the organization in *The Times*, and more than a thousand letters came from towns and villages wishing to set up similar bodies.

But the War Office read *The Times*, too. A telegram arrived : 'All unauthorized bodies to be at once disbanded.' He read it out on parade, following by the command 'Right turn ! Dismiss !' Once more, though, his point had been taken. An official volunteer force was quickly established and the unit, recognized as the first of its kind, became the Crowborough Company of the Fifth Royal Sussex Volunteer Regiment. No. 184343 Private Sir Arthur Conan Doyle – 'Ole Bill', as he termed himself – served in it all through the war.

A new adjutant, parading the company for the first time, spotted the burly private's South African medal.

'You have seen service, my man?'

'Yes, sir.'

'Good man!'

'Who is that big fellow on the right of the rear rank?' he asked the C.O. afterwards.

'That's Sherlock Holmes.'

'Good Lord! I hope he didn't mind my "my manning" him.'

'He just loves it.'

As in the matter of the knighthood, he turned to Holmes to grant him vicarious release. Sir Arthur Conan Doyle couldn't serve his country actively, but Mr Sherlock Holmes could, in the story *His Last Bow*. On 2 August, 1914, the date of this brief reunion between him and Watson to strike a blow for their country on the eve of war, Holmes was, in Watson's words, 'a tall, gaunt man of sixty', long since established in his solitary retirement. Sir Arthur Conan Doyle, on that date, was a gigantically-built man of fifty-five, a well-placed family man, prosperous, busy, though more with his crusades than with creative writing; the world's most widely-read storyteller, nevertheless: creator of the best known character in world fiction.

The stories collected in 1917 under the title *His Last Bow* add nothing much to the distinction of the canon of work which they had extended. It didn't matter. By then, the world, like the author, had graver preoccupations.

The following summaries are arranged in order of first magazine publication. This brief Preface is from the volume.

HIS LAST BOW

The friends of Mr Sherlock Holmes will be glad to learn that he is still alive and well, though somewhat crippled by occasional attacks of rheumatism. He has, for many years, lived in a small farm upon the downs five miles from Eastbourne, where his time is divided between philosophy and agriculture. During this period of rest he has refused the most princely offers to take up various cases, having determined that his retirement was a permanent one. The approach of the German war caused him, however, to lay his remarkable combination of intellectual and practical activity at the disposal of the government, with historical results which are recounted in *His Last Bow*. Several previous experiences which have lain long in my portfolio have been added to *His Last Bow* so as to complete the volume.

JOHN H. WATSON, M.D.

The Cardboard Box (*Strand*, Jan 1893, ill. S. Paget; *Harper's*, Jan 1893, ill. W. H. Hyde)

It is a blazing August day in the late 1880s, hot enough for Holmes to favour a straw boater for headgear; therefore, scarcely the ideal climate for him to be sitting on a garden bench in Croydon, flanked by Watson and Insp Lestrade, keenly examining a pair of human ears. Or rather, not a pair, as Holmes points out, which further rules out the possibility of a practical joke by medical students on their female recipient. He is convinced that there has been a shocking crime.

It is a case of three sisters; one of them good, another an angel, but the remaining one a devil, in the estimation of the man best suited to judge. He holds out his hands quietly enough for the darbies to be put on, and his long statement to the police moves Holmes to speculate solemnly on whether the universe is ruled by predestiny or the dread alternative, random chance.

Baker Street was like an oven, and the glare of the sunlight upon the yellow brickwork of the house across the road was painful to the eye. It was hard to believe that these were the same walls which loomed so gloomily through the fogs of winter. Our blinds were half-drawn, and Holmes lay curled upon the sofa, reading and re-reading a letter which he had received by the morning post. For myself, my term of service in India had trained me to stand heat better than cold, and a thermometer at ninety was no hardship. But the morning paper was uninteresting. Parliament had risen. Everybody was out of town, and I yearned for the glades of the New Forest or the shingle of Southsea. A depleted bank account had caused me to postpone my holiday, and as to my companion, neither the country nor the sea presented the slightest attraction to him. He loved to lie in the very centre of five millions of people, with his filaments stretching out and running through them, responsive to every little rumour or suspicion of unsolved crime. Appreciation of nature found no place among his many gifts, and his only change was when he turned his mind from the evil-doer of the town to track down his brother of the country.

Finding that Holmes was too absorbed for conversation I had tossed aside the barren paper, and leaning back in my chair I fell into a brown study. Suddenly my companion's voice broke in upon my thoughts:

'You are right, Watson,' said he. 'It does seem a most preposterous way of settling a dispute.'

'Most preposterous!' I exclaimed, and then suddenly realizing how he had echoed the inmost thought of my soul, I sat up in my chair and stared at him in blank amazement.

'What is this, Holmes?' I cried. 'This is beyond anything which I could have imagined.'

He laughed heartily at my perplexity.

'You remember,' said he, 'that some little time ago when I read you the passage in one of Poe's sketches in which a close reasoner follows the unspoken thoughts of his companion, you were inclined to treat the matter as a mere *tour-de-force* of the author. On my remarking that I was constantly in the habit of doing the same thing you expressed incredulity.'

'Oh, no!'

'Perhaps not with your tongue, my dear Watson, but certainly with your eyebrows. So when I saw you throw down your paper and enter upon a train of thought, I was very happy to have the opportunity of reading it off, and eventually of breaking into it, as a proof that I had been in rapport with you.'

But I was still far from satisfied. 'In the example which you read to me,' said I, 'the reasoner drew his conclusions from the actions of the man whom he observed. If I remember right, he stumbled over a heap of stones, looked up at the stars, and so on. But I have been seated quietly in my chair, and what clues can I have given you?'

'You do yourself an injustice. The features are given to man as the means by which he shall express his emotions, and yours are faithful servants.'

'Do you mean to say that you read my train of thoughts from my features?'

'Your features and especially your eyes. Perhaps you cannot yourself recall how your reverie commenced?'

'No, I cannot.'

'Then I will tell you. After throwing down your paper, which was the action which drew my attention to you, you sat for half a minute with a vacant expression. Then your eyes fixed themselves upon your newly framed picture of General Gordon, and I saw by the alteration in your face that a train of thought had been started. But it did not lead very far. Your eyes flashed across to the unframed portrait of Henry Ward Beecher which stands upon the top of your books. Then you glanced up at the wall, and of course your meaning was obvious. You were thinking that if the portrait were framed it would just cover that bare space and correspond with Gordon's picture over there.'

'You have followed me wonderfully!' I exclaimed.

'So far I could hardly have gone astray. But now your thoughts went back to Beecher, and you looked hard across as if you were studying the character in his features. Then your eyes ceased to pucker, but you continued to look across, and your face was thoughtful. You were recalling the incidents of Beecher's career. I was well aware that you could not do this without thinking of the mission which he undertook on behalf of the North at the time of the Civil War, for I remember your expressing your passionate indignation at the way in which he was received by the more turbulent of our people. You felt so strongly about it that I knew you could not think of Beecher without thinking of that also. When a moment later I saw your eyes wander away from the picture, I suspected that your mind had now turned to the Civil War, and when I observed that your lips set, your eyes sparkled, and your hands clenched I was positive that you were indeed thinking of the gallantry which was shown by both sides in that desperate struggle. But then, again, your face grew sadder; you shook your head. You were dwelling upon the sadness and horror and useless waste of life. Your hand stole towards your own old wound and a smile quivered on your lips, which showed me that the ridiculous side of this method of settling international questions had forced itself upon your mind. At this point I agreed with you that it was preposterous and was glad to find that all my deductions had been correct.'

'Absolutely!' said I. 'And now that you have explained it, I confess that I am as amazed as before.'

'It was very superficial, my dear Watson, I assure you.

'What say you, Watson? Can you rise superior to the heat and run down to Croydon with me on the off chance of a case for your annals?'

'I was longing for something to do.'

'You shall have it, then. Ring for our boots and tell them to order a cab. I'll be back in a moment when I have changed my dressing-gown and filled my cigar-case.'

Holmes and Watson

We had a pleasant little meal together, during which Holmes would talk about nothing but violins, narrating with great exultation how he had purchased his own Stradivarius, which was worth at least five hundred guineas, at a Jew broker's in Tottenham Court Road for fifty-five shillings. This led him to Paganini, and we sat for an hour over a bottle of claret while he told me anecdote after anecdote of that extraordinary man.

Watson

'I should prefer that you do not mention my name at all in connection with the case, as I choose to be only associated with those crimes which present some difficulty in their solution.'

Holmes

'As a medical man, you are aware, Watson, that there is no part of the body which varies so much as the human ear. Each ear is as a rule quite distinctive and differs from all other ones. In last year's *Anthropological Journal* you will find two short monographs from my pen upon the subject.'

Holmes

'What is the meaning of it, Watson?' said Holmes solemnly as he laid down the paper. 'What object is served by this circle of misery and violence and fear? It must tend to some end, or else our universe is ruled by chance, which is unthinkable. But what end? There is the great standing perennial problem to which human reason is as far from an answer as ever.'

Holmes

Wisteria Lodge (*Collier's*, Aug 1908, ill. F. D. Steele; *Strand*, Sep & Oct 1908, ill. Frank Wiles)

Watson, who is so easily blamed for any obscurities within the chronicles, is certainly at fault in assigning this case to the end of March, 1892. Holmes had gone missing at the Reichenbach Falls in May 1891, and did not reappear in England until three years later. The date is as impossible as the narrative attached to it, all of whose chief events are reported, rather than shared by the reader.

John Scott Eccles, another of Holmes's remarkably numerous bachelor clients, spends a night in Wisteria Lodge, the Surrey house of a new friend, a young man of Spanish descent named Garcia. It proves a disappointing evening, with his host nervously distracted. Next morning, Eccles discovers that Garcia and his footman and male cook are all gone.

Garcia had looked in on Eccles at 1 a.m., saying that he thought he had rung his bell; but it transpires perplexingly that the young foreigner had been murdered on Oxshott Common before that time. A fearful constable's glimpse of a dreadful face at a window, voodoo, and a woman with a twisted arm, are further elements in a tale of The Tiger of San Pedro.

'I suppose, Watson, we must look upon you as a man of letters. How do you define the word "grotesque"?'

'Strange – remarkable,' I suggested.

He shook his head at my definition.

'There is surely something more than that,' said he; 'some underlying suggestion of the tragic and the terrible. If you cast your mind back to some of those narratives with which you have afflicted a long-suffering public, you will recognize how often the grotesque has deepened into the criminal. Think of that little affair of the red-headed men. That was grotesque enough in the outset, and yet it ended in a desperate attempt at robbery. Or, again, there was that most grotesque affair of the five orange pips, which led straight to a murderous conspiracy. The word puts me on the alert.'

Holmes

'No woman would ever send a reply-paid telegram. She would have come.'

Holmes

'My mind is like a racing engine, tearing itself to pieces because it is not connected up with the work for which it was built. Life is commonplace; the papers are sterile; audacity and romance seem to have passed forever from the criminal world. Can you ask me, then, whether I am ready to look into any new problem, however trivial it may prove?'

Holmes

'If it were the devil himself a constable on duty should never thank God that he could not lay his hands upon him.'

Insp Baynes

'I'm sure, Watson, a week in the country will be invaluable to you. It is very pleasant to see the first green shoots upon the hedges and the catkins on the hazel once again. With a spud, a tin box, and an elementary book on botany, there are instructive days to be spent.'

Holmes

The Bruce-Partington Plans (*Strand*, Dec 1908, ill. Arthur Twidle; *Collier's* USA, Dec 1908, ill. F.D.Steele)

Mycroft Holmes makes one of his all too rare appearances, to urge his younger brother to use every effort to get back some top secret plans of the remarkable Bruce-Partington submarine. Arthur Cadogan West, a clerk at Woolwich Arsenal, has been found dead on the Underground railway with some of the documents in his pocket, but three vital ones are missing: 'The whole force of the State is at your back if you should need it,' Mycroft reaffirms, in supplying a list of suspect foreign agents in London. 'I'm afraid,' a smiling Holmes remarks to Watson, 'that all the queen's horses and all the queen's men cannot avail in this matter' (which is set in Baker Street's *annus mirabilis*, 1895).

Holmes's own alert consciousness provides the telling clue, from which it is possible to deduce backwards, on the old basis that when all other contingencies fail, whatever remains, however improbable, must be the truth. Yet again, the value of the newspaper agony column is demonstrated, and a man gets fifteen years for reading the *Daily Telegraph*.

Holmes declines to allow his name to go into the honours list, but is not so ungracious as to refuse one of those jewelled tie-pins which his Monarch liked to hand out to subjects who found her favour.

In the third week of November, in the year 1895, a dense yellow fog settled down upon London. From the Monday to the Thursday I doubt whether it was ever possible from our windows in Baker Street to see the loom of the opposite houses. The first day Holmes had spent in cross-indexing his huge book of references. The second and third had been patiently occupied upon a subject which he had recently made his hobby – the music of the Middle Ages. But when, for the fourth time, after pushing back our chairs from breakfast we saw the greasy, heavy brown swirl still drifting past us and condensing in oily drops upon the window-panes, my comrade's impatient and active nature could endure this drab existence no longer. He paced restlessly about our sitting-room in a fever of suppressed energy, biting his nails, tapping the furniture, and chafing against inaction.

'Nothing of interest in the paper, Watson?' he said.

I was aware that by anything of interest, Holmes meant anything of criminal interest. There was the news of a revolution, of a possible war, and of an impending change of government, but these did not come within the horizon of my companion. I could see nothing recorded in the shape of crime which was not commonplace and futile. Holmes groaned and resumed his restless meanderings.

'The London criminal is certainly a dull fellow,' said he in the querulous voice of the sportsman whose game has failed him. 'Look out of this window, Watson. See how the figures loom up, are dimly seen, and then blend once more into the cloud-bank. The thief or the murderer could roam London on such a day as the tiger does the jungle, unseen until he pounces, and then evident only to his victim.'

'There have,' said I, 'been numerous petty thefts.'

Holmes snorted his contempt.

'This great and sombre stage is set for something more worthy than that,' said he. 'It is fortunate for this community that I am not a criminal.'

'It is, indeed!' said I heartily.

'Suppose that I were Brooks or Woodhouse, or any of the fifty men who have good reason for taking my life, how long could I survive against my own pursuit? A summons, a bogus appointment, and all would be over. It is well they don't have days of fog in the Latin countries—the countries of assassination. By Jove! here comes something at last to break our dead monotony.'

It was the maid with a telegram. Holmes tore it open and burst out laughing.

'Well, well! What next?' said he. 'Brother Mycroft is coming round.'

'Why not?' I asked.

'Why not? It is as if you met a tram-car coming down a country lane. Mycroft has his rails and he runs on them. His Pall Mall lodgings, the Diogenes Club, Whitehall – that is his cycle. Once, and only once, he has been here. What upheaval can possibly have derailed him?'

Watson and Holmes

'Mycroft draws four hundred and fifty pounds a year, remains a subordinate, has no ambitions of any kind, will receive neither honour nor title, but remains the most indispensable man in the country.'

'But how?'

'Well, his position is unique. He has made it for himself. There has never been anything like it before, nor will be again. He has the tidiest and most orderly brain, with the greatest capacity for storing facts, of any man living. The same great powers which I have turned to the detection of crime he has used for this particular business. The conclusions of every department are passed to him, and he is the central exchange, the clearing-house, which makes out the balance. All other men are specialists, but his specialism is omniscience. We will suppose that a minister needs information as to a point which involves the Navy, India, Canada and the bimetallic question; he could get his separate advices from various departments upon each, but only Mycroft can focus them all, and say offhand how each factor would affect the other. They began by using him as a short-cut, a convenience; now he has made himself an essential. In that great brain of his everything is pigeon-holed and can be handed out in an instant. Again and again his word has decided the national policy. He lives in it. He thinks of nothing else save when, as an intellectual exercise, he unbends if I call upon him and ask him to advise me on one of my little problems. But Jupiter is descending today. What on earth can it mean? Who is Cadogan West, and what is he to Mycroft?'

Holmes and Watson

'Find an answer to all these questions, and you will have done good service for your country.'

'Why do you not solve it yourself, Mycroft? You can see as far as I.'

'Possibly, Sherlock. But it is a question of getting details. Give me your details, and from an armchair I will return you an excellent expert opinion. But to run here and run there, to cross-question railway guards, and lie on my face with a lens to my eye – it is not my *métier*. No, you are the only man who can clear the matter up. If you have a fancy to see your name in the next honours list – '

My friend smiled and shook his head.

'I play the game for the game's own sake,' said he. 'But the problem certainly presents some points of interest, and I shall be very pleased to look into it.

Mycroft Holmes and Holmes

It was one of my friend's most obvious weaknesses that he was impatient with less alert intelligences than his own.

Watson

His eager face still wore that expression of intense and high-strung energy, which showed me that some novel and suggestive circumstances had opened up a stimulating line of thought. See the foxhound with hanging ears and drooping tail as it lolls about the kennels, and compare it with the same hound as, with gleaming eyes and straining muscles, it runs upon a breast-high scent – such was the change in Holmes since the morning. He was a different man from the limp and lounging figure in the mouse-coloured dressing-gown who had prowled so restlessly only a few hours before round the fog-girt room.

Watson

Am dining at Goldini's Restaurant, Gloucester Road, Kensington. Please come at once and join me there. Bring with you a jemmy, a dark lantern, a chisel, and a revolver.

Holmes (note to Watson)

'Have you had something to eat? Then join me in a coffee and curaçao. Try one of the proprietor's cigars. They are less poisonous than one would expect.'

Holmes

One of the most remarkable characteristics of Sherlock Holmes was his power of throwing his brain out of action and switching all his thoughts on to lighter things whenever he had convinced himself that he could no longer work to advantage. I remember that during the whole of that memorable day he lost himself in a monograph which he had undertaken upon the Polyphonic Motets of Lassus. For my own part I had none of this power of detachment, and the day, in consequence, appeared to be interminable. The great national importance of the issue, the suspense in high quarters, the direct nature of the experiment which we were trying – all combined to work upon my nerve.

Watson

As to Holmes, he returned refreshed to his monograph upon the Polyphonic Motets of Lassus, which has since been printed for private circulation, and is said by experts to be the last word upon the subject. Some weeks afterwards I learned incidentally that my friend spent a day at Windsor, whence he returned with a remarkably fine emerald tie-pin. When I asked him if he had bought it, he answered that it was a present from a certain gracious lady in whose interests he had once been fortunate enough to carry out a small commission.

Watson

The Devil's Foot (*Strand*, Dec 1910, ill. Gilbert Holiday; *Strand*, New York, Jan & Feb 1911, ill. G. Holiday)

Overwork and some erratic habits have combined to threaten

'A straight left against a slogging ruffian.'

The Solitary Cyclist

(Below) 'There lay the unfortunate rider.'

The Priory School

'He sank down upon the sea-chest,
and looked helplessly from one of us
to the other.'

Black Peter

'He stood with slanting head
listening intently.'

Charles Augustus Milverton

'Lestrade took out his official note-book.'

The Six Napoleons

(Below) ' "He and his master dragged me to my room." '

Wisteria Lodge

'He examined them minutely.'

The Cardboard Box

(Below) 'We caught a glimpse of a dark, beautiful, horrified face.'

The Red Circle

Mr Mycroft Holmes

The Bruce-Partington Plans

'"Halloa, Watson! What is this?"'

The Bruce-Partington Plans

'"Put it down! Down, this instant, Watson – this instant, I say!"'

The Dying Detective

'The fellow gave a bellow of anger and sprang upon me like a tiger.'

The Disappearance of Lady Frances Carfax

'A remarkable wine, Watson. Our friend upon the sofa has
assured me that it is from Franz Josef's special cellar at the
Schoenbrunn Palace.'

His Last Bow

Holmes's health once more, in the spring of 1897. He and Watson have come to relax at a cottage near picturesque, elemental Poldhu Bay, on the extreme tip of the Cornish peninsula. It is an ideal place for Holmes to read up and ruminate on supposed Chaldean roots to the ancient language of Cornwall.

Even at this remote spot and time there occurs one of those singular tragedies which needs Holmes's unique powers to investigate and explain it, and which has elements *outré* enough to intrigue him. It nearly brings his death – though not from over-exertion – and Watson's, too, before what the press has dubbed 'The Cornish Horror' can be proved to have its roots in Africa.

In recording from time to time some of the curious experiences and interesting recollections which I associate with my long and intimate friendship with Mr Sherlock Holmes, I have continually been faced by difficulties caused by his own aversion to publicity. To his sombre and cynical spirit all popular applause was always abhorrent, and nothing amused him more at the end of a successful case than to hand over the actual exposure to some orthodox official, and to listen with a mocking smile to the general chorus of misplaced congratulation. It was indeed this attitude upon the part of my friend and certainly not any lack of interesting material which has caused me of late years to lay very few of my records before the public. My participation in some of his adventures was always a privilege which entailed discretion and reticence upon me.

It was, then, with considerable surprise that I received a telegram from Holmes last Tuesday – he has never been known to write where a telegram would serve – in the following terms:

Why not tell them of the Cornish horror – strangest case I have handled.

I have no idea what backward sweep of memory had brought the matter fresh to his mind, or what freak had caused him to desire that I should recount it; but I hasten, before another cancelling telegram may arrive, to hunt out the notes which give me the exact details of the case and to lay the narrative before my readers.

It was, then, in the spring of the year 1897 that Holmes's iron constitution showed some symptoms of giving way in the face of constant hard work of a most exacting kind, aggravated, perhaps, by occasional indiscretions of his own. In March of that year Dr Moore Agar, of Harley Street, whose dramatic introduction to Holmes I may some day recount, gave positive injunctions that the famous private agent lay aside all his cases and surrender himself to complete rest if he wished to avert an absolute breakdown. The state of his health was not a matter in which he himself took the faintest interest, for his mental detachment was absolute, but he was induced at last, on the threat of being permanently disqualified from work, to give himself a complete change of scene and air.

'I fear,' said Holmes, 'that if the matter is beyond humanity it is certainly beyond me.'

Holmes

It was not until long after we were back in Poldhu Cottage that Holmes broke his complete and absorbed silence. He sat coiled in his armchair, his haggard and ascetic face hardly visible among the blue swirl of his tobacco smoke, his black brows drawn down, his forehead contracted, his eyes vacant and far away. Finally he laid down his pipe and sprang to his feet.

'It won't do, Watson!' said he with a laugh. 'Let us walk along the cliffs together and search for flint arrows. We are more likely to find them than clues to this problem. To let the brain work without sufficient material is like racing an engine. It racks itself to pieces. The sea air, sunshine, and patience, Watson – all else will come.'

... I may have commented upon my friend's power of mental detachment, but never have I wondered at it more than upon that spring morning in Cornwall when for two hours he discoursed upon celts, arrowheads, and shards, as lightly as if no sinister mystery were waiting for his solution.

Watson and Holmes

'I followed you.'
'I saw no one.'
'That is what you may expect to see when I follow you.'

Holmes and Sterndale

The Red Circle (*Strand*, Mar & Apr 1911, ill. Pt 1, H.M.Brock, Pt 2, Joseph Simpson; *Strand* (New York), Apr & May 1911)

Another two-part, largely reported case involving enmity between Latins in England. No date is given nor clearly deducible, and it is of no matter.

Mrs Warren, whose profession is landlady, consults Holmes about her elusive lodger. He is one of those men, dear to fiction, who pay well, in advance, on condition that they are not disturbed and are given a house-key, to facilitate going and coming at all hours. Even his meals have to be left outside his door, where he in turn places cryptic notes of his wants, such as 'SOAP', 'MATCH', and 'DAILY GAZETTE'.

More seriously, Mrs Warren's husband is abducted in their road, clearly in mistake for someone else. Holmes uses a mirror to discover that the lodger is not the man he used to be. He reads a candle-code in

Italian and counterfeits a short message in it (which an American Sherlockian scholar worked out, by experiment, would have needed at least 477 passes of the candle, occupying the best part of five minutes). After that, it is fairly plain sailing, with some help from one of Pinkerton's American agents and some prosaic gestures by Insp Gregson.

Holmes was accessible upon the side of flattery, and also, to do him justice, upon the side of kindliness.

Watson

He had an almost hypnotic power of soothing when he wished.

Watson

He took down the great book in which, day by day, he filed the agony columns of the great London journals. 'Dear me!' said he, turning over the pages, 'what a chorus of groans, cries, and bleatings! What a rag-bag of singular happenings! But surely the most valuable hunting-ground that ever was given to a student of the unusual!'

Watson

'It is very curious and complex, Watson.'
'Why should you go further in it? What have you to gain from it?'
'What, indeed? It is art for art's sake, Watson. I suppose when you doctored you found yourself studying cases without thought of a fee?'
'For my education, Holmes.'
'Education never ends, Watson. It is a series of lessons with the greatest for the last.'

Holmes and Watson

'Our official detectives may blunder in the matter of intelligence, but never in that of courage. Gregson climbed the stair to arrest this desperate murderer with the same absolutely quiet and businesslike bearing with which he would have ascended the official staircase of Scotland Yard. The Pinkerton man had tried to push past him, but Gregson had firmly elbowed him back. London dangers were the privilege of the London force.'

Holmes

'But what I can't make head or tail of, Mr Holmes, is how on earth you got yourself mixed up in the matter.'
'Education, Gregson, education. Still seeking knowledge at the old university. Well, Watson, you have one more specimen of the tragic and grotesque to add to your collection. By the way, it is not eight o'clock, and a Wagner night

at Covent Garden ! If we hurry, we might be in time for the second act.'

Insp Gregson and Holmes

The Disappearance of Lady Frances Carfax (*Strand*, Dec 1911, ill. Alec Ball; *The American Magazine*, Dec 1911, ill. F.D.Steele)

Sent off alone on a holiday-cum-investigation in Switzerland, because Holmes is too busy to go, Watson might well have wondered whether there would be any repeat of the sly intervention of *The Hound of the Baskervilles* kind, or of the scornful criticism which his solo effort in *The Solitary Cyclist* case had earned. He, and the reader, will find out, though the answer has not much logic to it.

Watson is on the trail of Lady Frances Carfax, described somewhat ungallantly by Holmes as 'the last derelict of what only twenty years ago was a goodly fleet': he meant that she is her noble family's only surviving member. She is not more than forty and still handsome, but it is more likely to be her money that would attract an adventurer such as the savage-looking Englishman who is following her about Europe. Still, she has the shield of her religion, and the company of a saintly missionary, Dr Shlessinger, and his wife.

But why has she paid off her personal maid and disappeared? Watson is expected to find out, but he is searching in the wrong place, as Holmes's famous instinct should have told him: it makes it all the more unjust of him to tell his dogged friend, 'I cannot at the moment recall any possible blunder which you have omitted.'

'But why Turkish?' asked Mr Sherlock Holmes, gazing fixedly at my boots. I was reclining in a cane-backed chair at the moment, and my protruded feet had attracted his ever-active attention.

'English,' I answered in some surprise. 'I got them at Latimer's, in Oxford Street.'

Holmes smiled with an expression of weary patience.

'The bath!' he said; 'the bath! Why the relaxing and expensive Turkish rather than the invigorating home-made article?'

'Because for the last few days I have been feeling rheumatic and old. A Turkish bath is what we call an alterative in medicine – a fresh starting-point, a cleanser of the system.

'By the way, Holmes,' I added, 'I have no doubt the connection between my boots and a Turkish bath is a perfectly self-evident one to a logical mind, and yet I should be obliged to you if you would indicate it.'

'The train of reasoning is not very obscure, Watson,' said Holmes with a mischievous twinkle. 'It belongs to the same elementary class of deduction which I should illustrate if I were to ask you who shared your cab in your drive this morning.'

'I don't admit that a fresh illustration is an explanation,' said I with some asperity.

'Bravo, Watson! A very dignified and logical remonstrance. Let me see, what were the points? Take the last one first – the cab. You observe that you have some splashes on the left sleeve and shoulder of your coat. Had you sat in the centre of a hansom you would probably have had no splashes, and if you had they would certainly have been symmetrical. Therefore it is clear that you sat at the side. Therefore it is equally clear that you had a companion.'

'That is very evident.'

'Absurdly commonplace, is it not?'

'But the boots and the bath?'

'Equally childish. You are in the habit of doing up your boots in a certain way. I see them on this occasion fastened with an elaborate double bow, which is not your usual method of tying them. You have, therefore, had them off. Who has tied them? A bootmaker – or the boy at the bath. It is unlikely that it is the bootmaker, since your boots are nearly new. Well, what remains? The bath. Absurd, is it not?'

Holmes and Watson

'Single ladies must live, and their passbooks are diaries. She banks at Silvester's. I have glanced over her account.'

Holmes

'You know that I cannot possibly leave London while old Abrahams is in such mortal terror of his life. Besides, on general principles it is best that I should not leave the country. Scotland Yard feels lonely without me, and it causes an unhealthy excitement among the criminal classes. Go, then, my dear Watson, and if my humble counsel can ever be valued at so extravagant a rate as two pence a word, it waits your disposal night and day at the end of the Continental wire.'

Holmes

Like most lonely ladies, Lady Frances found her comfort and occupation in religion. Dr Shlessinger's remarkable personality, his whole-hearted devotion, and the fact that he was recovering from a disease contracted in the exercise of his apostolic duties affected her deeply. She had helped Mrs Shlessinger in the nursing of the convalescent saint. He spent his day, as the manager described it to me, upon a lounge-chair on the veranda, with an attendant lady upon either side of him. He was preparing a map of the Holy Land, with special reference to the kingdom of the Midianites, upon which he was writing a monograph.

Watson

Through the open sitting-room window I saw a huge, swarthy man with a bristling black beard walking slowly down the centre of the street and staring eagerly at the numbers of the houses. It was clear that, like myself, he was on the track of the maid. Acting upon the impulse of the moment, I rushed out and accosted him.

'You are an Englishman,' I said.
'What if I am?' he asked with a most villainous scowl.
'May I ask what your name is?'
'No, you may not,' said he with decision.
The situation was awkward.

Watson and Green

'Where is that coffin which was brought into your house?'
'What do you want with the coffin? It is in use. There is a body in it.'

Holmes and Peters

The Dying Detective (*Collier's*, Nov 1913, ill. F.D.Steele; *Strand*, Dec 1913, ill. Walter Paget)

Watson's reference to this unpleasant experience as having happened to him 'in the second year of my married life' suggests the late 1880s or 1890, during his second marriage; Holmes retired too soon after Watson's third marriage for it to have related to that. One might have expected the exact date to have been unforgettable by him, for, years before his Reichenbach 'bereavement', it was the day on which he was told that Sherlock Holmes was at death's door.

Mrs Hudson was the dread emissary. Hastening to Baker Street with her, Watson learned how her deplorable yet admired tenant had been stricken after being engaged on a case among infective dock workers. He finds Holmes in a desperate state, wasted, delirious, contagious by touch from an obscure Eastern disease.

Holmes's denigratory abuse of him must be put down to the affliction, which only one man, Culverton Smith, a Sumatran planter visiting London, might be able to cure. It is Watson's turn to play emissary, before being treated to a climactic demonstration of what some Americans used to call boondoggling.

Mrs Hudson, the landlady of Sherlock Holmes, was a long-suffering woman. Not only was her first-floor flat invaded at all hours by throngs of singular and often undesirable characters but her remarkable lodger showed an eccentricity and irregularity in his life which must have sorely tried her patience. His incredible untidiness, his addiction to music at strange hours, his occasional revolver practice within doors, his weird and often malodorous scientific experiments, and the atmosphere of violence and danger which hung around

him made him the very worst tenant in London. On the other hand, his pay-
ments were princely. I have no doubt that the house might have been purchased at the price which Holmes paid for his rooms during the years that I
was with him.

The landlady stood in the deepest awe of him and never dared to interfere
with him, however outrageous his proceedings might seem. She was fond of
him, too, for he had a remarkable gentleness and courtesy in his dealings with
women. He disliked and distrusted the sex, but he was always a chivalrous opponent. Knowing how genuine was her regard for him, I listened earnestly to
her story when she came to my rooms in the second year of my married life and
told me of the sad condition to which my poor friend was reduced.

'He's dying, Dr Watson,' said she.

Watson and Mrs Hudson

I have so deep a respect for the extraordinary qualities of Holmes that I have
always deferred to his wishes, even when I least understood them. By now all
my professional instincts were aroused. Let him be my master elsewhere, I at
least was his in a sick room.

'Holmes,' said I, 'you are not yourself. A sick man is but a child, and so I
will treat you. Whether you like it or not, I will examine your symptoms and
treat you for them.'

He looked at me with venomous eyes.

'If I am to have a doctor whether I will or not, let me at least have someone
in whom I have confidence,' said he.

'Then you have none in me?'

'In your friendship, certainly. But facts are facts, Watson, and, after all, you
are only a general practitioner with very limited experience and mediocre
qualifications. It is painful to have to say these things, but you leave me no
choice.'

I was bitterly hurt.

Watson and Holmes

'You mean well, Watson,' said the sick man with something between a sob
and a groan. 'Shall I demonstrate your own ignorance? What do you know,
pray, of Tapanuli fever? What do you know of the black Formosa corrup-
tion?'

'I have never heard of either.'

'There are many problems of disease, many strange pathological possibilities, in the East, Watson.' He paused after each sentence to collect his failing
strength. 'I have learned so much during some recent researches which have a
medico-criminal aspect. It was in the course of them that I contracted this
complaint. You can do nothing.'

Holmes and Watson

Unable to settle down to reading, I walked slowly round the room, examining
the pictures of celebrated criminals with which every wall was adorned.
Finally, in my aimless perambulation, I came to the mantelpiece. A litter of

pipes, tobacco-pouches, syringes, penknives, revolver-cartridges, and other débris was scattered over it.

Watson

Of all ruins, that of a noble mind is the most deplorable. I sat in silent dejection until the stipulated time had passed. He seemed to have been watching the clock as well as I, for it was hardly six before he began to talk with the same feverish animation as before.

'Now, Watson,' said he. 'Have you any change in your pocket?'

'Yes.'

'Any silver?'

'A good deal.'

'How many half-crowns?'

'I have five.'

'Ah, too few! Too few! How very unfortunate, Watson! However, such as they are you can put them in your watchpocket. And all the rest of your money in your left trouserpocket. Thank you. It will balance you so much better like that.'

This was raving insanity.

Watson and Holmes

'I cannot think why the whole bed of the ocean is not one solid mass of oysters, so prolific the creatures seem. Ah, I am wandering! Strange how the brain controls the brain!'

Holmes

'I never needed it more,' said Holmes as he refreshed himself with a glass of claret and some biscuits in the intervals of his toilet. 'However, as you know, my habits are irregular.'

Holmes

'Malingering is a subject upon which I have sometimes thought of writing a monograph.'

Holmes

'My correspondence, however, is, as you know, a varied one, and I am somewhat upon my guard against any packages which reach me.'

Holmes

'Thank you, Watson, you must help me on with my coat. When we have finished at the police-station I think that something nutritious at Simpson's would not be out of place.'

Holmes

His Last Bow: *An Epilogue of Sherlock Holmes*: (*Strand*, Sep 1917, ill. Albert Gilbert; *Collier's*, Sep 1917, ill. F.D.Steele)

It is the eve of the greatest war the world had ever known. Von Bork, unsurpassed among the Kaiser's agents in Europe, is preparing to return to the Fatherland from his home on the East Coast of England.

For much of four years this clifftop house has been the centre of 'half the mischief in England'. Its owner has hobnobbed in the highest circles as a sporting man-of-the-world, 'quite a decent fellow for a German'; all the while compiling a complete dossier on the country's defences, installations, industry, overseas commitments, and anything else that Germany could need to know. Only the updated naval signal codes are required, before Von Bork can follow his wife and household homeward to a hero's welcome.

The last documents are being brought him by a bitter Irish-American named Altamont, who has been glad to serve a German master against detested Britain. He comes as promised, 'bringing home the bacon'. There is some haggling from this tall, gaunt man of sixty, who so closely resembles caricatures of Uncle Sam, about payment of the boodle, to wit £500; neither man will trust the other to complete his part of the exchange first. Without knowing it, Von Bork is right to be wary. A cheque for that amount was a lot to give, in 1914, for a copy of *Practical Handbook of Bee Culture, with some Observations upon the Segregation of the Queen* – although one would fetch many times more than £500 today.

It was nine o'clock at night upon the second of August – the most terrible August in the history of the world. One might have thought already that God's curse hung heavy over a degenerate world, for there was an awesome hush and a feeling of vague expectancy in the sultry and stagnant air. The sun had long set, but one blood-red gash like an open wound lay low in the distant west. Above, the stars were shining brightly, and below, the lights of the shipping glimmered in the bay. The two famous Germans stood beside the stone parapet of the garden walk, with the long, low, heavily gabled house behind them, and they looked down upon the broad sweep of the beach at the foot of the great chalk cliff on which Von Bork, like some wandering eagle, had perched himself four years before. They stood with their heads close together, talking in low, confidential tones. From below the two glowing ends of their cigars might have been the smouldering eyes of some malignant fiend looking down in the darkness.

Von Bork laughed.

'They are not very hard to deceive,' he remarked. 'A more docile, simple folk could not be imagined.'

'I don't know about that,' said the other thoughtfully. 'They have strange limits and one must learn to observe them. It is that surface simplicity of theirs which makes a trap for the stranger. One's first impression is that they are entirely soft. Then one comes suddenly upon something very hard, and you know that you have reached the limit and must adapt yourself to the fact. They have, for example, their insular conventions which simply *must* be observed.'

'Meaning, "good form" and that sort of thing?' Von Bork sighed as one who had suffered much.

'Meaning British prejudice in all its queer manifestations.'

Von Bork and Von Herling

'Tut, my dear sir, we live in a utilitarian age. Honour is a mediaeval conception. Besides, England is not ready. It is an inconceivable thing, but even our special war tax of fifty million, which one would think made our purpose as clear as if we had advertised it on the front page of *The Times*, has not roused these people from their slumbers. Here and there one hears a question. It is my business to find an answer. Here and there also there is an irritation. It is my business to soothe it. But I can assure you that so far as the essentials go – the storage of munitions, the preparation for submarine attack, the arrangements for making high explosives – nothing is prepared. How, then, can England come in, especially when we have stirred her up such a devil's brew of Irish civil war, window-breaking Furies, and God knows what to keep her thoughts at home.'

'She must think of her future.'

'Ah, that is another matter. I fancy that in the future we have our own very definite plans about England, and that your information will be very vital to us. It is to-day or to-morrow with Mr John Bull. If he prefers to-day we are perfectly ready. If it is to-morrow we shall be more ready still. I should think they would be wiser to fight with allies than without them, but that is their own affair. This week is their week of destiny.'

Von Bork and Altamont

'Another glass, Watson!' said Mr Sherlock Holmes, as he extended the bottle of Imperial Tokay.

The thickset chauffeur, who had seated himself by the table, pushed forward his glass with some eagerness.

'It is a good wine, Holmes.'

'A remarkable wine, Watson. Our friend upon the sofa has assured me that it is from Franz Josef's special cellar at the Schoenbrunn Palace. Might I trouble you to open the window, for chloroform vapour does not help the palate.'

Holmes and Watson

'But you, Watson – I've hardly seen you in the light yet. How have the years used you? You look the same blithe boy as ever.'

'I feel twenty years younger, Holmes. I have seldom felt so happy as when I got your wire asking me to meet you at Harwich with the car. But you, Holmes – you have changed very little – save for that horrible goatee.'

'These are the sacrifices one makes for one's country, Watson,' said Holmes, pulling at his little tuft. 'To-morrow it will be but a dreadful memory.'

Holmes and Watson

'Exactly, Watson. . . . Here is the fruit of my leisured ease, the *magnum opus* of my latter years!' He picked up the volume from the table and read out the whole title, *Practical Handbook of Bee Culture, with Some Observations upon the Segregation of the Queen.* 'Alone I did it. Behold the fruit of pensive nights and laborious days when I watched the little working gangs as once I watched the criminal world of London.'

Holmes

'Though unmusical, German is the most expressive of all languages.'

Holmes

'I shall get level with you, Altamont,' he said, speaking with slow deliberation. 'If it takes me all my life I shall get level with you!'

'The old sweet song,' said Holmes. 'How often have I heard it in days gone by. It was a favourite ditty of the late lamented Professor Moriarty. Colonel Sebastian Moran has also been known to warble it. And yet I live and keep bees upon the South Downs.'

Von Bork and Holmes

'Good old Watson! You are the one fixed point in a changing age. There's an east wind coming all the same, such a wind as never blew on England yet. It will be cold and bitter, Watson, and a good many of us may wither before its blast. But it's God's own wind none the less, and a cleaner, better, stronger land will lie in the sunshine when the storm has cleared.'

Holmes

The Valley of Fear

In that fateful month of August 1914, in which 'Altamont' bested Von Bork, the *Strand Magazine* ran another of its favourite kind of announcement: 'CONAN DOYLE'S GREAT NEW SHERLOCK HOLMES SERIAL "THE VALLEY OF FEAR" THRILLING WITH INCIDENT AND EXCITEMENT WILL COMMENCE IN OUR NEXT NUMBER.' Below the proclamation appeared a facsimile of the heading and opening lines of the manuscript. Anyone who bothered to examine the erasures closely could have seen that it had started as a third-person narrative; afterwards, the impersonal 'said Dr Watson' style had been altered to the customary and more comfortable 'said I'.

The triumphal page was completed with a new portrait of Holmes, straight briar pipe in one hand, the other holding up a piece of paper bearing numerical symbols, which he studies intently. It was captioned 'What Sherlock Holmes found in the envelope.' It appeared again in the next issue, this time in full, dramatic colour and captioned 'The Cipher – and the man who solved it', as frontispiece to the serial's first episode. It illustrates the jacket of this present work.

The fact that Britain and a large part of the rest of the world were at war by this time was no damper on the story's prospects. At that time of eagerness to get into the fight, with long lines of excited volunteers for 'Fred Karno's ragtime infantry', and stage revues with such titles as *On Duty* and *Business as Usual*, a brand new serial story about the omniscient man who never lost his battles against the agents of lawlessness and oppression could not have been more opportune: All this, and Sherlock Holmes, too!

Furthermore, the yarn turned out to be a cracker. Holmes scintillates from the start, swiftly sensing the evil shadow of Moriarty over the hurried communication from an informant within the Professor's organization: demonstrating how, even without a key, Sherlock Holmes can crack any code, however abstruse; ribbing Watson for his development of an unexpected vein of pawky humour which is delightfully evident.

The Holmes-Watson relationship, so important to the spirit of the stories, and so missed when it is disregarded or fumbled, shows at its best in this one. More clearly than perhaps anywhere else, they revel in the extent and harmony of their friendship and rapport. The notion of the glacial know-all, contemptuously putting down his ingenuous, bumbling acolyte, could never be conceived by anyone beginning by reading this tale. They are pals, buddies, equals in their differing moulds. For a large portion of this longest of the Sherlock Holmes stories they are off-stage; but when they are on, they play to each other admirably. It is a story whose author clearly enjoyed writing it.

He began it in the winter of 1913, to give Greenhough Smith a new serial to keep up the momentum of success from the adventure-fantasies, *The Lost World* (*Strand*, April–November 1912) and *The Poison Belt* (March–July 1913), whose central figure was another notable creation of self-portraiture, Professor Challenger. With series, serials, single stories, articles, and contributions to symposia, Doyle's name had seldom been missing from the magazine since its foundation in 1891. When there was nothing by him on hand they printed something *about* him.

One of the many visitors to Windlesham in that last pre-war year had been William J.Burns, by reputation America's greatest private detective at the time. They talked of Crippen, whose trial in 1910 Doyle had attended, alert for any flaw in an apparently open-and-shut prosecution; and the case of Oscar Slater, a dissolute German-Jew imprisoned in 1909 after a reprieve from hanging for murder, for whom he would fight on at personal expense until 1927 to prove mistaken identity; and of Sherlock Holmes, the real reason for so many celebrated people coming to meet the man who had created him. In turn, Doyle drew Burns out on the workings of his mentors, the Pinkerton Detective Agency, of Chicago, who had hounded Butch Cassidy and the Sundance Kid, and the Jesse James and Renos and Youngers gangs, and whose emblem was an ever-open eye, with the motto 'We Never Sleep'.

The other side of the Pinkertons' activities had been to give personal protection to the rich and powerful, and act for them to put down labour organizations such as the Molly Maguires, a sharp thorn in the sides of employers in the Pennsylvania coalfields in the 1870s. Doyle got hold of the book *The Molly Maguires and the Detectives*, 1877, by Allan Pinkerton, the agency's Glasgow-born founder. As he read it he formulated a fictional organization, The Scowrers, a violent lodge of the Ancient Order of Freemen, holding sway in a similarly fictional Vermissa Valley, under the rule of hardnosed Councillor Jack McGinty. In real life, a Pinkerton agent, James McPharlan had penetrated the

Molly Maguires. In the story which was to be called *The Valley of Fear* it is Birdy Edwards, using the alias Jack McMurdo, who infiltrates the Scowrers.

A dramatic detective tale set in a rough-tough American mining community was an irresistible idea to Conan Doyle; but he had the notion of making it two tales, beginning with Sherlock Holmes investigating the murder of the American tenant of an ancient moated manor house in Sussex, whose wife and best male friend have some explanation to hide from the police which is not the obvious one.

Holmes's investigation is brilliant, carried out with all the flair and impudence, especially towards the police, which go with his best spirits. The story within the story, a flashback explanation of the American background to the case, takes up more than half of the novel's length. It is just another rough melodrama, with none of the panache of what has preceded it. It could have been expressed in one page, or even one paragraph; but it was the primary reason for the story's having been written at all, so we must be grateful, even if we skip it. The late Adrian Conan Doyle always insisted that its climactic line, 'Birdy Edwards is here. I am Birdy Edwards!' was the most dramatic one his father ever wrote.

Conan Doyle must have known that the story would lose its impact with the shift from Sussex and Sherlock Holmes to America and the Scowrers. He had acknowledged in print that his Huguenot story *The Refugees* suffered a similar 'defect inherent in my plan of showing the causes which led to the disruption as well as its consequences to individuals.' Like it, *The Valley of Fear* was 'really two books with the Atlantic rolling between them.' It is why it has been less regarded than most of the Sherlock Holmes stories; yet, in essentials and in exuberance of spirit, it is among the best.

He finished writing it in April 1914. The *Strand's* serialization, from September to May 1915, was pre-empted in terms of completion by its syndication in American Sunday newspapers from September 20 to November 22, 1914, with 12 illustrations by Arthur I. Keller. American book publication was also first, in March 1915, by George H. Doran Co, New York, with seven of Keller's drawings. The British edition, that June, by Smith, Elder & Co, used only Frank Wiles's frontispiece.

The September 1914 issue of the *Strand*, in which the serial began, carried elsewhere in its pages a feature with the notably relevant title, *The Latest Methods of Tracking Criminals*. It was a study of a 'system of detective science' formulated by an Austrian, Dr Hans Gross, who had established chairs in his subject at several universities, himself occupying the one at Graz. Gross, born in 1847 (he died in 1915, the year after the *Strand* article's appearance), had been a lawyer and examining judge. He had devoted himself over many years to the new science of 'criminalistics', based largely on his own 'Gross system'. The article described the system, which an editorial introduction pointed out would remind readers 'at every step of the methods of Sherlock Holmes'. The writer, Waldemar Kaempffert, 'who was commissioned to go to Graz and make a personal investigation', reported Dr Gross's criteria for a 'criminalist', whether detective, lawyer, or judge :

> He should be a linguist and a draughtsman. He should know what a physician can tell him, what he should ask him ; he must know the wiles of the poacher as well as those of the stock speculator ; he should discern how a will was forged, and what was the sequence of events in a railway accident ; he must know how professional gamblers cheated, how a boiler exploded, and how a lying horse-dealer rejuvenated a broken-down animal ; he must be familiar with book-keeping, so that he can intelligently examine a merchant's accounts ; he must understand the jargon of the underworld, must be capable of translating cipher messages, and must know the methods and tools of all artisans.

'It is safe to say,' his interviewer commented, after detailing some of Gross's methods and experiments, 'that fifty per cent of these laboratory methods – methods now adopted by the most enlightened police officials of Europe are of Gross's devising.' What he did not add was that a good many of them were nothing new to Sherlock Holmes's numberless followers. Conan Doyle did not glean his ideas about the imprint of a man's trade and habits on his clothing and skin from Gross ; he didn't need a textbook to tell him that blood smears at the scene of a crime might have been planted there to mislead, or that a hanging man must not necessarily have either committed suicide or been murdered ; or that there is nothing so eloquent as a footprint, and that old superstitions live long. Gross did not need to tell Doyle these things, because, to a considerable extent, Doyle had said them first.

Hans Gross's textbook on 'criminalistics', the first work ever to detail such procedures as examination of stains and blood, looking for signs of faked illness, how to preserve footprints, to burgle, to counterfeit, to break ciphers and secret writing, and much more, was published, in German, in 1891. The first version in English, *Criminal Investigation*, was an adapted one made by John Adam, Crown and Public Prosecutor at Madras, and published there in 1906. *A Study in Scarlet* had been published in 1887 and *The Sign of the Four* in 1890. Sherlock Holmes and his methods were established before Gross first published, and were familiar throughout the world by the time Adams completed his English version. That is not to say that Gross knew of them, and learned from them, but merely to remark that Arthur Conan Doyle, through Sherlock Holmes, anticipated many of the basic methods of detection and of forensic science. Eminent criminologists have confirmed it; and when the French Sûreté Générale's laboratories at Lyon were named after Conan Doyle in tribute they, at least, got the name right.

It is a pity that the *Strand's* writer, so grandiloquently 'commissioned to go to Graz' (from how far away is not stated), didn't ask the Herr Professor what he thought of Holmes? Perhaps it would have seemed undignified to do so; Holmes is not mentioned in the body of the article, although it might almost have been about him.

Gross's book became a standard work for police. The Sherlock Holmes stories, too, were made required reading by some forces. Many individual policemen, not only ones engaged in the cerebral side of the work, readily acknowledge his spiritual influence even now. I remember the menacing spectacle of a trio of weapon-laden Chicago patrolmen who found me loitering with intent in a television station passageway. They stayed to watch my broadcast about the man who had inspired two of them to become cops in the first place – so they said.

Arthur Conan Doyle was a natural detective genius, who systematized his methods, partly on lines absorbed from Joe Bell, and demonstrated them through Sherlock Holmes. It takes a genius to portray another so convincingly. It was something quite other than literary skill that made him able to invent crimes and their solutions, then reason backwards to recreate their details, and forward again to show Holmes's methods at work. If some of the plots seem old hat today, it is because they have been imitated and adapted so many times, and made over-familiar, in all sorts of guises. If some seem far-fetched, one has only to open any newspaper to read of people still falling for the same kind of confidence tricks (personally and nationally), still proving unable to temper passion with sanity, still being beastly to anyone and anything that it is in their power to oppress. The types of people and crimes which repelled Sherlock Holmes are still with us, and the most sophisticated techniques available against them are in large part derived from the pioneering principles evolved for him by his creator.

The Valley of Fear (*Strand*, Sep 1914 to May 1915, ill. Frank Wiles; Philadelphia Press, Sep to Nov 1914, ill. A.I.Keller)

It is some time in the late 1880s, an early January morning. Holmes, Watson and big, bright Inspector MacDonald of the Yard sit in the parlour of 221B Baker Street. They are discussing Prof Moriarty (of whom, it may be remembered, Watson has professedly never heard when told about him by Holmes a few years later, in 1891, according to his perhaps distraught account of *The Final Problem*).

Holmes has just decoded a cipher message from an informant in the Moriarty organization, Porlock, which has warned him of imminent danger to someone named Douglas at a place called Birlstone; but Inspector Mac's errand is to tell Holmes of just such a tragedy, and to ask him to investigate some peculiar circumstances reported by the Sussex Constabulary.

John Douglas and his wife, Ivy, have lived for five years in the ancient moated manor of Birlstone, on the Kent-Sussex border. A frequent visitor is Douglas's only friend from his obscure past in America, Cecil Barker. The Douglases are rich and locally popular, with no apparent apprehensions. Yet someone has waited concealed in Douglas's study at night, blasted him faceless with a sawn-off shotgun, and got clean away, despite the raised drawbridge and the moat. There are plenty of clues, notably a card bearing a scrawled symbol, 'V.V. – 341', and a brand-mark on the deceased's arm. His wedding ring is missing, although a ring which he had always worn *above* it is still in place.

There is, in fact, a clue too many, and another one, most important of them all, which only Holmes notices. His interest in a dumb-bell and his insistence that the police investigators really ought to take more account of local history, seem to them maddeningly irrelevant, compared with finding out just what is going on between Cecil Barker and the astonishingly merry widow. The mystery is solved with a little help from Watson's umbrella, and we travel back a few years to happenings in the Valley of Fear itself.

'I am inclined to think...' said I.
'I should do so,' Sherlock Holmes remarked impatiently.

Watson and Holmes

'You have heard me speak of Professor Moriarty?'
'The famous scientific criminal, as famous among crooks as...'
'My blushes, Watson!' Holmes murmured in a deprecating voice.
'I was about to say, as he is unknown to the public.'

'A touch! A distinct touch!' cried Holmes. 'You are developing a certain unexpected vein of pawky humour, Watson, against which I must learn to guard myself. But in calling Moriarty a criminal you are uttering libel in the eyes of the law – and there lie the glory and the wonder of it! The greatest schemer of all time, the organizer of every deviltry, the controlling brain of the underworld, a brain which might have made or marred the destiny of nations – that's the man! But so aloof is he from general suspicion, so immune from criticism, so admirable is his management and self-effacement, that for those very words that you have uttered he could hale you to a court and emerge with your year's pension as a solatium for his wounded character. Is he not the celebrated author of *The Dynamics of an Asteroid*, a book which ascends to such rarefied heights of pure mathematics that it is said that there was no man in the scientific press capable of criticizing it? Is this a man to traduce? Foul-mouthed doctor and slandered professor – such would be your respective rôles! That's genius, Watson. But if I am spared by lesser men, our day will surely come.'

Holmes and Watson

'There are many ciphers which I would read as easily as I do the apocrypha of the agony column: such crude devices amuse the intelligence without fatiguing it.'

Holmes

'The vocabulary of Bradshaw is nervous and terse, but limited. The selection of words would hardly lend itself to the sending of general messages. We will eliminate Bradshaw. The dictionary is, I fear, inadmissible for the same reason. What then is left?'

'An almanac!'

'Excellent, Watson! I am very much mistaken if you have not touched the spot. An almanac! Let us consider the claims of Whitaker's Almanac. It is in common use. It has the requisite number of pages. It is in double column. Though reserved in its earlier vocabulary, it becomes, if I remember right, quite garrulous towards the end.'

Holmes and Watson

Holmes had the impersonal joy of the true artist in his better work, even as he mourned darkly when it fell below the high level to which he aspired.

Watson

Inspector MacDonald smiled, and his eyelid quivered as he glanced towards me. 'I won't conceal from you, Mr Holmes, that we think in the C.I.D. that you have a wee bit of a bee in your bonnet over this professor. I made some inquiries myself about the matter. He seems to be a very respectable, learned, and talented sort of man.'

'I'm glad you've got so far as to recognize the talent.'

'Man, you can't but recognize it! After I heard your view I made it my business to see him. I had a chat with him on eclipses. How the talk got that way I canna think; but he had out a reflector lantern and a globe, and made it all clear in a minute. He lent me a book; but I don't mind saying that it was a bit above my head, though I had a good Aberdeen upbringing. He'd have made a grand meenister with his thin face and gray hair and solemn-like way of talking. When he put his hand on my shoulder as we were parting, it was like a father's blessing before you go out into the cold, cruel world.'

Holmes chuckled and rubbed his hands. 'Great!' he said. 'Great!'

Inspector MacDonald and Holmes

'I thought you told me once, Mr Holmes, that you had never met Professor Moriarty.'

'No, I never have.'

'Then how do you know about his rooms?'

'Ah, that's another matter. I have been three times in his rooms, twice waiting for him under different pretexts and leaving before he came. Once – well, I can hardly tell about the once to an official detective. It was on the last occasion that I took the liberty of running over his papers – with the most unexpected results.'

'You found something compromising?'

'Absolutely nothing. That was what amazed me. However, you have now seen the point of the picture. It shows him to be a very wealthy man. How did he acquire wealth? He is unmarried. His younger brother is a station master in the west of England. His chair is worth seven hundred a year. And he owns a Greuze.'

'Well?'

'Surely the inference is plain.'

'You mean that he has a great income and that he must earn it in an illegal fashion?'

'Exactly. Of course I have other reasons for thinking so – dozens of exiguous threads which lead vaguely up toward the centre of the web where the poisonous, motionless creature is lurking. I only mention the Greuze because it brings the matter within the range of your own observation.'

'Well, Mr Holmes, I admit that what you say is interesting: it's more than interesting – it's just wonderful. But let us have it a little clearer if you can. Is it forgery, coining, burglary – where does the money come from?'

'Have you ever read of Jonathan Wild?'

'Well, the name has a familiar sound. Someone in a novel, was he not? I don't take much stock of detectives in novels – chaps that do things and never let you see how they do them. That's just inspiration: not business.'

'Jonathan Wild wasn't a detective, and he wasn't in a novel. He was a master criminal, and he lived last century – 1750 or thereabouts.'

'Then he's no use to me. I'm a practical man.'

'Mr Mac, the most practical thing that you ever did in your life would be to shut yourself up for three months and read twelve hours a day at the annals of crime. Everything comes in circles – even Professor Moriarty. Jonathan Wild was the hidden force of the London criminals, to whom he sold his brains and his organization on a fifteen per cent commission. The old wheel turns, and the same spoke comes up. It's all been done before, and will be again. I'll tell you one or two things about Moriarty which may interest you.'

'You'll interest me, right enough.'

'I happen to know who is the first link in his chain – a chain with this Napoleon-gone-wrong at one end, and a hundred broken fighting men, pick-pockets, blackmailers, and card sharpers at the other, with every sort of crime in between. His chief of staff is Colonel Sebastian Moran, as aloof and guarded and inaccessible to the law as himself. What do you think he pays him ?'

'I'd like to hear.'

'Six thousand a year. That's paying for brains, you see – the American busi-ness principle. I learned that detail quite by chance. It's more than the Prime Minister gets. That gives you an idea of Moriarty's gains and of the scale on which he works. Another point: I made it my business to hunt down some of Moriarty's cheques lately – just common innocent cheques that he pays his household bills with. They were drawn on six different banks. Does that make any impression on your mind ?'

'Queer, certainly ! But what do you gather from it ?'

'That he wanted no gossip about his wealth. No single man should know what he had. I have no doubt that he has twenty banking accounts ; the bulk of his fortune abroad in the Deutsche Bank or the Crédit Lyonnais as likely as not. Sometime when you have a year or two to spare I commend to you the study of Professor Moriarty.'

Inspector MacDonald and Holmes

'Moriarty rules with a rod of iron over his people. His discipline is tremen-dous. There is only one punishment in his code. It is death.'

Holmes

He brightened and rubbed his thin hands together as he listened to the meagre but remarkable details. A long series of sterile weeks lay behind us, and here at last was a fitting object for those remarkable powers which, like all special gifts, become irksome to their owner when they are not in use. That razor brain blunted and rusted with inaction.

Sherlock Holmes's eyes glistened, his pale cheeks took a warmer hue, and his whole eager face shone with an inward light when the call for work reached him.

Watson

'I go into a case to help the ends of justice and the work of the police. If I have ever separated myself from the official force, it is because they have first separ-ated themselves from me. I have no wish ever to score at their expense.'

Holmes

He was in his most cheerful and debonair humour. 'My dear Watson, when I have exterminated that fourth egg I shall be ready to put you in touch with the whole situation.'

He sat with his mouth full of toast and his eyes sparkling with mischief, watching my intellectual entanglement. The mere sight of his excellent appetite was an assurance of success; for I had very clear recollections of days and nights without a thought of food, when his baffled mind had chafed before some problem while his thin, eager features became more attenuated with the asceticism of complete mental concentration. Finally he lit his pipe, and sitting in the inglenook of the old village inn he talked slowly and at random about his case, rather as one who thinks aloud than as one who makes a considered statement.

Watson

'I am not a whole-souled admirer of womankind, as you are aware, Watson, but my experience of life has taught me that there are few wives, having any regard for their husbands, who would let any man's spoken word stand between them and that husband's dead body. Should I ever marry, Watson, I should hope to inspire my wife with some feeling which would prevent her from being walked off by a housekeeper when my corpse was lying within a few yards of her.'

Holmes

'There is an appalling directness about your questions, Watson,' said Holmes, shaking his pipe at me. 'They come at me like bullets.'

Holmes

'I shall sit in that room and see if its atmosphere brings me inspiration. I am a believer in the genius loci.'

Holmes

'Darkness and Dr Watson's umbrella – my wants are simple.'

Holmes

'Breadth of view, my dear Mr Mac, is one of the essentials of our profession. The interplay of ideas and the oblique uses of knowledge are often of extraordinary interest.'

Holmes

'What are we here for at all? I really think that you might treat us with more frankness.'

Holmes laughed. 'Watson insists that I am the dramatist in real life,' said he. 'Some touch of the artist wells up within me, and calls insistently for a well staged performance. Surely our profession, Mr Mac, would be a drab and sordid one if we did not sometimes set the scene so as to glorify our results. The blunt accusation, the brutal tap upon the shoulder – what can one make of such a *dénouement*? But the quick inference, the subtle trap, the clever forecast of coming events, the triumphant vindication of bold theories – are these not the pride and the justification of our life's work? At the present moment you thrill with the glamour of the situation and the anticipation of the hunt. Where would be that thrill if I had been as definite as a timetable? I only ask a little patience, Mr Mac, and all will be clear to you.'

'Well, I hope the pride and justification and the rest of it will come before we all get our death of cold,' said the London detective with comic resignation.

Inspector MacDonald and Holmes

'If criminals would always schedule their movements like railway trains, it would certainly be more convenient for all of us.'

Holmes

Two months had gone by, and the case had to some extent passed from our minds. Then one morning there came an enigmatic note slipped into our letterbox. 'Dear me, Mr Holmes. Dear me !' said this singular epistle. There was neither superscription nor signature.

Watson

'There is a master hand here. It is no case of sawed-off shotguns and clumsy six-shooters. You can tell an old master by the sweep of his brush. I can tell a Moriarty when I see one.'

Holmes

'Do you say that no one can ever get level with this king devil ?'
'No, I don't say that,' said Holmes, and his eyes seemed to be looking far into the future. 'I don't say that he can't be beat. But you must give me time – you must give me time !'

Cecil Barker and Holmes

13

The Case Book of Sherlock Holmes

The moated Birlstone Manor of *The Valley of Fear* is based on Groombridge Manor. The village of Groombridge stands on the border in such a way that some residents use Kent in their addresses, while others' homes are in Sussex.

Some years ago its late owner, Mr Sidney Mountain, told me about a former ghost-in-residence there – the family's departed chauffeur. He had not been seen since sometime in the 1920s, when a visitor had abducted him and smuggled him away in the luggage compartment of a car.

I wish now I had been more inquisitive at the time. There are so many questions which ought to have been asked. How was the abduction managed? Was the ghost dragged from the house, wailing and protesting? Did the kidnapper steer it by the arm, unobtrusively but firmly, murmuring, 'Keep walking, and look natural, or you're a dead man'?

The point of this inconclusive anecdote is that the alleged spirit-snatcher was Sir Arthur Conan Doyle.

To the Inspector Lestrades of this world, that wraps the case up. All the circumstantial evidence points in a single direction. Conan Doyle was an enthusiastic motorist. He had represented his country in an international rally, the Prince Henry of Prussia's tour from Homburg, in Hesse-Nassau, to London, in 1911. His home at Crowborough was less than five miles from the scene of the abduction, a reasonable distance to transport a cooped-up ghost. He was an occasional visitor to the house, which he knew well enough to make it Birlstone Manor.

He had the means and the opportunity. Motive? To anyone of the school of deduction which produces its results by starting with a theory, and selecting facts to fit it, the answer would be obvious: Conan Doyle *needed* a ghost. He wanted every obtainable token of proof that life exists in other forms.

He had become the figurehead, the chief crusader, of the spiritualist movement. He was devoting his time, his fortune, his health to carrying a message of comfort and reassurance to a war-bereaved world.

He had foreseen the war and its new methods of carnage, and published deeply convinced warnings of it. He had visited some of the war fronts and had seen the appalling mess for himself. The rumble of the guns in France was heard clearly at Crowborough. He had lost a son, Capt Kingsley Conan Doyle, his closest brother and companion of Southsea days, Brig-Gen Innes Doyle, and several other relatives, including Jean's favourite brother, Capt Malcolm Leckie.

Although he felt in his physical prime, he was too old for the army. There was still something he could do, though. He had been investigating spiritualism since his college days. Suddenly, in 1916, that which remained after the impossible had been excluded represented the most important truth he had ever faced. He was convinced, and wanted to convince everyone else.

It marked the end of his career as a popular storyteller. The fiction he produced in his last decade on earth included a number of effectively creepy short stories, and two more series with Professor Challenger in them, though not centrally. *The Land of Mist* ran in the *Strand* from July 1925 to March 1926, and *The Maracot Deep* from October 1927 to February 1928. There were no more big historical undertakings, and the last Sherlock Holmes stories, appearing at scattered intervals during the 1920s, while showing some gleams of the old brilliance, were mostly so far below the old standard that the provenance of some of them has been called into question.

The collection under the title *The Case Book of Sherlock Holmes* comprises the final twelve. One of them appeared first in Britain, in 1921, three were published simultaneously in Britain and America, in 1922–24, and the remaining eight appeared first in the USA, in 1925–27, including a series of six in *Liberty* magazine in 1926–27.

Three of the last twelve stories, *The Veiled Lodger, Shoscombe Old Place* and *The Retired Colourman*, have their own little mystery attached. When they appeared in the *Strand*, in 1927, they were illustrated by Frank Wiles, whose last work for the magazine had been in 1914–15, on *The Valley of Fear*.

Wiles was an active artist during 1912–30. He illustrated some of Angela Brazil's school tales and contributed to some of the Blackie Annuals. He *could* have been engaged to do three isolated Holmes stories in 1926, for publication in 1927; but it seems most unlikely, in that Howard Elcock, a fairly frequent *Strand* artist of the 1920s, who had worked on other Conan Doyle pieces, including *Memories and Adventures*, 1923–24, was available. Indeed, he illustrated seven of the other *Case Book* series.

Might we deduce, then, that *The Veiled Lodger, Shoscombe Old Place* and

The Retired Colourman were stories which Doyle had written before the war, but that after Wiles had completed his work on them Doyle had had second thoughts and asked for them to be held back as not being up to his top standard of writing? Certainly, the first and last are nothing to shout about, though *Shoscombe* has some endearing points. Did the editor of *Liberty* beg for a series for 1926–27, to which a preoccupied Doyle responded by letting his agent release these three rejects? To make a series of six, did he write up cursorily some of those stories which over the years hopeful imitators, American as well as British, had sent him and he had bought and put aside? These three, *The Blanched Soldier*, *The Three Gables*, and *The Lion's Mane*, are sub-standard works, the first two of them displaying many Americanisms of language and style.

In this, as in detection, it is a capital mistake to theorize before one has all the evidence. Like others who have puzzled over the assemblage which is *The Case Book of Sherlock Holmes*, I can only echo, 'The faculty of deduction is certainly contagious, Watson . . .'

THE CASE BOOK OF SHERLOCK HOLMES

I FEAR that Mr Sherlock Holmes may become like one of those popular tenors who, having outlived their time, are still tempted to make repeated farewell bows to their indulgent audiences. This must cease and he must go the way of all flesh, material or imaginary. One likes to think that there is some fantastic limbo for the children of imagination, some strange, impossible place where the beaux of Fielding may still make love to the belles of Richardson, where Scott's heroes still may strut, Dickens's delightful Cockneys still raise a laugh, and Thackeray's worldlings continue to carry on their reprehensible careers. Perhaps in some corner of such a Valhalla, Sherlock and his Watson may for a time find a place, while some more astute sleuth with some even less astute comrade may fill the stage which they have vacated.

His career has been a long one – though it is possible to exaggerate it; decrepit gentlemen who approach me and declare that his adventures formed the reading of their boyhood do not meet the response from me which they seem to expect. One is not anxious to have one's personal dates handled so unkindly . . .

. . . He began his adventures in the very heart of the later Victorian era, carried it through the all-too-short reign of Edward, and has managed to hold his own little niche even in these feverish days. Thus it would be true to say that those who first read of him, as young men, have lived to see their own grown-up children following the same adventures in the same magazine. It is a striking example of the patience and loyalty of the British public.

... And so, reader, farewell to Sherlock Holmes! I thank you for your past constancy, and can but hope that some return has been made in the shape of that distraction from the worries of life and stimulating change of thought which can only be found in the fairy kingdoms of romance.

ARTHUR CONAN DOYLE

The Mazarin Stone (*Strand*, Oct 1921, ill. A. Gilbert; *Hearst's International*, Nov 1921, ill. F.D. Steele)

A case full of (recorded) sound and (impotent) fury.

Holmes, viewed by some third person, uses the old *Empty House* device of an effigy of himself to lure an attacker, though this time there are up-to-date amplifications. There seem also to have been architectural changes to 221B Baker Street. Altogether, we feel ourselves on thoroughly unfamiliar territory.

'When will you be pleased to dine, Mr Holmes?' Mrs Hudson asked. 'Seven-thirty, the day after to-morrow,' said he.

Mrs Hudson and Holmes

'I'm expecting something this evening.'
    'Expecting what?'
    'To be murdered, Watson.'
    'No, no, you are joking, Holmes!'
    'Even my limited sense of humour could evolve a better joke than that. But we may be comfortable in the meantime, may we not? Is alcohol permitted? The gasogene and cigars are in the old place. Let me see you once more in the customary armchair. You have not, I hope, learned to despise my pipe and my lamentable tobacco? It has to take the place of food these days.'
    'But why not eat?'
    'Because the faculties become refined when you starve them. Why, surely,

as a doctor, my dear Watson, you must admit that what your digestion gains in the way of blood supply is so much lost to the brain. I am a brain, Watson. The rest of me is a mere appendix.'

Holmes and Watson

'Your morals don't improve, Watson. You have added fibbing to your other vices.'

Holmes

'I can't possibly leave you.'
   'Yes, you can, Watson. And you will, for you have never failed to play the game. I am sure you will play it to the end.'

Watson and Holmes

'Really, sir, you compliment me. Old Baron Dowson said the night before he was hanged that in my case what the law had gained the stage had lost. And now you give my little impersonations your kindly praise.'

Holmes to Sylvius

Thor Bridge (*Strand*, Feb and Mar 1922, ill. A. Gilbert; *Hearst's International*, Feb and Mar 1922, ill. G. Patrick Nelson)

The since-famous, and seemingly bottomless, tin dispatch-box in the vaults of Cox & Co's bank, Charing Cross branch, is opened for the first time to supply this rather painful tale. A passionate wife, driven to tragic desperation by the fading of her allure and the spectacle of her husband being drawn to another woman, is not a theme which would have suited the family readership of the *Strand Magazine's* earlier days. The same might be said of several of the *Case Book* accounts.

   It is a good case, though, with an explanation which it would be improper to give away. Our heroes are in excellent form, and Mr J. Neil Gibson, 'the greatest financial power in the world', is another bully for Holmes to diminish. The most tantalizing feature is the brief glimpse of other goodies in Watson's box, alas, never revealed further by him.

   In his 1930 *Strand* article, 'Some Letters of Conan Doyle', Greenhough Smith claimed this to be the only idea from an outside source, other than that for *The Hound of the Baskervilles*, that Doyle ever found 'strike fire' in him. It came from Smith himself, who passed on the particulars of a German case he had read about.

Somewhere in the vaults of the bank of Cox and Co, at Charing Cross, there is a travel-worn and battered tin dispatch-box with my name, John H. Watson, M.D., Late Indian Army, painted upon the lid. It is crammed with papers, nearly all of which are records of cases to illustrate the curious problems which Mr Sherlock Holmes had at various times to examine. Some, and not the least interesting, were complete failures, and as such will hardly bear narrating, since no final explanation is forthcoming. A problem without a solution may interest the student, but can hardly fail to annoy the casual reader. Among these unfinished tales is that of Mr James Phillimore, who, stepping back into his own house to get his umbrella, was never more seen in this world. No less remarkable is that of the cutter *Alicia*, which sailed one spring morning into a small patch of mist from where she never again emerged, nor was anything further ever heard of herself and her crew. A third case worthy of note is that of Isadora Persano, the well-known journalist and duellist, who was found stark staring mad with a match box in front of him which contained a remarkable worm said to be unknown to science. Apart from these unfathomed cases, there are some which involve the secrets of private families to an extent which would mean consternation in many exalted quarters if it were thought possible that they might find their way into print. I need not say that such a breach of confidence is unthinkable, and that these records will be separated and destroyed now that my friend has time to turn his energies to the matter. There remain a considerable residue of cases of greater or less interest which I might have edited before had I not feared to give the public a surfeit which might react upon the reputation of the man whom above all others I revere. In some I was myself concerned and can speak as an eye-witness, while in others I was either not present or played so small a part that they could only be told as by a third person. The following narrative is drawn from my own experience.

It was a wild morning in October, and I observed as I was dressing how the last remaining leaves were being whirled from the solitary plane tree which graces the yard behind our house. I descended to breakfast prepared to find my companion in depressed spirits, for, like all great artists, he was easily impressed by his surroundings. On the contrary, I found that he had nearly finished his meal, and that his mood was particularly bright and joyous, with that somewhat sinister cheerfulness which was characteristic of his lighter moments.

'You have a case, Holmes?' I remarked.

'The faculty of deduction is certainly contagious, Watson,' he answered. 'It has enabled you to probe my secret. Yes, I have a case. After a month of trivialities and stagnation the wheels move once more.'

'Might I share it?'

'There is little to share, but we may discuss it when you have consumed the two hard-boiled eggs with which our new cook has favoured us. Their condition may not be unconnected with the copy of the *Family Herald* which I observed yesterday upon the hall-table. Even so trivial a matter as cooking an egg demands an attention which is conscious of the passage of time and incompatible with the love romance in that excellent periodical.'

Watson and Holmes

'Let me say right here, Mr Holmes, that money is nothing to me in this case. You can burn it if it's any use in lighting you to the truth. This woman is innocent and this woman has to be cleared, and it's up to you to do it. Name your figure!'

'My professional charges are upon a fixed scale,' said Holmes coldly. 'I do not vary them, save when I remit them altogether.'

Gibson and Holmes

'Well, Watson, we have helped a remarkable woman, and also a formidable man. Should they in the future join their forces, as seems not unlikely, the financial world may find that Mr Neil Gibson has learned something in that schoolroom of sorrow where our earthly lessons are taught.'

Holmes

The Creeping Man (*Strand*, Mar 1923, ill. H.K.Elcock; *Hearst's International*, Mar 1923, ill. F.D.Steele)

This is another out of the tin box, but one which, unfortunately, might as well have been left there. Watson is by turns grumpy, clumsy and forgetful. The prose shows signs of having been tinkered with, at the least.

Prof Presbury, the famous 'Camford' physiologist, is behaving oddly. It is not unheard of for a man of 61 to become engaged to a colleague's young daughter; he must be envied, for she is 'a very perfect girl both in mind and body'. It is a little less conventional of him to scuttle about on all fours, taunt a chained wolfhound face-to-face, and swarm up an ivied house wall, to peer in at his daughter's bedroom window.

The explanation lies as far off as Prague and the Himalayan slopes.

The relations between us in those latter days were peculiar. He was a man of habits, narrow and concentrated habits, and I had become one of them. As an institution I was like the violin, the shag tobacco, the old black pipe, the index books, and others perhaps less excusable. When it was a case of active work and a comrade was needed upon whose nerve he could place some reliance, my role was obvious. But apart from this I had uses. I was a whetstone for his mind, I stimulated him. He liked to think aloud in my presence. His remarks could hardly be said to be made to me – many of them would have been as appropriately addressed to his bedstead – but none the less, having formed the habit, it had become in some way helpful that I should register and interject. If I irritated him by a certain methodical slowness in my mentality, that irritation served only to make his own flame-like intuitions and impressions flash up the more vividly and swiftly. Such was my humble role in our alliance.

Watson

'I have serious thoughts of writing a small monograph upon the uses of dogs in the work of the detective.'

'But surely, Holmes, this has been explored,' said I. 'Bloodhounds – sleuth-hounds – '

'No, no, Watson, that side of the matter is, of course, obvious. But there is another which is far more subtle. You may recollect that in the case which you, in your sensational way, coupled with the Copper Beeches, I was able, by watching the mind of the child, to form a deduction as to the criminal habits of the very smug and respectable father.'

'Yes, I remember it well.'

'My line of thoughts about dogs is analogous. A dog reflects the family life. Whoever saw a frisky dog in a gloomy family, or a sad dog in a happy one? Snarling people have snarling dogs, dangerous people have dangerous ones. And their passing moods may reflect the passing moods of others.'

Holmes and Watson

'Good, Watson. You always keep us flat-footed on the ground.'

Holmes

'To-morrow will certainly see us in Camford. There is, if I remember right, an inn called the Chequers where the port used to be above mediocrity and the linen was above reproach. I think, Watson, that our lot for the next few days might lie in less pleasant places.'

Holmes

'Excellent, Watson! Compound of the Busy Bee and Excelsior. We can but try – the motto of the firm.'

Holmes

'When one tries to rise above Nature one is liable to fall below it. The highest type of man may revert to the animal if he leaves the straight road of destiny ... Consider, Watson, that the material, the sensual, the worldly would all prolong their worthless lives. The spiritual would not avoid the call to something higher. It would be the survival of the least fit. What sort of cesspool may not our poor world become?'

Holmes

The Sussex Vampire (*Strand*, Jan 1924, ill. H.K. Elcock; *Hearst's International*, Jan 1924, ill. W.T. Benda)

Efforts have been made in recent years to link Sherlock Holmes with Count Dracula and his milieu. Happily, they have not matured.

Holmes is contemptuous of the suggestion that a vampire might have caused the throat injuries to the infant son of one of Watson's old rugger opponents, 'Big Bob' Ferguson, of Lamberley, Sussex. Yet, the exotic Mrs Ferguson has been behaving strangely to both this child and to her older stepson, and has even been seen with blood around her lips.

Holmes finds it all relatively simple, although his exposition rather conceals it: 'It has been a case for intellectual deduction, but when this original intellectual deduction is confirmed point by point by quite a number of independent incidents, then the subjective becomes objective and we can say confidently that we have reached our goal.'

Ferguson puts his big hand to his furrowed forehead. 'For heaven's sake, Holmes,' says he hoarsely; and no wonder.

All the same, there are some enjoyably idiosyncratic touches to a rather *outré* narrative, the one which includes mention of that other, sadly missing one, of the ship *Matilda Briggs* and the giant rat of Sumatra.

'Matilda Briggs was not the name of a young woman, Watson. It was the name of a ship which is associated with the giant rat of Sumatra, a story for which the world is not yet prepared.'

Holmes

It was one of the peculiarities of his proud, self-contained nature that though he docketed any fresh information very quietly and accurately in his brain, he seldom made any acknowledgement to the giver.

Watson

'I never get your limits, Watson. There are unexplored possibilities about you.'

Holmes

'One forms provisional theories and waits for time or fuller knowledge to explode them. A bad habit, Mr Ferguson, but human nature is weak. I fear that your old friend here has given an exaggerated view of my scientific methods.'

Holmes

The Three Garridebs (*Collier's*, Oct 1924, ill. J.R. Flanagan ; *Strand*, Jan 1925, ill. H.K. Elcock)

Birmingham seems to be the place to despatch a dupe to, in order to get him out of the way for a time : it was so in the case of *The Stockbroker's Clerk*, and it is in this instance. The inference is elusive ; what might be suggested today cannot necessarily apply to 1902, the year in which Holmes refused a knighthood.

We are also back in *Red-Headed League* vein for a study in cupidity, in which two men with the rare surname of Garrideb need only locate a third, in order to share with him an eccentric American's $15 million estate. The scholarly old Nathan Garrideb does not normally leave his home, but as a collector who fancies becoming recognized as the Hans Sloane (1660–1753) of his age he is open to persuasion that a day return to Birmingham should reward him handsomely.

It may have been a comedy, or it may have been a tragedy. It cost one man his reason, it cost me a blood-letting, and it cost yet another man the penalties of the law. Yet there was certainly an element of comedy. Well, you shall judge for yourselves.

I remember the date very well, for it was the same month that Holmes refused a knighthood for services which may perhaps some day be described. I only refer to the matter in passing, for in my position of partner and confidant I am obliged to be particularly careful to avoid any indiscretion. I repeat, however, that this enables me to fix the date, which was the latter end of June, 1902, shortly after the conclusion of the South African War. Holmes had spent several days in bed, as was his habit from time to time, but he emerged that morning with a long foolscap document in his hand and a twinkle of amusement in his austere gray eyes.

Watson

'I have been down to see friend Lestrade at the Yard. There may be an occasional want of imaginative intuition down there, but they lead the world for thoroughness and method.'

Holmes

'He nearly fainted at the sudden shock of it,
but he bit his lip . . .'

The Valley of Fear

'"I heard him cock the gun, but I had got
hold of it before he could fire."'

The Valley of Fear

The Illustrious Client

'His face turned upon us with a glare of baffled rage, which gradually softened into a rather shamefaced grin as he realized that two pistols were pointed at his head.'

The Three Garridebs

'"It took some violence to do that,' said Holmes, gazing at the chip on the ledge. With his cane he struck the ledge several times without leaving a mark. "Yes, it was a hard knock."'

Thor Bridge

'The Professor spat out some atrocious word at me and hurried on down the staircase.'

The Creeping Man

'There was something in the woman's voice which arrested Holmes's attention. He turned swiftly upon her.
  "Your life is not your own," he said. "Keep your hands off it."'

The Veiled Lodger

'Holmes released the spaniel, and with a joyous cry it dashed
forward to the carriage and sprang upon the step.'

Shoscombe Old Place

Professor James Moriarty

Col. Sebastian Moran

Charles Augustus Milverton

Baron Adelbert Gruner

'You're not hurt, Watson? For God's sake, say that you are not hurt!'

It was worth a wound – it was worth many wounds – to know the depth of loyalty and love which lay behind that cold mask. The clear, hard eyes were dimmed for a moment, and the firm lips were shaking. For the one and only time I caught a glimpse of a great heart as well as of a great brain. All my years of humble but single-minded service culminated in that moment of revelation.

'It's nothing, Holmes. It's a mere scratch.'

He had ripped up my trousers with his pocket-knife.

'You are right,' he cried with an immense sigh of relief. 'It is quite superficial.'

Holmes and Watson

The Illustrious Client (*Collier's*, Nov 1924, ill. John Richard Flanagan; *Strand*, May 1925, ill. Howard K. Elcock)

The Client does not appear, and is discreetly not named, but it is pretty certain that he was that same Edward of the 'all-too-short reign', and that this is a case from 1902, probably not long after his postponed coronation. He is not himself in trouble, though. He is concerned for the welfare of the beautiful, passionate daughter of General de Merville, of Khyber fame. That fine old gentleman is broken with concern, for his Violet is besotted with love of a handsome Austrian adventurer. Baron Adelbert Gruner is 'said to have the whole sex at his mercy and to have made ample use of the fact,' not to mention being thought to have disposed of his last wife over a cliff. That is why the tactful intermediary, Col Sir James Damery, has come to seek Holmes's help.

Warnings and threats are useless. Baron Gruner has prepared his inamorata against any slander she might hear of him, so the example of a surviving victim, Kitty Winter, cannot dissuade her. A murderous attack on Holmes almost puts him out of the contest; but so long as the London Library stands in St James's Square there will always be a means towards diversionary connoisseurship, and Watson, deputed to go solo again, can be relied on to rise at least halfway to an emergency.

Sir Arthur Conan Doyle reckoned this among his half-dozen best Sherlock Holmes stories, and rightly so. The female characters are stronger and more realistic than any of their predecessors, while Gruner is a more plausible villain than Moriarty, Moran, or Milverton. His confrontations with Holmes and with Watson do not need a single word changing, nor an emphasis stressing, to keep their dramatic strength in any modern medium.

Both Holmes and I had a weakness for the Turkish bath. It was over a smoke in the pleasant lassitude of the drying-room that I have found him less reticent and more human than anywhere else. On the upper floor of the Northumberland Avenue establishment there is an isolated corner where two couches lie side by side, and it was on these that we lay upon September 3, 1902, the day when my narrative begins. I had asked him whether anything was stirring, and for answer he had shot his long, thin, nervous arm out of the sheets which enveloped him and had drawn an envelope from the inside pocket of the coat which hung beside him.

Watson

'I am accustomed to have mystery at one end of my cases, but to have it at both ends is too confusing.'

Holmes

'A complex mind. All great criminals have that. My old friend Charlie Peace was a violin virtuoso. Wainwright was no mean artist. I could quote many more.'

Holmes

'Woman's heart and mind are insoluble puzzles to the male. Murder might be condoned or explained, and yet some smaller offence might rankle.'

Holmes

'A purring cat who thinks he sees prospective mice. Some people's affability is more deadly than the violence of coarse souls.'

Holmes

'I tell you, Mr Holmes, this man collects women, and takes a pride in his collection, as some men collect moths or butterflies. He had it all in the book. Snapshot photographs, names, details, everything about them. It was a beastly book – a book no man, even if he had come from the gutter, could have put together. But it was Adelbert Gruner's book all the same. "Souls I have ruined." He could have put that on the outside if he had been so minded.'

Kitty Winter

'At half-past five a cab deposited us outside 104 Berkeley Square, where the old soldier resides – one of those awful gray London castles which would make a church seem frivolous.'

Holmes

'I don't quite know how to make her clear to you, Watson. Perhaps you may meet her before we are through, and you can use your own gift of words. She is beautiful, but with the ethereal other-world beauty of some fanatic whose thoughts are set on high. I have seen such faces in the pictures of the old masters of the Middle Ages. How a beastman could have laid his vile paws upon such a being of the beyond I cannot imagine. You may have noticed how extremes call to each other, the spiritual to the animal, the cave-man to the angel. You never saw a worse case than this.

'She knew what we had come for, of course – that villain had lost no time in poisoning her mind against us. Miss Winter's advent rather amazed her, I think, but she waved us into our respective chairs like a reverend abbess receiving two rather leprous mendicants. If your head is inclined to swell, my dear Watson, take a course of Miss Violet de Merville.'

Holmes

'I was sorry for her, Watson. I thought of her for the moment as I would have thought of a daughter of my own. I am not often eloquent. I use my head, not my heart. But I really did plead with her with all the warmth of words that I could find in my nature. I pictured to her the awful position of the woman who only wakes to a man's character after she is his wife – a woman who has to submit to be caressed by bloody hands and lecherous lips.'

Holmes

'I'll tell you who I am. I am his last mistress. I am one of a hundred that he has tempted and used and ruined and thrown into the refuse heap, as he will you also. *Your* refuse heap is more likely to be a grave, and maybe that's the best. I tell you, you foolish woman, if you marry this man he'll be the death of you. It may be a broken heart or it may be a broken neck, but he'll have you one way or the other. It's not out of love for you I'm speaking. I don't care a tinker's curse whether you live or die. It's out of hate for him and to spite him and to get back on him for what he did for me. But it's all the same, and you needn't look at me like that, my fine lady, for you may be lower than I am before you are through with it.'

Kitty Winter

I think I could show you the very paving-stone upon which I stood when my eyes fell upon the placard, and a pang of horror passed through my very soul. It was between the Grand Hotel and Charing Cross Station, where a one-legged newsvendor displayed his evening papers. The date was just two days after the last conversation. There, black upon yellow, was the terrible news-sheet:

MURDEROUS ATTACK UPON
SHERLOCK HOLMES

Watson

There was a curious secretive streak in the man which led to many dramatic effects, but left even his closest friend guessing as to what his exact plans might be. He pushed to an extreme the axiom that the only safe plotter was he who plotted alone. I was nearer him than anyone else, and yet I was always conscious of the gap between.

Watson

'I am here to be used, Holmes.'

'Well, then, spend the next twenty-four hours in an intensive study of Chinese pottery.'

He gave no explanations and I asked for none. By long experience I had learned the wisdom of obedience. But when I had left his room I walked down Baker Street, revolving in my head how on earth I was to carry out so strange an order. Finally I drove to the London Library in St James's Square, put the matter to my friend Lomax, the sublibrarian, and departed to my rooms with a goodly volume under my arm.

It is said that the barrister who crams up a case with such care that he can examine an expert witness upon the Monday has forgotten all his forced knowledge before the Saturday. Certainly I should not like now to pose as an authority upon ceramics. And yet all that evening, and all that night with a short interval for rest, and all the next morning, I was sucking in knowledge and committing names to memory. There I learned of the hall-marks of the great artist-decorators, of the mystery of cyclical dates, the marks of the Hung-wu and the beauties of the Yung-lo, the writings of Tang-ying, and the glories of the primitive period of the Sung and the Yuan.

Watson

When an object is good and a client is sufficiently illustrious, even the rigid British law becomes human and elastic.

Watson

The Three Gables (*Liberty*, Sep 1926, ill. F.D.Steele ; *Strand*, Oct 1926, ill. H.K.Elcock)

A black bruiser, Steve Dixie, warns Holmes off his current inquiry into the doings of a gang of intimidators. A chance request to him to advise the widow of an old client, who has been offered a large sum for the immediate sale of her house and all its contents, brings him up against one of the very gang's operations.

This is the most outlandish and seemingly alien tale of the entire canon. Holmes withholds criminal evidence in return for a payment of £5,000 to his client by an adversary of whom Watson so far forgets himself as to write : 'So roguish and exquisite did she look as she stood before us with a challenging smile that I felt of all Holmes's criminals this was the one whom he would find it hardest to face.'

The Blanched Soldier (*Liberty*, Oct 1926, ill. F.D.Steele ; *Strand*, Nov 1926, ill. H. K. Elcock)

Holmes narrates a case himself – or purports to. It is a not very credible account of an upstanding young ex-Serviceman searching for his elusive mate from Boer War days. He finds him, though in incommunicado state due to a coincidental visitation of ichthyosis, whose most apparent symptom is a face as white as cheese.

(The future may be a closed book to Dr Watson, and perhaps he does embroider facts to attain dramatic and romantic results in his narratives, but when it comes to chronicling the past he has nothing to fear from this level of competition.)

The Lion's Mane (*Liberty*, Nov 1926, ill. F.D.Steele ; *Strand*, Dec 1926, ill. H.K.Elcock)

The coastline of Sussex, where it forms that majestic, chalky outline called the Seven Sisters, is crumbling away at the rate of one yard each year. Allowing for extra during unusually severe storms and winters, it seems to be inferred that Holmes's retirement home, nestling a little way inland, is now the best part of one hundred yards closer to the sea than it was in the year of this post-retirement case, 1909. The tortuous, steep and slippery path, down to the beach where Fitzroy McPherson met his death, has been long effaced. Harold Stackhurst's well-known coaching establishment, The Gables, is no more. Only Sherlock Holmes endures.

This is his own telling of a seaside mystery which he happened to be on hand to solve. 'I am an omnivorous reader with a strangely retentive memory for trifles,' he explains. If he had not chanced to take in *Out of Doors : A Selection of Original Articles on Practical Natural History*, 1874, by the Rev. J.G.Wood (1827–89), there might have been no explaining done, and Maudie Bellamy might have felt twice bereaved.

It is a most singular thing that a problem which was certainly as abstruse and unusual as any which I have faced in my long professional career should have come to me after my retirement, and be brought, as it were, to my very door. It occurred after my withdrawal to my little Sussex home, when I had given myself up entirely to that soothing life of Nature for which I had so often yearned during the long years spent amid the gloom of London. At this period of my life the good Watson had passed almost beyond my ken. An occasional week-end visit was the most that I ever saw of him. Thus I must act as my own chronicler.

Holmes

The Retired Colourman (*Liberty*, Dec 1926, ill. F.D.Steele ; *Strand*, Jan 1927, ill. F.Wiles)

Scotland Yard have called on Holmes's help often enough, but it is rare for them to refer a client to him – 'just as medical men occasionally send their incurables to a quack.'

Josiah Amberley, retired manufacturer of artistic materials, has mislaid his wife, twenty years his junior. It seems that he has been deprived of her by his frequent chess opponent, Dr Ray Ernest, who is more adept than he is at another game. They have even taken the old man's deed-box with them.

Holmes is busy with the unrecorded case of the two Coptic Patriarchs, so Watson goes it alone again, but is once more cynically used by Holmes.

The only shaft of interest on a weak story is the appearance of another private investigator, Barker, referred to by Holmes as 'my hated rival upon the Surrey shore.' We never meet him again.

'What did you think of him ?'

'A pathetic, futile, broken creature.'

'Exactly, Watson. Pathetic and futile. But is not all life pathetic and futile ? Is not his story a microcosm of the whole ? We reach. We grasp. And what is left in our hands at the end ? A shadow. Or worse than a shadow – misery.'

Holmes and Watson

'I must admit to you that the case, which seemed to me to be so absurdly simple as to be hardly worth my notice, is rapidly assuming a very different aspect. It is true that though in your mission you have missed everything of importance, yet even those things which have obtruded themselves upon your notice give rise to serious thought.'

'What have I missed?'

'Don't be hurt, my dear fellow. You know that I am quite impersonal. No one else would have done better. Some possibly not so well.'

Holmes and Watson

'With your natural advantages, Watson, every lady is your helper and accomplice. What about the girl at the post-office, or the wife of the green-grocer? I can picture you whispering soft nothings with the young lady at the Blue Anchor, and receiving hard somethings in exchange. All this you have left undone.'

'It can still be done.'

'It has been done. Thanks to the telephone and the help of the Yard, I can usually get my essentials without leaving this room.'

Holmes and Watson

'Let us escape from this weary workaday world by the side door of music. Carina sings to-night at the Albert Hall, and we still have time to dress, dine and enjoy.'

Holmes

'Amberley excelled at chess – one mark, Watson, of a scheming mind.'

Holmes

'Burglary has always been an alternative profession had I cared to adopt it, and I have little doubt that I should have come to the front.'

Holmes

The Veiled Lodger (*Liberty*, Jan 1927, ill. F.D.Steele; *Strand*, Feb 1927, ill. F.Wiles)

Once again, the case mentioned within the case – this time, that concerning the politician, the lighthouse, and the trained cormorant – sounds more promising than the case itself. Titles can be deceptive, however, and we shall never know.

Mrs Merrilow, a buxom Brixton landlady, does not mind Watson's filthy habits, but she is concerned about her long-term lodger. Mrs Ronder has never uncovered her face in seven years, except inadvertently, and one of those occasions was enough to cause the milkman to drop his pail. Now she seems to be wasting away, and has taken to crying 'Murder!' She will not consult the police or the clergy, but has allowed Mrs Merrilow to fetch Holmes to her.

There is nothing for him to do except listen to a moving confession: 'Poor girl! Poor girl! The ways of fate are indeed hard to understand. If there is not some compensation hereafter, then the world is a cruel jest.'

When one considers that Mr Sherlock Holmes was in active practice for twenty-three years, and that during seventeen of them I was allowed to co-operate with him and to keep notes of his doings, it will be clear that I have a mass of material at my command. The problem has always been not to find but to choose. There is the long row of yearbooks which fill a shelf, and there are the dispatch-cases filled with documents, a perfect quarry for the student not only of crime but of the social and official scandals of the late Victorian era. Concerning these latter, I may say that the writers of agonized letters, who beg that the honour of their families or the reputation of famous forebears may not be touched, have nothing to fear. The discretion and high sense of professional honour which have always distinguished my friend are still at work in the choice of these memoirs, and no confidence will be abused. I deprecate, how- ever, in the strongest way the attempts which have been made lately to get at and to destroy these papers. The source of these outrages is known, and if they are repeated I have Mr Holmes's authority for saying that the whole story con- cerning the politician, the lighthouse, and the trained cormorant will be given to the public. There is at least one reader who will understand.

Watson

Sherlock Holmes threw himself with fierce energy upon the pile of common- place books in the corner. For a few minutes there was a constant swish of the leaves, and then with a grunt of satisfaction he came upon what he sought. So excited was he that he did not rise, but sat upon the floor like some strange Buddha, with crossed legs, the huge books all round him, and one open upon his knees.

Watson

'There is a cold partridge on the sideboard, Watson, and a bottle of Montra- chet. Let us renew our energies before we make a fresh call upon them.'

Holmes

We sat in silence for some time after the unhappy woman had told her story.

Then Holmes stretched out his long arm and patted her hand with such a show of sympathy as I had seldom known him to exhibit.

'Poor girl!' he said. 'Poor girl! The ways of fate are indeed hard to understand. If there is not some compensation hereafter, then the world is a cruel jest.'

Watson and Holmes

We had risen to go, but there was something in the woman's voice which arrested Holmes's attention. He turned swiftly upon her.

'Your life is not your own,' he said. 'Keep your hands off it.'

'What use is it to anyone?'

'How can you tell? The example of patient suffering is in itself the most precious of all lessons to an impatient world.'

The woman's answer was a terrible one. She raised her veil and stepped forward into the light.

'I wonder if you would bear it,' she said.

Eugenia Ronder and Holmes

Shoscombe Old Place (*Liberty*, Mar 1927, ill. F.D.Steele ; *Strand*, Apr 1927, ill. F.Wiles)

Sir Robert Norberton, of Shoscombe Old Place, Berkshire, is by reputation a dangerous man of the turf: he once horsewhipped Sam Brewer, the well-known Curzon Street moneylender, on Newmarket Heath, almost killing him. Now he is the one in danger. If his fancied colt, Shoscombe Prince, does not win the Derby, and restore his fortune through his bets, he will be sold up by Brewer and others.

Then, why has he fallen out with Lady Beatrice Falder, his sister, with whom he lives and on whom he depends? Why choose this time to give away her pet spaniel to a neighbouring publican? As for the lady, why has she stopped looking in on Shoscombe Prince, or letting herself be seen at all, except when taking her drive with her maid?

The solution is reached through the dog and a bone. But the bone is not the dog's – it is, according to Watson, the upper condyle of a human femur.

'By the way, Watson, you know something of racing?'

'I ought to. I pay for it with half my wound pension.'

Holmes and Watson

14

Who's Who of Characters

All characters with significance to their stories – those who would be billed players, for speaking parts, in any dramatization – are included. Most of them have an apposite quote attached, not so much descriptive as relevant to what they are or do. Their fates, destinies, and other concluding circumstances which might give too much away are not stated.

There are just a few extra entries, such as names of off-stage characters of some significance and of restaurants notably used by Holmes and Watson. No references are made to other places, fictional or real, or to real-life people.

Only those quotations which seem to need attribution to their speaker have been given it. I have abbreviated story titles by omitting the definite or indefinite article.

ACHMET. Bearer of the Agra Treasure; murdered for it. *Sign of Four*

ACTON. One of the Reigate squires, in protracted litigation with Cunningham. Victim of a singular burglary. *Reigate Squires*

ADAIR, HON RONALD. Second son of the Earl of Maynooth. Shot dead in his locked room at his Park Lane home. 'The youth moved in the best society – had, so far as was known, no enemies and no particular vices.' – Watson, *Empty House*

ADLER, IRENE. Former operatic contralto, born New Jersey, USA, 1858. While prima donna at the Imperial Opera of Warsaw she became closely associated with the Crown Prince of Bohemia, who was compromisingly photographed with her. 'He (Holmes) used to make merry over the cleverness of women, but I have not heard him do it of late. And when he speaks of Irene Adler, or when he refers to her photograph, it is always under the honourable title of *the* woman.' – Watson, *Scandal in Bohemia*

AKBAR, DOST. One of the Four. *Sign of Four*

ALLEN, MRS. Housekeeper at Birlstone Manor. *Valley of Fear*

ALTAMONT. Irish-American alias of Holmes. 'Sometimes I assure you I can hardly understand him. He seems to have declared war on the King's English as well as on the English king.' – Von Bork, *His Last Bow*

AMBERLEY, JOSIAH. Retired manufacturer of artists' materials. His much younger wife disappeared, in company with his chess opponent, Dr Ray Ernest. 'He made his little pile, retired from business at the age of sixty-one, bought a house at Lewisham, and settled down to rest after a life of ceaseless grind. One would think his future was tolerably assured.' – Holmes, *Retired Colourman*

AMES. Butler at Birlstone Manor. 'Ten years with Sir Charles Chandos – as solid as a rock.' – Insp MacDonald, *Valley of Fear*

ANGEL, HOSMER. City cashier. Fiancé of Mary Sutherland. He disappeared on their wedding morning. 'A flush stole over Miss Sutherland's face, and she picked nervously at the fringe of her jacket. "I met him first at the gasfitters' ball," she said.' – Watson, *Case of Identity*

ANDERSON, P.C. Sussex Constabulary. Fulworth village constable. 'A big, ginger-moustached man of the slow, solid Sussex breed – a breed which covers much good sense under a heavy, silent exterior.' – Holmes, *Lion's Mane*

ANNA. Russian nihilist, betrayed by her husband, whom she tracked to England. 'She was brown with the dust and draped with the cobwebs which had come from the walls of her hiding-place. Her face, too, was streaked with grime, and at the best she never could have been handsome.' – Watson, *Golden Pince-Nez*

ANSTRUTHER, DR. Occasional locum tenens to Watson. *Boscombe Valley Mystery*

ARMITAGE, JAMES. See TREVOR.

ARMSTRONG, DR LESLIE. One of the heads of Cambridge University Medical School. Scientific thinker of European reputation. 'A man of energy and character. I have not seen a man who, if he turns his talents that way, was more calculated to fill the gap left by the illustrious Moriarty.' – Holmes, *Missing Three-Quarter*

BAKER, HENRY. Scholar, and frequenter of the Alpha Inn, near the British Museum. Owner of the hat and Christmas goose brought to Holmes by Peterson. 'He is a man who leads a sedentary life, goes out little, is out of training entirely, is middle-aged, has grizzled hair which he has had cut within the last few days, and which he anoints with lime-cream. These are the more patent facts which are to be deduced from his hat. Also, by the way, that it is extremely improbable that he has gas laid on in his house.' – Holmes, *Blue Carbuncle*

BAKER STREET IRREGULARS. 'The unofficial force': a gang of urchins who sometimes work for Holmes. 'I could hear Mrs Hudson, our landlady, raising her voice in a wail of expostulation and dismay... There came a swift pattering of naked feet upon the stairs, a clatter of high voices, and in rushed a dozen dirty and ragged little street Arabs. There was some show of discipline among them, despite their tumultuous entry, for they instantly drew up in line and stood facing us with expectant faces.' – Watson, *Sign of Four*

BALDWIN, TED. Alias Hargrave (or Hargrove). A leading member of the Scowrers. Sometime suitor of Ettie Shafter, and sworn enemy of his rival for her, Jack McMurdo. *Valley of Fear*

BANNISTER. Servant to Hilton Soames at St Luke's College. Formerly butler to Gilchrist's father. *Three Students*

BARCLAY, COL. JAMES. Officer Commanding 1st Bn the Royal Mallows (or Munsters). Commissioned from the ranks for bravery in the Indian Mutiny. Married to Nancy Devoy, a colour-sergeant's daughter. Found dead, in suspicious circumstances, in his quarters at Aldershot. 'He was a dashing, jovial old soldier in his usual mood, but there were occasions on which he seemed to show himself capable of considerable violence and vindictiveness. This side of his nature, however, appears never to have been turned towards his wife.' – Holmes, *Crooked Man*

BARDLE, INSP. Sussex Constabulary officer in charge of the Murdoch killing investigation. *Lion's Mane*

BARKER. Private investigator into the disappearance of Dr Ray Ernest. 'He is my hated rival upon the Surrey shore.' – Holmes, *Retired Colourman*

BARKER, CECIL JAMES. Former gold-mining partner of John Douglas in California. Chief witness at the Birlstone Manor shooting scene. 'An easy-going, free-handed gentleman. But, my word! I had rather not be the man that crossed him!' – Ames, *Valley of Fear*

BARNES, JOSIAH. Landlord of the Green Dragon, Shoscombe. 'A sporting host, Josiah Barnes, entered eagerly into our plans for the extirpation of the fish of the neighbourhood.' – Watson, *Shoscombe Old Place*

BARRYMORE, JOHN AND ELIZA, *née* Selden. Married butler and housekeeper at Baskerville Hall. 'Her telltale eyes were red and glanced at me from between swollen lids. It was she, then, who wept in the night, and if she did so her husband must know it. Yet he had taken the obvious risk of discovery in declaring that it was not so . . . Already round this pale-faced, handsome, black-bearded man there was gathering an atmosphere of mystery and of gloom. It was he who had been the first to discover the body of Sir Charles, and we had only his word for all the circumstances.' – Watson, *Hound of the Baskervilles*

BASKERVILLE, SIR HENRY, Bart. Nephew and heir to the late Sir Charles Baskerville, Bart, of Baskerville Hall, Dartmoor. Gave up a farming career in Canada in his twenties to inherit the accursed estate after his uncle's mysterious death. 'There is no devil in hell, Mr Holmes, and there is no man upon earth who can prevent me from going to the home of my own people.' *Hound of the Baskervilles*

BATES, MARLOW. J. Neil Gibson's estate manager, who alerts Holmes to his employer's true nature. 'Well! Well! Mr Gibson seems to have a nice loyal household.' – Holmes *Thor Bridge*

BAYNES, INSP. Surrey Constabulary. Praised by Holmes for his investigation into the Garcia murder on Oxshott Common. 'Your powers, if I may say so without offence, seem superior to your opportunities.' *Wisteria Lodge*

BECHER. See FERGUSON. *Engineer's Thumb*

BEDDINGTON. See PINNER. *Stockbroker's Clerk*

BEDDOES. See TREVOR. '*Gloria Scott*'

BELLAMY, MAUD. Daughter of Tom Bellamy, boat and bathing-cot proprietor, Fulworth, Sussex. Fiancée of the late Fitzroy McPherson. 'Women have seldom been an attraction to me, for my brain has always governed my heart, but I could not look upon her perfect clear-cut face, with all the soft freshness of the downlands in her delicate colouring, without realizing that no young man would cross her path unscathed.' – Holmes, *Lion's Mane*

BELLINGER, LORD. Twice Prime Minister of Great Britain. Brings his European Secretary, Trelawney Hope, to consult Holmes. 'The Premier sprang to his feet with that quick, fierce gleam of his deep-set eyes before which a Cabinet had cowered.' – Watson, *Second Stain*

BENNETT, TREVOR (JACK). Assistant and secretary to Prof Presbury. Engaged to his daughter Edith. *Creeping Man*

BEPPO. Italian art-work jobber. 'He was a well-known ne'er-do-well among the Italian colony. He had once been a skilful sculptor and had earned an honest living, but he had taken to evil courses and had twice already been in jail.' – Watson, *Six Napoleons*

BERNSTONE, MRS: Housekeeper at Pondicherry Lodge. *Sign of Four*

BILLY. Occasional page-boy at 221B Baker Street. There seem to have been two Billies, perhaps required to use the same name, at different periods. *Valley of Fear, Thor Bridge, Mazarin Stone*

BLACK PETER. See CAREY. *Black Peter*

BLESSINGTON (real name Sutton). Patron and resident patient of Dr Percy Trevelyan. 'I'll take the house, furnish it, pay the maids, and run the whole place. All you have to do is just wear out your chair in the consulting-room. I'll let you have pocket-money and everything. Then you hand over to me three quarters of what you earn.' – Blessington, *Resident Patient*

BOHEMIA, KING OF. Wilhelm Gottsreich Sigismond von Ormstein, Grand Duke of Cassel-Felstein; incognito, Count von Kramm. Betrothed to Clotilde Lothman von Saxe-Meningen, second daughter of the King of Scandinavia. Sometime close friend of Irene Adler, with whom he was injudiciously photographed. 'Would she not have made an admirable queen? Is it not a pity that she was not on my level?' – Wilhelm, *Scandal in Bohemia*

BOONE, HUGH. See ST CLAIR. *Man with the Twisted Lip*

BRACKENSTALL, LADY, *née* Mary Fraser, of Adelaide. Widow of the murdered Sir Eustace Brackenstall, of the Abbey Grange, Marsham, Kent. 'I suppose that it is no use my attempting to conceal that our marriage has not been a happy one ... I was brought up in the freer, less conventional atmosphere of South Australia, and this English life, with its proprieties and its primness, is not congenial to me.' – Lady Brackenstall, *Abbey Grange*

BRADSTREET, INSP. Scotland Yard officer concerned in *Man with the Twisted Lip, Engineer's Thumb* and *Blue Carbuncle*

BRECKINRIDGE. Poultry seller in Covent Garden Market. 'When you see a man with whiskers of that cut and the "Pink 'Un" protruding out of his pocket, you can always draw him by a bet.' – Holmes, *Blue Carbuncle*

BREWER, SAM. London moneylender. Once publicly horse-whipped by Sir Robert Norberton; now his chief creditor. *Shoscombe Old Place*

BROWN, JOSIAH. Owner of one of the smashed busts. *Six Napoleons*

BROWN, SILAS. Trainer of Lord Backwater's racehorse Desborough at Capleton, Dartmoor. 'A more perfect compound of the bully, coward and sneak than Master Silas Brown I have seldom met with.' – Holmes, *Silver Blaze*

BROWNER, JAMES. Ship's steward. Married Mary Cushing, who disappeared while afloat with another sailor. 'He would always take drink when he was ashore, and a little drink would send him stark, staring mad.' – Susan Cushing, *Cardboard Box*

BRUNTON, RICHARD. Butler for 20 years to Reginald Musgrave. Accomplished linguist and musician. Formerly engaged to Rachel Howells. 'The butler at Hurlstone is always a thing that is remembered by all who visit us. But this paragon has one fault. He is a bit of a Don Juan, and you can imagine that for a man like him it is not a very difficult part to play in a quiet country district. When he was married it was all right, but since he has been a widower we have had no end of trouble with him.' – Musgrave, *Musgrave Ritual*

BURNET, MISS. Governess to the children of Henderson. Incognito of Signora Victor Durando, British-born widow of the late San Pedro Minister in London. 'He little knew that the woman who faced him at every meal was the woman whose husband he had hurried at an hour's notice into eternity.' – Miss Burnet, *Wisteria Lodge*

BURNWELL, SIR GEORGE. Gambler and womanizer. Close friend of Arthur Holder, and even closer friend of Mary Holder. 'A man of the world to his finger-tips, one who had been everywhere, seen everything, a brilliant talker, and a man of great personal beauty. Yet when I think of him in cold blood, far away from the glamour of his presence, I am convinced from his cynical speech and the look which I have caught in his eyes that he is one who should be deeply distrusted.... So, too, thinks my little Mary, who has a woman's quick insight into character.' – Alexander Holder, *Beryl Coronet*

CAIRNS, PATRICK. Harpooner, formerly under Capt Peter Carey. 'His face gets between me and my sleep.' – Cairns, *Black Peter*

CALHOUN, CAPT JAMES. American sea captain and murder gang leader. *Five Orange Pips*

CANTLEMERE, LORD. Government representative in the Mazarin diamond investigation. 'I can get along with the Prime Minister, and I've nothing against the Home Secretary, who seemed a civil, obliging sort of man, but I can't stand his Lordship.' – Billy, the pageboy, *Mazarin Stone*

CAREY, CAPT PETER. Retired sealer and whaler. Settled with his wife and daughter near Forest Row, Sussex, and was found harpooned there. 'The man was an intermittent drunkard, and when he had the fit on him he was a perfect fiend. He has been known to drive his wife and daughter out of doors in the middle of the night and flog them through the park until the whole village outside the gates was aroused by their screams.' – Insp Hopkins, *Black Peter*

CARFAX, LADY FRANCES. Wealthy spinster and last survivor of the direct family of the Earl of Rufton. Disappeared while travelling on the Continent. 'One of the most dangerous classes in the world is the drifting and friendless woman. She is the most harmless and often the most useful of mortals, but she is the inevitable inciter of crime in others. She is helpless. She is migratory. She has sufficient means to take her from country to country and from hotel to hotel. She is lost, as often as not, in a maze of obscure *pensions* and boarding-houses. She is a stray chicken in a world of foxes. When she is gobbled up she is hardly missed.' – Holmes, *Disappearance of Lady Frances Carfax*

CARRUTHERS, BOB. Employer of Miss Violet Smith as his daughter's music teacher at Farnham, Surrey. 'It may be a mere fancy of mine; but it had seemed to me sometimes that my employer, Mr Carruthers, takes a great deal of interest in me. We are thrown rather together. I play his accompaniments in the evening. He has never said anything. He is a perfect gentleman. But a girl always knows.' – Violet Hunter, *Solitary Cyclist*

CARTWRIGHT. Messenger boy used by Holmes to trace a mutilated copy of *The Times* and to bring him food and information on Dartmoor. 'He has given me an extra pair of eyes upon a very active pair of feet.' – Holmes, *Hound of the Baskervilles*

CHARPENTIER, ARTHUR. Sub-lieutenant, RN. Son of Mme

Charpentier, proprietress of a Camberwell boarding house, and brother of Alice. Arrested on suspicion of Drebber's murder. 'He (Drebber) then turned to Alice, and before my very face, proposed to her that she should fly with him. "You are of age," he said, "and there is no law to stop you. I have money enough and to spare. Never mind the old girl here, but come along with me now straight away ... What happened then I do not know. I heard oaths and the confused sounds of a scuffle.... I saw Arthur standing in the doorway laughing, with a stick in his hand. "I don't think that fellow will trouble us again," he said.' – Mme Charpentier, *Study in Scarlet*

CLAY, JOHN. Thief, smasher, forger, and murderer : in Holmes's estimation, fourth smartest man in London, and, for daring, possibly third. *Red-Headed League*

CLAYTON, JOHN. London cabby who drives the bearded man following Sir Henry Baskerville. *Hound of the Baskervilles*

CORAM, PROF. Elderly, invalid scholar and cigarette-smoker, of Yoxley Old Place, near Chatham, Kent. 'Bad, sir, very bad, but an old man has few pleasures. Tobacco and my work – that is all that is left to me.' – Coram, *Golden Pince-Nez*

COVENTRY, SGT. Hampshire Constabulary. Local policeman called to the scene of the Maria Gibson shooting. *Thor Bridge*

CROKER, CAPT JACK. Former first officer of SS *Rock of Gibraltar*, aboard which he met Mary Fraser, later Lady Brackenstall. 'His record was magnificent. There was not an officer in the fleet to touch him. As to his character, he was reliable on duty, but a wild, desperate fellow off the deck of his ship.' – Watson, *Abbey Grange*

CUBITT, MRS ELSIE, *née* Patrick. Wife of Hilton Cubitt, of Ridling Thorpe Manor, Norfolk, country gentleman. Former fiancée of Abe Slaney. Recipient of messages in 'dancing men' cipher devised by her Chicago gangster father. 'If you take me, Hilton, you will take a woman who has nothing that she need be personally ashamed of; but you will have to be content with my word for it.' Elsie Cubitt, *Dancing Men*

CUMMINGS, JOYCE. Grace Dunbar's defending counsel. *Thor Bridge*

CUNNINGHAM, J.P. One of the Reigate squires, with one son, Alec. Their coachman, William Kirwan, was killed, apparently tackling burglars. 'The one was an elderly man, with a strong, deep-lined, heavy-eyed face; the other a dashing young fellow, whose bright, smiling expression and showy dress were in strange contrast with the business which had brought us there.' – Watson, *Reigate Squires*

CUSACK, CATHERINE. The Countess of Morcar's maid at the time of the jewel robbery. *Blue Carbuncle*

CUSHING, MARY. See BROWNER. *Cardboard Box*

CUSHING, SARAH. Spinster sister of Susan Cushing and Mary Browner. 'That's all right, my lass,' said I, putting out my hand towards her in a kindly way, but she had it in both hers in an instant, and they burned as if they were in a fever. I looked into her eyes and I read it all there.' – Jim Browner, *Cardboard Box*

CUSHING, SUSAN, of Croydon. Spinster elder sister of Sarah Cushing and Mary Browner. Recipient through the post of two salted human ears. 'It is a rare event for her to receive anything through the post.' – Daily Chronicle, *Cardboard Box*

DAMERY, COL SIR JAMES. The 'Illustrious Client's' emissary to Holmes. 'He has rather a reputation for arranging delicate matters which are to be kept out of the papers.' – Holmes, *Illustrious Client*

DARBYSHIRE, WILLIAM. See STRAKER. *Silver Blaze*

DE MERVILLE, VIOLET. Daughter of Gen. de Merville, of Khyber fame. Her father's health was wrecked by her infatuation with Baron Gruner. 'I have been fortunate enough to win the entire affection of this lady. This was given to me in spite of the fact that I told her very clearly of all the unhappy incidents in my past life. I also told her that certain wicked and designing persons – I hope you recognize yourself – would come to her and tell her these things, and I warned her how to treat them. You have heard of post-hypnotic treatment, Mr Holmes? Well, you will see how it works.' – Gruner, *Illustrious Client*

DEVINE, MARIE. Formerly personal maid to Lady Frances Carfax. Fiancée of Jules Vibart, head waiter of the National Hotel, Lausanne. *Disappearance of Lady Frances Carfax*

DIOGENES CLUB. A haven for unclubbable gentlemen in Pall Mall, of which Mycroft Holmes was a founder-member. Members may not recognize one another, and talking is allowed only in the Stranger's Room. *Greek Interpreter* and *Bruce-Partington Plans*

DIXIE, STEVE. Boxer and gangster. *Three Gables*

DOBNEY, SUSAN. Lady Frances Carfax's old governess and regular correspondent who reported her missing. *Disappearance of Lady Frances Carfax*

DODD, JAMES M. Stockbroker. Concerned for his friend from the South African War, Godfrey Emsworth. 'A big, fresh, sunburned, upstanding Briton.' *Blanched Soldier*

DOLORES. Peruvian maid to Mrs Robert Ferguson since before her marriage. 'Then your wife's character would really be better known by Dolores than by you?' – Holmes, *Sussex Vampire*

DORAN, HATTY. Californian heiress, due to marry Lord St Simon. She disappeared from her wedding celebrations, believed abducted and murdered. 'There will soon be a call for protection in the marriage market, for the present free-trade principle appears to tell heavily against our home product. One by one the management of the noble houses of Great Britain is passing into the hands of our fair cousins from across the Atlantic.' – Gossip paragraph, *Noble Bachelor*

DOUGLAS, JOHN. Irish-born tenant of the Manor House, Birlstone, Sussex. Former gold-miner in California, where he married his late wife, Ettie Shafter. (See EDWARDS, BIRDY). He subsequently married an Englishwoman, Ivy. 'It was remarked sometimes, however, by those who knew them best, that the confidence between the two did not appear to be complete, since the wife was either very reticent about her husband's past life, or else, as seemed more likely, was imperfectly informed about it.' – Watson, *Valley of Fear*

DOWNING, P.C. Surrey Constabulary. Severely bitten about the thumb when apprehending a suspect. *Wisteria Lodge*

DREBBER, ENOCH J. Mormon from Salt Lake City, Utah. Widower of the late Lucy Ferrier. Found murdered in a empty house in Lauriston Gardens, Brixton, London. 'He was coarse in his habits and brutish in his ways. The very night of his arrival he became very much the worse for drink, and, indeed, after twelve o'clock in the day he could hardly ever be said to be sober. His manners towards the maidservants were disgustingly free and familiar. Worst of all, he speedily assumed the same attitude towards my daughter, Alice, and spoke to her more than once in a way which, fortunately, she is too innocent to understand.' – Mme Charpentier, *Study in Scarlet*

DUNBAR, GRACE. Governess to the Gibsons, of Thor Place. Arrested for the murder of Mrs Neil Gibson, whose husband was attracted to her. 'I can never forget the effect which Miss Dunbar produced upon me. It was no wonder that even the masterful millionaire had found in her something more powerful than himself.' – Watson, *Thor Bridge*

DURANDO, SRA VICTOR. See BURNET. *Wisteria Lodge*

ECCLES, JOHN SCOTT. Suspect for the murder of Aloysius Garcia, whose bachelor home he had been visiting at the time. 'I am a bachelor, and being of a sociable turn I cultivate a large number of friends . . . I met some weeks ago a young fellow named Garcia. He was, I understood, of Spanish descent and connected in some way with the embassy. He spoke perfect English, was pleasing in his manners, and as good-looking a man as ever I saw in my life. In some way we struck up quite a friendship, this young fellow and I. He seemed to take a fancy to me.' – Eccles, *Wisteria Lodge*

EDWARDS, BIRDY. Pinkerton detective, under the alias John McMurdo. Lodged with Jacob Shafter in the Vermissa Valley and married his daughter, Ettie. After her death he settled in England as John Douglas. 'Birdy Edwards is here. I am Birdy Edwards !' *Valley of Fear*

ELISE. German woman who warned Victor Hatherley of danger from her male colleagues. *Engineer's Thumb*

ELMAN, REV J.C. Vicar, and red herring, of Mossmoor-cum-Little Purlington, near Frinton, Essex. 'A big, solemn, rather pompous clergyman.' – Watson, *Retired Colourman*

EMSWORTH, GODFREY. Son of Col Emsworth, Crimean VC, of Tuxbury Old Park, near Bedford. Served with Jimmie Dodd in South African War (lance-corporal), until wounded (elephant gunshot). 'There was something shocking about the man, Mr Holmes. It wasn't merely that ghastly face glimmering as white as cheese in the darkness. It was more subtle than that – something slinking, something furtive, something guilty – something very unlike the frank, manly lad that I had known.' – Dodd, *Blanched Soldier*

ERNEST, DR RAY. See AMBERLEY. *Retired Colourman*

ESCOTT. A rising plumber. Holmes's alias in wooing Milverton's housemaid. 'I have walked out with her each evening, and I have talked with her. Good heavens, those talks!' – Holmes, *Charles Augustus Milverton*

EVANS, KILLER. See GARRIDEB, JOHN. *Three Garridebs*

FAIRBAIRN, ALEC. Seafaring man who disappeared while boating with Jim Browner's wife. 'Mary would go round to have tea with her sister and him. How often she went I don't know, but I followed her one day, and as I broke in at the door Fairbairn got away over the back garden wall.' – Browner, *Cardboard Box*

FALDER, LADY BEATRICE. Sir Robert Norberton's sister and financier. *Shoscombe Old Place*

FERGUSON. Alias of Dr Becher, posing as secretary and manager to Col Lysander Stark. 'Dr Becher is an Englishman, and there isn't a man in the parish who has a better-lined waistcoat.' – Eyford station-master, *Engineer's Thumb*

FERGUSON, ROBERT. Tea broker, of Cheeseman's, Lamberley, Sussex. One son, Jacky, by his first wife, and an infant son from his second marriage to a Peruvian merchant's daughter. As 'Big Bob' Ferguson, he had been a rugby-playing acquaintance of Watson's younger days. 'Hullo, Watson. You don't look quite the man you did when I threw you over the ropes into the crowd at the Old Deer Park.' *Sussex Vampire*

FERRIER, LUCY. Adopted daughter of John Ferrier, a Mormon farmer of Utah. After he was shot dead she was forcibly married (polygamously) to Enoch J. Drebber, but died within a month. Her wedding ring was found with Drebber's murdered body in London. 'There were some words between young Drebber and young Stangerson as to which was to have her. They'd both been in the party that followed them, and Stangerson had shot her father, which seemed to give him the best claim; but when they argued it out in council, Drebber's party was the stronger, so the prophet gave her over to him.' – Jefferson Hope, *Study in Scarlet*

FORBES. Scotland Yard officer on the *Naval Treaty* case.

FORRESTER, MRS CECIL. Mary Morstan's employer, as governess, whom Holmes had once assisted. *Sign of Four*

FORRESTER, INSP. Surrey Constabulary officer on the *Reigate Squires* case.

FOUR, THE. Conspirators to steal the Agra Treasure: Jonathan Small, Mahomet Singh, Abdulla Khan, Dost Akbar. *Sign of Four*

FOURNAYE, MME. Wife, and murderess, of Eduardo Lucas. *Second Stain*

FRANKLAND. Occupant of Lafter Hall, Dartmoor. Estranged father of Laura Lyons. Amateur astronomer, student of old manorial and communal rights. 'His passion is for the British law, and he has spent a large fortune in litigation. He fights for the mere pleasure of fighting and is equally ready to take up either side of a question, so that it is no wonder that he has found it a costly amusement. Sometimes he will shut up a right of way and defy the parish to make him open it. At others he will with his own hands tear down some other man's gate and declare that a path has existed there from time immemorial, defying the owner to prosecute him for trespass.' – Watson, *Hound of the Baskervilles*

GARCIA, ALOYSIUS. Bachelor son of the former highest dignitary of the South American Republic of San Pedro. Murdered on Oxshott Common, Surrey, while attached to the Spanish Embassy and residing at Wisteria Lodge. 'He lived with a faithful servant, a countryman of his own, who looked after all his needs. This fellow could speak English and did his housekeeping for him. Then there was a wonderful cook, he said, a half-breed whom he had picked up in his travels, who could serve an excellent dinner. I remember that he remarked what a queer household it was to find in the heart of Surrey, and that I agreed with him, though it has proved a good deal queerer than I thought.' – Eccles, *Wisteria Lodge*

GARCIA, BERYL. See STAPLETON. *Hound of the Baskervilles*

GARRIDEB, JOHN. Alias of Killer Evans, of Chicago, murderer. Escaped to London, where he killed (in self defence) the Chicago forger and coiner, Rodger Prescott. 'His accent was American, but was not accompanied by any eccentricity of speech.' – Watson, *Three Garridebs*

GARRIDEB, NATHAN. London antiquarian and collector. Expectant beneficiary under the will of the late Alexander Hamilton Garrideb, of Kansas. 'Just think what I could do with five million dollars. Why, I have the nucleus of a national collection. I shall be the Hans Sloane of my age.' – Nathan Garrideb, *Three Garridebs*

GIBSON, J. NEIL. Gold-mining magnate and former US senator, of Thor Place, Hampshire. His wife, formerly Maria Pinto, daughter of a Brazilian government official, was found shot to death on a bridge in their grounds, presumably murdered by their desirable governess, Grace Dunbar. 'Now, I make no pretence to be more moral than my neighbours, and I will admit to you that I could not live under the same roof with such a woman and in daily contact with her without feeling a passionate regard for her.' – Gibson, *Thor Bridge*

GILCHRIST. Sporting student at St Luke's College. Son of the late, ruined racing man, Sir Jabez Gilchrist. 'My scholar has been left very poor, but he is hard-working and industrious.' – Hilton Soames, *Three Students*

GOLDINI'S. Restaurant in the Gloucester Road used by Holmes and Watson. *Bruce-Partington Plans*

GORGIANO, GIUSEPPE ('Black Gorgiano'). A leading official of the notorious Neapolitan society, the Red Circle, specializing in blackmail and murder. Stabbed to death through the throat in a London flat. 'Not only was his body that of a giant but everything about him was grotesque, gigantic, and terrifying ... a man who had earned the name of "Death" in the south of Italy, for he was red to the elbow in murder!' – Emilia Lucca, *Red Circle*

GREEN, HON PHILIP. Son of a distinguished admiral. Reformed voluptuary, searching for Lady Frances Carfax, whose love he had squandered in his youth. 'Her mind was pure as snow. She could not bear a shadow of coarseness. So, when she came to hear of things that I had done, she would have no more to say to me. And yet she loved me – that is the wonder of it! – loved me well enough to remain single all her sainted days just for my sake alone.' – Green, *Disappearance of Lady Frances Carfax*

GREGORY, INSP. Officer investigating the *Silver Blaze* case.

GREGSON, INSP TOBIAS. Considered by Holmes the smartest member of Scotland Yard, although 'normally out of his depth.' Concerned in *Study in Scarlet, Greek Interpreter, Red Circle, Wisteria Lodge.*

GRUNER, BARON ADELBERT. Austrian-born collector of books, pictures, porcelain, and women. Author of a standard work on Ming, and compiler of the 'lust diary' ('This horrible book' – Sir James Damery; 'A beastly book – a book no man, even if he had come from the gutter, could have put together' – Kitty Winter). Widower, and prospective husband of Violet de Merville. 'He is an excellent antagonist, cool as ice, silky voiced and soothing as one of your fashionable consultants, and poisonous as a cobra. He has breeding in him – a real aristocrat of crime, with a superficial suggestion of afternoon tea and all the cruelty of the grave behind it.' – Holmes, *Illustrious Client*

HARKER, HORACE. Journalist, bewildered by the murder on his doorstep of Pietro Venucci. 'If I had come in here as a journalist, I should have interviewed myself and had two columns in every evening paper. As it is, I am giving away valuable copy by telling my story over and over to a string of different people.' – Harker, *Six Napoleons*

HARRIS. Holmes's alias, as an accountant, in *Stockbroker's Clerk*

HARRISON, ANNIE and JOSEPH. Percy Phelps's fiancée and her brother. 'She is a good sort, or I am mistaken. She and her brother are the only children of an iron-master up Northumberland way. He got engaged to her when travelling last winter, and she came down to be introduced to his people, with her brother as escort. Then came the smash, and she stayed on to nurse her lover, while brother Joseph, finding himself pretty snug, stayed on.' – Holmes, *Naval Treaty*

HATHERLEY, VICTOR. Hydraulic engineer. Victim of assault, while on professional call, resulting in the loss of a thumb.

'When I came to I found that it was still bleeding, so I tied one end of my handkerchief very tightly round the wrist and braced it up with a twig.'

'Excellent! You should have been a surgeon.'

'It is a question of hydraulics.'

– Hatherley and Watson, *Engineer's Thumb*

HAYES, REUBEN. Former head coachman to the Duke of Holdernesse. Landlord of the Fighting Cock inn, near Mackleton, Derbyshire. 'The sooner you pay your score and get out of this the better I shall be pleased.' – Hayes, *Priory School*

HAYTER, COL. Friend of Watson, who had attended him in Afghanistan. Host to Watson and Holmes at his home near Reigate, Surrey, at the time of William Kirwan's murder.

HEBRON, JOHN. Deceased first husband of Effie Munro. Father of Lucy. *Yellow Face*

HENDERSON. Alias of the deposed Central American dictator, Don Juan Murillo, 'The Tiger of San Pedro', while in England. 'Strong, fearless, and energetic, he had sufficient virtue to enable him to impose his odious vices upon a cowering people for ten or twelve years.' – Watson, *Wisteria Lodge*

HOLDER, ALEXANDER and **ARTHUR.** Prominent London banker, who accepted the Beryl Coronet as security against a loan; and his son, whom he suspected of stealing it. 'My God, what shall I do! I have lost my honour, my gems, and my son in one night.' – Alexander Holder, *Beryl Coronet*

HOLDER, MARY. Niece (adopted daughter) of Alexander Holder; fascinated by Sir George Burnwell. 'Disregarding my presence, she went straight to her uncle and passed her hand over his head with a sweet womanly caress.' – Watson, *Beryl Coronet*

HOLDERNESSE, SIXTH DUKE OF, KG, PC, etc. Baron Beverley, Earl of Carston, Lord-Lieutenant of Hallamshire from 1900, Lord of the Admiralty, 1872, etc, etc. Married (1888) Edith, daughter of Sir

Charles Appledore. Heir, Lord Saltire. 'His Grace is not in the habit of posting letters himself.' – James Wilder, *Priory School*

HOLDHURST, LORD. Foreign Secretary at the time the Naval Treaty was stolen. Uncle of Percy Phelps. 'With his slight, tall figure, his sharp features, thoughtful face, and curling hair prematurely tinged with gray, he seemed to represent that not too common type, a nobleman who is in truth noble.' – Watson, *Naval Treaty*

HOLMES, MYCROFT. Sherlock Holmes's elder brother by seven years. Government accountant and inter-departmental adviser. Founder-member of the Diogenes Club, Pall Mall. *Greek Interpreter* and *Bruce-Partington Plans.*'Heavily built and massive, there was a suggestion of uncouth physical inertia in the figure, but above this unwieldy frame there was perched a head so masterful in its brow, so alert in its steel-gray, deep-set eyes, so firm in its lips, and so subtle in its play of expression, that after the first glance one forgot the gross body and remembered only the dominant mind.' – Watson, *Bruce-Partington Plans*

HOLMES, SHERLOCK. Consulting detective. Born c. 1854. University education (unspecified). Commenced practice c. 1878. Met Watson 1 (?) Jan, 1881, and took lodgings with him at 221B Baker Street, London W. (prop Mrs Hudson). Missing, believed killed, 4 May, 1891. Resumed practice c. April 1894. Offered knighthood (refused) 1902. Retired to Sussex coast 1903. 'I think that I may go so far as to say, Watson, that I have not lived wholly in vain. If my record were closed tonight I could still survey it with equanimity. The air of London is the sweeter for my presence : in over a thousand cases I am not aware that I have ever used my powers upon the wrong side.' – Holmes, *Final Problem*

HOPE, JEFFERSON. Californian pioneer, betrothed to the late Lucy Ferrier. After her death he followed those responsible to London, where he worked as a cab driver. 'Year passed into year, his black hair turned grizzled, but still he wandered on, a human bloodhound, with his mind wholly set upon the one object to which he had devoted his life.' *Study in Scarlet*

HOPE, RT HON TRELAWNEY and **LADY HILDA.** Secretary for European Affairs, and his wife, daughter of the Duke of Belminster. A vital document was stolen from a locked despatch-box on their dressing-table. 'I am a light sleeper, and so is my wife. We are both prepared to swear that no one could have entered the room during the night.' – Hope, *Second Stain*

HOPKINS, INSP STANLEY. Scotland Yard Officer held in modified esteem by Holmes. 'I am disappointed in Stanley Hopkins. I had hoped for better things from him.' Associated with the cases of *Golden Pince-Nez, Black Peter, Missing Three-Quarter* and *Abbey Grange*.

HORNER, JOHN. Plumber. Arrested for theft of the Countess of Morcar's famous jewel. *Blue Carbuncle*

HOWELLS, RACHEL. Second housemaid to Reginald Musgrave. Formerly engaged to his butler, Brunton. 'She was of Welsh blood, fiery and passionate.' – Musgrave, *Musgrave Ritual*

HUDSON. Former seaman. Survivor of the wrecked convict transport *Gloria Scott*. Sometime gardener, then butler, to James Trevor, JP. 'The maids complained of his drunken habits and his vile language. The dad raised their wages all round to compensate them for the annoyance.' – Victor Trevor, '*Gloria Scott*'

HUDSON, MORSE. Art dealer. An unidentified man smashed a bust of Napoleon in his shop. *Six Napoleons*

HUDSON, MRS. Landlady to Holmes, and sometimes Watson, at 221B Baker Street. 'Mrs Hudson, the landlady of Sherlock Holmes, was a long-suffering woman. Not only was her first-floor flat invaded at all hours by throngs of singular and often undesirable characters but her remarkable lodger showed an eccentricity and irregularity in his life which must have sorely tried her patience. His incredible untidiness, his addiction to music at strange hours, his occasional revolver practice within doors, his weird and often malodorous scientific experiments, and the atmosphere of violence and danger which hung around him made him the very worst tenant in London.' – Watson, *Dying Detective*

HUNTER, NED. Stable lad at King's Pyland, drugged by means of curried mutton. *Silver Blaze*

HUNTER, VIOLET. Governess, hired on unconventional terms by Jephro Rucastle, and consulted Holmes. 'I confess that it is not the situation which I should like to see a sister of mine apply for.' – Holmes, *Copper Beeches*

HUXTABLE, DR THORNEYCROFT. Founder and principal of the Priory School, near Mackleton, Derbyshire. Author of *Huxtable's Sidelights On Horace*.'His card, which seemed too small to carry the weight of his academic distinctions, preceded him by a few seconds.' – Watson, *Priory School*

JACKSON. Occasional locum tenens to Watson. *Crooked Man*

JOHNSON, SHINWELL ('Porky'). Ex-convict, retained by Holmes as informant and underworld contact. 'With the glamour of his two convictions upon him, he had the *entrée* of every night club, doss house and gambling den in the town.' – Watson, *Illustrious Client*

JOHNSON, SIDNEY. Senior clerk and draughtsman in the Submarine Section at Woolwich Arsenal. 'The place is disorganized. The Chief dead, Cadogan West dead, our papers stolen. And yet, when we closed our door on Monday evening we were as efficient an office as any in the Government service.' – Johnson, *Bruce-Partington Plans*

JONES, ATHELNEY. Scotland Yard detective on the case of *The Sign of the Four.*

JONES, PETER. Scotland Yard inspector involved in the case of the *Red-Headed League.*

KHAN, ABDULLAH. One of the Four. *Sign of Four*

KEMP, WILSON. Latimer's associate. 'A man of the foulest antecedents.' – Holmes, *Greek Interpreter*

KIRWAN, WILLIAM. Murdered coachman to the Cunninghams. *Reigate Squires*

KLEIN, ISADORA. Pernambucan-born rich widow. Subject of a novel by her lover, Douglas Maberley. *Three Gables*

KRATIDES, PAUL and SOPHY. Athenian brother and sister, of wealthy family, who fell into the clutches of Wilson Kemp and Harold Latimer. *Greek Interpreter*

LANNER, INSP. Scotland Yard officer investigating the death of Mr Blessington. *Resident Patient*

LA ROTHIÈRE, LOUIS. Member of London's corps of international agents. *Second Stain* and *Bruce-Partington Plans*

LATIMER, HAROLD. Kidnapper, with Wilson Kemp, of Paul Kratides, brother of Sophy, whom Latimer had led astray. *Greek Interpreter*

LESTRADE, G. (pron Lestrayed). Scotland Yard inspector concerned in many of Holmes's cases. A quick and energetic worker, despite his adherence to the rule book and conventional methods. Humoured by Holmes, who regarded him and Insp Gregson as 'the pick of a bad lot'. 'Although he is absolutely devoid of reason, he is as tenacious as a bulldog when he once understands what he has to do, and, indeed, it is just this tenacity which has brought him to the top at Scotland Yard.' – Holmes, *Cardboard Box*

LEVERTON. Detective from Pinkerton's Agency, Chicago, in London in pursuit of Giuseppe Gorgiano. 'A quiet, business-like young man, with a clean shaven, hatchet face.' – Watson, *Red Circle*

LOMAX. Watson's sub-librarian friend at the London Library. *Illustrious Client*

LOPEZ. Alias Lucas. Murillo's secretary. *Wisteria Lodge*

LOWENSTEIN,H. Rejuvenation therapist, of Prague. *Creeping Man*

LUCAS, EDUARDO. International agent, and one of the best amateur tenors in England. Spent much of this time in Paris with his wife, a Creole of excitable temperament. 'He kept his life in watertight compartments.' – Lestrade, *Second Stain*

LUCCA, EMILIA and GENNARO. New York-Italian couple, hunted in London by Giuseppe Gorgiano. ' "You have killed him!" she muttered. "Oh, *Dio mio*, you have killed him!" ... Round and round the room she danced, her hands clapping, her dark eyes gleaming with delighted wonder, and a thousand pretty Italian exclamations pouring from her lips. It was terrible and amazing to see such a woman so convulsed with joy at such a sight.' – Watson, *Red Circle*

LYONS, MRS LAURA. Frankland's daughter, cast off by him and deserted by her artist husband. She was helped by Sir Charles Baskerville, whom she had asked to meet her on the night he died. 'If I can see this Mrs Laura Lyons, of equivocal reputation, a long step will have been made towards clearing one incident in this chain of mysteries.' – Watson, *Hound of the Baskervilles*

MABERLEY, MARY, of The Three Gables, Harrow Weald. Widowed mother of the late Douglas Maberley, British Attaché at Rome, minor novelist, and lover of Isadora Klein. *Three Gables*.

McCARTHY, JAMES. Farmer's son, arrested on suspicion of having murdered his father, Charles McCarthy, beside Boscombe Pool. 'In the surgeon's deposition it was stated that the posterior third of the left parietal bone and the left half of the occipital bone had been shattered by a heavy blow from a blunt weapon. I marked the spot upon my own head. Clearly such a blow must have been struck from behind. That was to some extent in favour of the accused, as when seen quarrelling he was face to face with his father. Still, it did not go for very much, for the older man might have turned his back.' – Watson, *Boscombe Valley Mystery*

MacDONALD, ALEC. Young and able Aberdonian inspector at Scotland Yard. 'Holmes was not prone to friendship, but he was tolerant of the big Scotchman, and smiled at the sight of him.' – Watson, *Valley of Fear*

McFARLANE, JOHN HECTOR. Suspected murderer of his benefactor, Jonas Oldacre. 'You mentioned your name, as if I should recognize it, but I assure you that, beyond the obvious facts that you are a bachelor, a solicitor, a Freemason, and an asthmatic, I know nothing whatever about you.' – Holmes, *Norwood Builder*

McGINTY, JOHN ('Black Jack'). Saloon keeper at Vermissa, USA. Bodymaster of Lodge 341, Vermissa Valley, Ancient Order of Freemen, and Boss of the Scowrers. 'Drink and politics had made the Boss a very rich as well as powerful man.' *Valley of Fear*

MacKINNON, INSP. Scotland Yard officer on the *Norwood Builder* case.

McLAREN, MILES. Student at St Luke's College. One of three suspected of examination cheating. 'One of the brightest intellects of the University: but he is wayward, dissipated, and unprincipled.' – Soames, *Three Students*

McMURDO and WILLIAMS. Prize-fighter porters at Pondicherry Lodge. Williams had been lightweight champion of England. 'Not Mr Sherlock Holmes! God's truth! how could I have mistook you? If instead o' standin' there so quiet you had just stepped up and given me that cross-hit of yours under the jaw, I'd ha' known you without a question.' – McMurdo, *Sign of Four*

McMURDO, JOHN. See EDWARDS, BIRDY. *Valley of Fear*

McPHERSON, FITZROY. Science master at Stackhurst's coaching establishment. Fiancé of Maud Bellamy. Died mysteriously after swimming. 'A fine upstanding young fellow whose life had been crippled by heart trouble following rheumatic fever. He was a natural athlete, however.' – Holmes, *Lion's Mane*

MacPHERSON. P.C. Impressionable police officer on guard at the murdered Eduardo Lucas's house. 'I meant no harm, sir, I'm sure. The young woman came to the door last evening – mistook the house, she did. And then we got talking. It's lonesome, when you're on duty here all day.' – MacPherson, *Second Stain*

MARCINI'S. London restaurant used by Holmes and Watson. *Hound of the Baskervilles*

MARTHA. Holmes's elderly female accomplice, planted as one of Von Bork's servants. (She is *not* Mrs Hudson.) 'A dear old ruddy-faced woman in a country cap. She was bending over her knitting and stopping occasionally to stroke a large black cat.' *His Last Bow*

MARVIN, TEDDY. New captain of the Coal and Iron Police, Vermissa Valley, USA. 'What are you but the paid tool of the men of capital, hired by them to club or to shoot your poorer fellow-citizens?' – McGinty, *Valley of Fear*

MASON, JOHN. Head trainer at Shoscombe stables. Consulted Holmes about Sir Robert Norberton's strange new habits. 'Well, sir, when a man does one queer thing, or two queer things, there may be a meaning to it, but when everything he does is queer, then you begin to wonder.' – Mason, *Shoscombe Old Place*

MASON, MRS. The Fergusons' baby's nurse. *Sussex Vampire*

MASON, WHITE. Chief detective of Sussex Constabulary, investigating the Birlstone Manor killing. 'White Mason is a smart man. No local job has ever been too much for White Mason.' – Sgt Wilson, *Valley of Fear*

MELAS. Greek-born linguist, twice abducted by Harold Latimer. 'He earns his living partly as interpreter in the law courts and partly by acting as guide to any wealthy Orientals who may visit the Northumberland Avenue hotels.' – Mycroft Holmes, *Greek Interpreter*

MERTON, SAM. Boxer and associate of Count Sylvius. 'Sam's not a shark, he is a great big silly bull-headed gudgeon.' – Holmes, *Mazarin Stone*

MEUNIER, OSCAR. Sculptor in wax, of Grenoble, who modelled Holmes. 'It really is rather like me, is it not?' – Holmes, *Empty House*

MILLAR, FLORA. Former *danseuse* at The Allegro and close friend of Lord St Simon; she created a disturbance at his wedding breakfast. 'I have not treated her ungenerously, and she had no just cause of complaint against me, but you know what women are, Mr Holmes.' – St Simon, *Noble Bachelor*

MILVERTON, CHARLES AUGUSTUS. Blackmailer, of Appledore Towers, Hampstead. Termed by Holmes the worst man in London. 'A round, plump, hairless face, a perpetual frozen smile, and two keen gray eyes, which gleamed brightly from behind broad, gold-rimmed glasses. There was something of Mr Pickwick's benevolence in his appearance, marred only by the insincerity of the fixed smile and by the hard glitter of those restless and penetrating eyes. His voice was as smooth and suave as his countenance.' – Watson, *Charles Augustus Milverton*

MORIARTY, PROF JAMES. London's grand master of crime. Of good birth and education, at the age of 21 he wrote a treatise on the Binomial Theorem which enjoyed European vogue and earned him a provincial university chair of mathematics. Author of *The Dynamics of an Asteroid* ('ascends to such rarefied heights of pure mathematics that it is said that there was no man in the scientific press capable of criticizing it.' – Holmes, *Valley of Fear*). Adverse rumours compelled him to resign his chair and set up in London as an army coach and 'Napoleon of crime'. A bachelor, he had two brothers, one a colonel, also named James, the other a West Country station master. 'My nerves are fairly proof, Watson, but I must confess to a start when I saw the very man who had been so much in my thoughts standing there on my threshold. His appearance was quite familiar to me. He is extremely tall and thin, his forehead domes out in a white curve, and his two eyes are deeply sunken in his head. He is clean-shaven, pale, and ascetic-looking, retaining something of the professor in his features. His shoulders are rounded from much study, and his face protrudes forward and is forever slowly oscillating from side to side in a curiously reptilian fashion.' – Holmes, *Final Problem*

MORPHY, ALICE and PROF. See PRESBURY.

MORTIMER, JAMES, MRCS. Medical attendant and personal friend of the late Sir Charles Baskerville, and sponsor of Sir Henry. 'Mister, sir, Mister – a humble M.R.C.S.' – Mortimer, *Hound of the Baskervilles*

MORTON, CYRIL. Electrical engineer. Violet Smith's fiancé. *Solitary Cyclist*

MORTON, INSP. Scotland Yard officer in the Dying Detective affair.

MOSER, M. Manager of the Hôtel National at Lausanne, interviewed by Watson. *Disappearance of Lady Frances Carfax*

MOULTON, FRANCIS HAY. Sometime gold prospector married to Hatty Doran. 'Well, we talked it over, and he had fixed it all up so nicely, with a clergyman all ready in waiting, that we just did it right there; and then Frank went off to seek his fortune, and I went back to pa.' – Hatty Doran, *Noble Bachelor*

MOUNT-JAMES, LORD. Godfrey Staunton's uncle; one of

England's richest misanthropes. 'The old boy is nearly eighty – cram full of gout, too. They say he could chalk his billiard-cue with his knuckles.' – Cyril Overton, *Missing Three-Quarter*

MUNRO, GRANT (JACK). Hop merchant. Married to Effie, widow of John Hebron, of New Jersey. Her uncharacteristic behaviour caused him to consult Holmes. 'One does not like to speak of one's domestic affairs to strangers. It seems dreadful to discuss the conduct of one's wife with two men whom I have never seen before. It's horrible to have to do it.' – Munro, *Yellow Face*

MURDOCH, IAN. Mathematical coach at Stackhurst's coaching establishment. 'He seemed to live in some high, abstract region of surds and conic sections with little to connect him with ordinary life.' – Holmes, *Lion's Mane*

MURILLO, DON JUAN. See HENDERSON, *Wisteria Lodge*

MURRAY. Watson's orderly at the battle of Maiwand, who conducted him to safety, on a packhorse, after he had been wounded. *Study in Scarlet*

MUSGRAVE, REGINALD, MP, of Hurlstone Manor, West Sussex. Member of one of the oldest families in the kingdom, who befriended Holmes at university. 'Something of his birth-place seemed to cling to the man, and I never looked at his pale, keen face or the poise of his head without associating him with gray archways and mullioned windows and all the venerable wreckage of a feudal keep.' – Holmes, *Musgrave Ritual*

NELIGAN, JOHN HOPLEY. Unprepossessing young man suspected of killing Capt Peter Carey. 'It seems to me to have only one drawback, Hopkins, and that is that it is intrinsically impossible. Have you tried to drive a harpoon through a body? No? Tut, tut, my dear sir, you must really pay attention to these details.' – Holmes, *Black Peter*

NORBERTON, SIR ROBERT, of Shoscombe Old Place, Berkshire. Owner of the Derby outsider, Shoscombe Prince, and financially dependent on it, in default of his sister, Lady Beatrice Falder. 'He is about the most dare-devil rider in England – second in the Grand National a few years back. He is one of those men who have overshot their true generation. He should have been a buck in the days of the Regency – a boxer, an athlete, a plunger on the turf, a lover of fair ladies, and, by all account, so far down Queer Street that he may never find his way back again.' – Watson, *Shoscombe Old Place*

NORLETT, MR AND MRS. Lady Beatrice Falder's confidential maid and her actor husband. *Shoscombe Old Place*

NORTON, GODFREY. Lawyer, of the Inner Temple, who married Irene Adler. *Scandal in Bohemia*

OAKSHOTT, MRS MAGGIE. Poultry raiser. James Ryder's sister. *Blue Carbuncle*

OBERSTEIN, HUGO ('PIERROT'). Foreign agent involved in the Bruce-Partington case. 'There are numerous small fry, but few who would handle so big an affair.' – Holmes, *Bruce-Partington Plans*

OLDACRE, JONAS ('MR CORNELIUS'). Prosperous builder. Benefactor to John Hector McFarlane, who was suspected of his murder. 'I was engaged to him, Mr Holmes, when I heard a shocking story of how he had turned a cat loose in an aviary, and I was so horrified at his brutal cruelty that I would have nothing more to do with him.' – McFarlane's mother, *Norwood Builder*

OPENSHAW, JOHN. Son of John Openshaw and nephew of Col Elias Openshaw, both of whom, like him, met sudden death after receiving five orange pips through the post. 'To tell the truth, I have felt helpless. I have felt like one of those poor rabbits when the snake is writhing towards it. I seem to be in the grasp of some resistless, inexorable evil, which no foresight and no precautions can guard against.' – Openshaw, *Five Orange Pips*

ORMSTEIN. See BOHEMIA.

OVERTON, CYRIL. Captain of Cambridge University Rugby Football XV. 'An enormous young man, sixteen stone of solid bone and muscle, who spanned the doorway with his broad shoulders.' – Watson, *Missing Three-Quarter*

PARR, LUCY. Second waiting-maid in Alexander Holder's household. Suspected, with her one-legged greengrocer sweetheart, Francis Prosper, of stealing the Beryl Coronet. 'She is a very pretty girl, and has attracted admirers who have occasionally hung about the place.' – Holder, *Beryl Coronet*

PETERS, HENRY ('HOLY'). See SHLESSINGER. *Disappearance of Lady Frances Carfax*

PETERSON. London commissionaire, who handed in the mislaid hat and goose to Holmes. 'A very honest fellow.' – Holmes, *Blue Carbuncle*

PHELPS, PERCY ('TADPOLE'). Civil Servant, formerly at school with Watson. Nephew of Lord Holdhurst, for whom he was copying a secret treaty when it was stolen from his office. 'This gaudy relationship did him little good at school. On the contrary, it seemed rather a piquant thing to us to chevy him about the playground and hit him over the shins with a wicket.' – Watson, *Naval Treaty*

PIKE, LANGDALE. London gossip-writer consulted by Holmes. *Three Gables*

PINNER, ARTHUR AND HARRY. Known to police as Beddington. London agent and managing director of the Franco-Midland Hardware Co, who engaged Hall Pycroft. 'Of course you expect two brothers to be alike, but not that they should have the same tooth stuffed in the same way.' – Pycroft, *Stockbroker's Clerk*

PORLOCK, FRED. An informant inside the Moriarty organization, employed by Holmes. A code message from him warned of danger to John Douglas, of Birlstone Manor. 'Porlock, Watson, is a nom-de-plume, a mere identification mark; but behind it lies a shifty and evasive personality. In a former letter he frankly informed me that the name was not his own, and defied me ever to trace him among the teeming millions of this great city. Porlock is important, not for himself, but for the great man with whom he is in touch. Picture to yourself the pilot fish with the shark, the jackal with the lion – anything that is insignificant in companionship with what is formidable.' – Holmes, *Valley of Fear*

PRENDERGAST, JACK. Leader of the convict seizure of the *Gloria Scott*, transporting them to Australia. 'Now, you don't think it likely that a man who could do anything is going to wear his breeches out sitting in the stinking hold of a rat-gutted, beetle-ridden, mouldy old coffin of a China coaster? – Prendergast, *'Gloria Scott'*

PRESBURY, PROF. Eminent Camford University physiologist, engaged to be married to the much younger Alice Morphy. His daughter, Edith Presbury, is engaged to her father's assistant and secretary, Trevor (Jack) Bennett. 'He is sixty-one years of age, but he became engaged to the daughter of Professor Morphy, his colleague in the chair of comparative anatomy. It was not, I understand, the reasoned courting of an elderly man but rather the passionate frenzy of youth, for no one could have shown himself a more devoted lover.' – Holmes, *Creeping Man*

PRICE. Watson's alias, as a clerk. *Stockbroker's Clerk*

PYCROFT, HALL. Stockbroker's clerk, unexpectedly offered the post of business manager of the Franco-Midland Hardware Co. 'No one knows how these things are worked. Some people say that the manager just plunges his hand into the heap and takes the first that comes. Anyhow it was my innings that time.' – Pycroft, *Stockbroker's Clerk*

RANCE, PC JOHN. Officer who found Drebber's body but ignored his killer. 'I've seen many a drunk chap in my time, but never anyone so cryin' drunk as that cove. He was at the gate when I came out, a-leanin' up ag'in the railings, and a-singin' at the pitch o' his lungs about Columbine's New-fangled Banner, or some such stuff.' – Rance, *Study in Scarlet*

RAS, DAULAT. Indian student at St Luke's College and possible Greek examination cheat. 'A quiet, inscrutable fellow; as most of those Indians are. He is well up in his work, though his Greek is his weak subject.' – Soames, *Three Students*

RONDER, EUGENIA. Widow of Ronder, of Ronder's Wild Beasts, who met his death in circumstances implicating a lion, Sahara King. 'From keeping beasts in a cage, the woman seemed, by some retribution of Fate, to have become herself a beast in a cage.' – Watson, *Veiled Lodger*

ROSS, COL. Owner of King's Pyland training stable, on Dartmoor, from where Silver Blaze was stolen. *Silver Blaze*

ROSS, DUNCAN. Founder of the Red-Headed League, with headquarters at 7 Pope's Court, Fleet Street, and employer on its behalf of Jabez Wilson. 'He seized my hair in both his hands, and tugged until I yelled with the pain. "There is water in your eyes," said he as he released me. "I perceive that all is as it should be. But we have to be careful, for we have twice been deceived by wigs and once by paint. I could tell you tales of cobbler's wax which would disgust you with human nature.' – Wilson, *Red-Headed League*

ROUNDHAY, REV. Vicar of Tredannick Wollas, Cornwall. Mortimer Tregennis lodged in his vicarage. 'Something of an archaeologist, and as such Holmes made his acquaintance. He was a middle-aged man, portly and affable, with a considerable fund of local lore.' – Watson, *Devil's Foot*

ROYLOTT, DR GRIMESBY. Last of the Roylotts of Stoke Moran, Surrey, one of England's oldest Saxon families. Practised medicine in Calcutta until his imprisonment for beating his native butler to death. Later returned to Stoke Moran with his wife and twin stepdaughters, Helen and Julia Stoner. His wife was killed in a railway accident. 'A series of disgraceful brawls took place, two of which ended in the police-court, until at last he became the terror of the village, and the folks would fly at his approach, for he is a man of immense strength, and absolutely uncontrollable in his anger.' – Helen Stoner, *Speckled Band*

RUCASTLE, JEPHRO, of The Copper Beeches, near Winchester. Employer of Violet Hunter as governess to his son Edward, by his second wife. 'A child who may some day play a considerable part in the history of the country . . . one dear little romper just six years old. Oh, if you could see him killing cockroaches with a slipper! Smack! smack! smack! Three gone before you could wink!' – Rucastle, *Copper Beeches*

RYDER, JAMES. Head attendant at the Hotel Cosmopolitan when the Countess of Morcar's priceless jewel was stolen. Brother of Maggie Oakshott. 'The little man stood glancing from one to the other of us with half-frightened, half-hopeful eyes, as one who is not sure whether he is on the verge of a windfall or of a catastrophe.' – Watson, *Blue Carbuncle*

ST CLAIR, NEVILLE. Former actor and journalist. Believed murdered by a City matchseller, Hugh Boone, at the Bar of Gold opium den, Upper Swandam Lane, in the East End dock area. 'The prisoner lay with his face towards us . . . He was, as the inspector had said, extremely dirty, but the grime which covered his face could not conceal its repulsive ugliness. A broad wheal from an old scar ran right across it from eye to chin, and by its contraction had turned up one side of the upper lip.' – Watson, *Man with the Twisted Lip*

ST CLAIR, MRS. Neville St Clair's wife (or widow?). 'On the very day that I saw him last he cut himself in the bedroom, and yet I in the dining-room rushed upstairs instantly with the utmost certainty that something had happened. Do you think that I would respond to such a trifle and yet be ignorant of his death?' *Man with the Twisted Lip*

ST SIMON, LORD ROBERT WALSINGHAM DE VERE. Former Under-Secretary for the Colonies. Thwarted bridegroom of Hatty Doran. 'I may be forced to acquiesce in these recent developments, but I can hardly be expected to make merry over them.' – St Simon, *Noble Bachelor*

SALTIRE, LORD ARTHUR. Heir and only legitimate child of the Duke of Holdernesse. He disappeared suddenly from his school in Derbyshire, at the same time as the German master, Heidegger. 'The boy was fully dressed when he fled. Therefore, he foresaw what he would do. But the German went without his socks. He certainly acted on very short notice.' – Holmes, *Priory School*

SANDEFORD. Owner of the sixth bust of Napoleon investigated by Holmes. *Six Napoleons*

SAN PEDRO, 'TIGER OF'. See HENDERSON.

SCANLAN. Scowrer pal of John McMurdo. *Valley of Fear*

SCOWRERS. Members of Lodge 341, Vermissa Valley, USA, a violent breakaway branch of the generally law-abiding Ancient Order of Freemen. *Valley of Fear*

SELDEN. The 'Notting Hill murderer', escaped from Dartmoor Prison, where he had been serving a life sentence for a crime so atrocious that the death penalty had been commuted on the grounds of possible insanity. 'From crime to crime he sank lower and lower until it is only the mercy of God which has snatched him from the scaffold; but to me, sir, he was always the little curly-headed boy that I had nursed and played with as an elder sister would.' – Mrs Barrymore, *Hound of the Baskervilles*

SERGIUS. See CORAM. *Golden Pince-Nez*

SHAFTER, ETTIE. Daughter of Jacob Shafter, boarding house keeper at Vermissa, USA. McMurdo lodged there and fell in love with her. 'McMurdo was a man who made his mark quickly ... On the second day he told her that he loved her.' *Valley of Fear*

SHERMAN. Taxidermist and kennel keeper who lent Watson his accomplished dog for Holmes's use. 'A queer mongrel with a most amazing power of scent. I would rather have Toby's help than that of the entire detective force of London.' – Holmes, *Sign of Four*

SHLESSINGER, REV DR. Missionary and bible scholar. Alias of 'Holy' Peters, of Australia and South America, operating with his 'wife', Annie Fraser. 'One of the most unscrupulous rascals that Australia has ever evolved – and for a young country it has turned out some very finished types.' – Holmes, *Disappearance of Lady Frances Carfax*

SHOLTO, THADDEUS. Twin brother of Bartholomew Sholto: sons of the late Maj John Sholto, possessor of the Agra Treasure. Bartholomew Sholto was murdered at his home, Pondicherry Lodge, Upper Norwood, before Thaddeus could confront him with Mary Morstan, heiress to a share of the treasure. 'Your servant, gentlemen. Pray step into my little sanctum. A small place, miss, but furnished to my own liking. An oasis of art in the howling desert of South London.' – Thaddeus Sholto. *Sign of Four*

SIMPSON'S. Strand restaurant used by Holmes and Watson. *Dying Detective* and *Illustrious Client*

SIMPSON, FITZROY. Amateur bookmaker who had squandered his education and upbringing on the turf. Arrested on suspicion of kidnapping Silver Blaze and killing his trainer, John Straker. 'When confronted with his cravat he turned very pale and was utterly unable to account for its presence in the hand of the murdered man ... His stick, which was a penang-lawyer weighted with lead, was just such a weapon as might, by repeated blows, have inflicted the terrible injuries to which the trainer had succumbed.' – Watson, *Silver Blaze*

SINGH, MAHOMET. One of the Four. *Sign of Four*

SLANEY, ABE. Former fiancé of Elsie Cubitt, while a member of her father's gang. 'The most dangerous crook in Chicago.' – Wilson Hargreave, NY Police Bureau, *Dancing Men*

SMALL, JONATHAN. One of the Four. While a soldier in the 3rd Buffs, serving in India, he lost a leg to a crocodile. Invalided out, he became labour overseer on an indigo plantation. He survived the siege of Agra by Mutineers and was concerned with three Indians in the murder of a jewel courier, Achmet, for the Agra Treasure. Serving life imprisonment in the Andaman Islands for the crime, he escaped by canoe with a native, Tonga, and made his way to London, seeking return of the treasure. 'It does seem a queer thing that I, who have a fair claim to half a million of money, should spend the first half of my life building a breakwater in the Andamans, and am like to spend the other half digging drains at Dartmoor.' – Small, *Sign of Four*

SMITH, CULVERTON. Planter in Sumatra, and expert on tropical diseases. Uncle of Victor Savage, who died of an obscure Asiatic disease contracted in the heart of London. Fetched by Watson to try to save Holmes from a fatal complaint caught from Chinese seamen at Rotherhithe. 'I caught a glimpse of his face in the mirror over the mantelpiece. I could have sworn that it was set in a malicious and abominable smile. Yet I persuaded myself that it must have been some nervous contraction which I had surprised, for he turned to me an instant later with genuine concern upon his features.' – Watson, *Dying Detective*

SMITH, MORDECAI. Thames boat proprietor (Smith's Wharf, opposite Millbank.) Owner of the steam launch *Aurora*, concerned in the Agra Treasure chase. 'At that moment who should come down but Mordecai Smith, the missing owner. He was rather the worse for liquor. I should not, of course, have known him, but he bellowed out his name and the name of the launch.' – Holmes, *Sign of Four*

SMITH, VIOLET. Music teacher to the daughter of Bob Carruthers, of Chiltern Grange, Surrey, a supposed friend of her late Uncle Ralph, of Johannesburg. 'It is part of the settled order of Nature that such a girl should have followers, but for choice not on bicycles in lonely country roads.' – Holmes, *Solitary Cyclist*

SMITH, WILLOUGHBY. Prof Coram's secretary. Found dying of a stab wound, clutching a pair of pince-nez. 'Wanted, a woman of good address, attired like a lady. She has a remarkably thick nose, with eyes which are set close upon either side of it. She has a puckered forehead, a peering expression, and probably rounded shoulders. There are indications that she has had recourse to an optician at least twice during the last few months. As her glasses are of remarkable strength, and as opticians are not very numerous, there should be no difficulty in tracing her.' – Holmes (after examining the glasses), *Golden Pince-Nez*

SOAMES, HILTON. Tutor and lecturer at St Luke's College who took his suspicions of examination cheating to Holmes. 'Either I must find the man or else the examination must be postponed until fresh papers are prepared, and since this cannot be done without explanation, there will ensue a hideous scandal, which will throw a cloud not only on the college, but on the university.' – Soames, *Three Students*

SPAULDING, VINCENT. Jabez Wilson's pawnbroking assistant. Alias of John Clay. 'Never was such a fellow for photography. Snapping away with a camera when he ought to be improving his mind, and then diving down into the cellar like a rabbit into its hole to develop his pictures. That is his main fault, but on the whole he's a good worker. There's no vice in him.' – Wilson, *Red-Headed League*

STACKHURST, HAROLD. Proprietor of The Gables scholastic coaching establishment near Holmes's retirement cottage in Sussex. 'He and I were always friendly from the day I came to the coast, and he was the one man who was on such terms with me that we could drop in on each other in the evenings without an invitation.' – Holmes, *Lion's Mane*

STAMFORD. A dresser (surgeon's assistant) at St Bartholomew's Hospital while Watson was studying there, and later. A chance reunion in the Criterion Bar, Piccadilly Circus, resulted in his introducing Watson and Holmes. 'The sight of a friendly face in the great wilderness of London is a pleasant thing indeed to a lonely man. In old days Stamford had never been a particular crony of mine, but now I hailed him with enthusiasm.' – Watson, *Study in Scarlet*

STANGERSON, JOSEPH. Mormon, and murderer of John Ferrier; from Salt Lake City, Utah, travelling as private secretary to Enoch J. Drebber. Murdered at Halliday's Private Hotel, Little George Street, London. 'We have come at the advice of our fathers to solicit the hand of your daughter for whichever of us may seem good to you and to her. As I have but four wives and Brother Drebber here has seven, it appears to me that my claim is the stronger one.' – Stangerson (to Ferrier), *Study in Scarlet*

STAPLETON, JOHN and **BERYL,** of Merripit House, on the Grimpen Mire, Dartmoor. A keen naturalist, he discovered the Vandaleur Moth (Vandaleur was his own name at the time). Headmaster of a private school which subsequently failed. It was Beryl Stapleton who warned Sir Henry Baskerville to stay away from Dartmoor. 'His gray clothes and jerky, zigzag, irregular progress made him not unlike some huge moth himself . . . There could not have been a greater contrast between brother and sister, for Stapleton was neutral tinted, with light hair and gray eyes, while she was darker than any brunette whom I have seen in England . . . With her perfect figure and elegant dress she was, indeed, a strange apparition upon a lonely moorland path.' – Watson, *Hound of the Baskervilles*

STARK, COL LYSANDER (FRITZ). German murderer and counterfeiter who engaged Victor Hatherley in his capacity as hydraulic engineer. 'Of course, I was glad, for the fee was at least tenfold what I should have asked had I set a price upon my own services . . . On the other hand, the face and manner of my patron had made an unpleasant impression upon me.' – Hatherley, *Engineer's Thumb*

STARR, DR LYSANDER. Late mayor of Topeka, invented by Holmes. 'Good old Dr Starr! His name is still honoured.' – John Garrideb, *Three Garridebs*

STAUNTON, GODFREY. The missing three-quarter of Cambridge University Rugby XV. Nephew and heir of Lord Mount-James. 'I didn't think there was a soul in England who didn't know Godfrey Staunton, the crack three-quarter, Cambridge, Blackheath, and five Internationals. Good Lord! Mr Holmes, where *have* you lived ?' – Cyril Overton, *Missing Three-Quarter*

STEILER, PETER (THE ELDER). Landlord of the Englischer Hof hotel, Meiringen, below the Reichenbach Falls. 'Our landlord was an intelligent man and spoke excellent English, having served for three years as waiter at the Grosvenor Hotel in London.' – Watson, *Final Problem*

STERNDALE, DR LEON. Famous lion-hunter and explorer in Africa. A distant cousin of the Cornish Tregennis family. 'The huge body, the craggy and deeply seamed face with the fierce eyes and hawk-like nose, the grizzled hair which nearly brushed our cottage ceiling, the beard – golden at the fringes and white near the lips, save for the nicotine stain from his perpetual cigar – all these were as well known in London as in Africa.' – Watson, *Devil's Foot*

STOCKDALE, SUSAN. Maid to Mrs Mary Maberley. Her husband, Barney, was a member of the Spencer John gang. *Three Gables*

STONER, HELEN. Daugher of the late Maj-Gen Stoner. Twin sister of the late Julia Stoner. Stepdaughter of Dr Grimesby Roylott. Engaged to Percy Armitage, an old friend. 'Very sorry to knock you up, Watson, but it's the common lot this morning. Mrs Hudson has been knocked up, she retorted upon me, and I on you ... It seems that a young lady has arrived in a considerable state of excitement, who insists upon seeing me. She is waiting now in the sitting-room. Now, when young ladies wander about the metropolis at this hour of the morning, and knock sleepy people up out of their beds, I presume that it is something very pressing which they have to communicate.' – Holmes, *Speckled Band*

STOPER, MISS. Manager of Westaway's agency for governesses. *Copper Beeches*

STRAKER, JOHN. Retired jockey; trainer at King's Pyland stables, Dartmoor. Believed to have been murdered trying to prevent the kidnapping of the racehorse, Silver Blaze. Also known (though not at home) as William Darbyshire (or Derbyshire). 'When I returned to London I called upon the milliner, who had recognized Straker as an excellent customer of the name of Derbyshire, who had a very dashing wife, with a strong partiality for expensive dresses.' – Holmes, *Silver Blaze*

STRAUBENZEE. Maker of Count Sylvius's airgun. *Mazarin Stone*

SUTHERLAND, MARY. Stepdaughter of James Windibank and fiancée of Hosmer Angel. 'He was in dreadful earnest and made me swear, with my hands on the Testament, that whatever happened I would always be true to him. Mother said he was quite right to make me swear, and that it was a sign of his passion. Mother was all in his favour from the first and was even fonder of him than I was.' – *Case of Identity*

SYLVIUS, COUNT NEGRETTO. Big-game hunter, cardplayer, man-about-town, and potential murderer of Holmes. 'Half-Italian, you know, and with the Southern graces of manner when in the mood, but a devil incarnate in the other mood.' – Holmes, *Mazarin Stone*

TANGEY, SGT AND MRS. Foreign Office commissionaire asleep on duty when the naval treaty was stolen. His wife was suspected. 'We have set one of our women on to her. Mrs Tangey drinks, and our woman has been with her twice when she was well on, but she could get nothing out of her.' – Forbes, *Naval Treaty*

TAVERNIER. French modeller of a wax bust of Holmes. *Mazarin Stone*

TOLLER, MR AND MRS. Rucastle's groom and housekeeper. *Copper Beeches*

TONGA. Native of the Andaman Islands who enabled Jonathan Small to escape from the penal settlement. He shared Small's travels, allowing himself to be exhibited at English fairgrounds as 'The Black Cannibal'. 'He was staunch and true, was little Tonga. No man ever had a more faithful mate.' – Small, *Sign of Four*

TREGELLIS, JANET. Daughter of Musgrave's head gamekeeper. In love with Brunton, the butler. *Musgrave Ritual*

TREGENNIS, BRENDA, GEORGE AND OWEN, of Tredannick Wartha, Cornwall. Victims of 'The Cornish Horror'. 'The sister lay back stone-dead in her chair, while the two brothers sat on each side of her laughing, shouting, and singing, the senses stricken clean out of them.' – Rev Roundhay, *Devil's Foot*

TREGENNIS, MORTIMER. Brother of Brenda, George and Owen, subsequently sharing his sister's fate. 'We are devil-ridden, Mr Holmes! My poor parish is devil-ridden! Satan himself is loose in it! We are given over into his hands!' – Rev Roundhay, *Devil's Foot*

TREVELYAN, DR PERCY. An impecunious medical man, until he was enabled to set up in private practice, through the patronage of a stranger, Blessington. 'I am sure that you will not think that I am unduly singing my own praises if I say that my student career was considered by my professors to be a very promising one. After I had graduated I continued to devote myself to research, occupying a minor position in King's College Hospital, and I was fortunate enough to

excite considerable interest by my research into the pathology of catalepsy, and finally to win the Bruce Pinkerton prize and medal by the
monograph on nervous lesions to which your friend has just alluded.' –
Trevelyan, *Resident Patient*

TREVOR, JAMES, JP., of Donnithorpe, Norfolk. Formerly James
Armitage, one of few survivors of the convict transport *Gloria Scott*, he
became a goldminer and pugilist in Australia. Father of Victor Trevor.
'He was a man of little culture, but with a considerable amount of rude
strength, both physically and mentally. He knew hardly any books,
but he had travelled far, had seen much of the world, and had remembered all that he had learned.' – Holmes, *'Gloria Scott'*

TREVOR, VICTOR. Son of James Trevor and college friend of
Holmes. 'He was the only friend I made during the two years I was at
college ... He was a hearty, full-blooded fellow, full of spirits and
energy, the very opposite to me in most respects, but we had some subjects in common, and it was a bond of union when I found that he was
as friendless as I.' Holmes, *'Gloria Scott'*

TURNER, ALICE. Daughter of John Turner. Friend since childhood of James McCarthy. 'There rushed into the room one of the most
lovely young women that I have ever seen in my life. Her violet eyes
shining, her lips parted, a pink flush upon her cheeks, all thought of her
natural reserve lost in her overpowering excitement and concern. "Oh,
Mr Sherlock Holmes!" she cried, glancing from one to the other of us,
and finally, with a woman's quick intuition, fastening upon my companion.' – Watson, *Boscombe Valley Mystery*

TURNER, JOHN. Alice's father. Landowner, of Boscombe Valley,
near Ross-on-Wye, Herefordshire. Made his money in Australia,
where he became acquainted with Charles McCarthy, later one of his
tenants. 'Black Jack of Ballarat was the name I went under.' – Turner,
Boscombe Valley Mystery

TURNER, MRS. 'Our landlady' at 221B Baker Street at the time of *A
Scandal in Bohemia*. One of Watson's chronicling errors, or a temporary
stand-in for an absent Mrs Hudson?

VANDELEUR. See STAPLETON, *Hound of the Baskervilles*

VENUCCI, PIETRO. Italian gangster in London, found stabbed to
death. His sister Lucretia had stolen the black pearl of the Borgias from
her mistress, the Princess of Colonna. *Six Napoleons*

VERNER. Physician relative of Holmes, who used him to buy Watson
out of his Kensington practice. *Disappearance of Lady Frances Carfax*

VON BORK. Principal German secret agent in Britain for four years up to the outbreak of the First World War. 'A remarkable man this Von Bork – a man who could hardly be matched among all the devoted agents of the Kaiser. It was his talents which had first recommended him for the English mission, the most important mission of all, but since he had taken it over those talents had become more and more manifest to the half-dozen people in the world who were really in touch with the truth.' *His Last Bow*

VON HERDER. Blind German maker (to Moriarty's order) of the airgun used by Col Moran. *Empty House*

VON HERLING, BARON. Chief Secretary of the German Legation in London up to World War I. *His Last Bow*

WALTER, SIR JAMES. Head of the Submarine Department at Woolwich Arsenal when the Bruce-Partington plans were stolen. 'He has grown gray in the service, is a gentleman, a favoured guest in the most exalted houses, and, above all, a man whose patriotism is beyond suspicion.' – Mycroft Holmes, *Bruce-Partington Plans*

WALTERS, PC. Surrey Constabulary. Constable on watch at Wisteria Lodge. 'I was sitting reading in the chair. I don't know what made me look up, but there was a face looking in at me through the lower pane. Lord, sir, what a face it was! I'll see it in my dreams.' *Wisteria Lodge*

WARREN, MRS. Bloomsbury landlady concerned about a new lodger of elusive habits. 'Why, bless you, Mrs Warren, if I were your lodger you would often not see me for weeks on end.' – Holmes, *Red Circle*

WEST, ARTHUR CADOGAN. Clerk at Woolwich Arsenal, found dead beside a railway line just outside Aldgate Underground station with secret papers on him. 'Once or twice it seemed to me that he was on the point of telling me something. He spoke one evening of the importance of the secret, and I have some recollection that he said that he had no doubt foreign spies would pay a great deal to have it.' – Violet Westbury, *Bruce-Partington Plans*.

WESTBURY, VIOLET. Arthur Cadogan West's fiancée. He had left her abruptly, on their way to the theatre, a few hours before his body was found beside the Underground railway line. 'The call must have been very pressing, since he left his girl standing in the fog.' – Holmes, *Bruce-Partington Plans*

WHITNEY, ISA. Husband of an old school friend of the first Mrs Watson. Opium addict. 'Having read De Quincey's description of his dreams and sensations, he had drenched his tobacco in laudanum in an attempt to produce the same effects. He found, as so many more had done, that the practice is easier to attain than to get rid of.' – Watson, *Man with the Twisted Lip*

WIGGINS. Spokesman of the Baker Street Irregulars. 'One of their number, taller and older than the others, stood forward with an air of lounging superiority which was very funny in such a disreputable little scarecrow.' – Watson, *Sign of Four*

WATSON, JOHN H., MD. Medical practitioner and author. Born c 1852. MD, 1878. Army Medical Dept, 1878–80 Service in Afghanistan, att. Northumberland Fusiliers and Berkshires. Wounded at Battle of Maiwand, 7 July 1880. Arrived back in England, late Nov 1880, and left service. Introduced to Sherlock Holmes by Stamford at Bart's Hospital chemical laboratory, 1 (?) Jan, 1881. Took lodgings with him at 221 B, Baker Street, London W (prop Mrs Hudson). Married (i) Nov 1886, wife's name unrecorded (dec'd 1887 or 1888; (ii) c 1887–89, probably to Mary Morstan (dec'd c 1891–94); (iii) c 1902, wife's name unrecorded. In medical practice: (i) Kensington, 1886–88; (ii) Paddington, 1889–90; (iii) Kensington, 1890–94; (iv) Queen Anne St, Marylebone, 1902–? 'Watson, you excel yourself. I am bound to say that in all the accounts which you have been so good as to give of my own small achievements you have habitually underrated your own abilities. It may be that you are not yourself luminous, but you are a conductor of light.' – Holmes, *Hound of the Baskervilles*

WILDER, JAMES. Natural son of, and secretary to, the sixth Duke of Holdernesse; half-brother to Lord Saltire. 'I could see that there were other questions which Holmes would have wished to put, but the nobleman's abrupt manner showed that the interview was at an end. It was evident that to his intensely aristocratic nature this discussion of his intimate family affairs with a stranger was most abhorrent, and that he feared lest every fresh question would throw a fiercer light into the discreetly shadowed corners of his ducal history.' – Watson, *Priory School*

WILLIAMSON. Tenant of Charlington Hall, near Farnham, Surrey. 'There is some rumour that he is or has been a clergyman, but one or two incidents of his short residence at the Hall struck me as peculiarly unecclesiastical.' – Holmes, *Solitary Cyclist*

WILSON, JABEZ. Pawnbroker with a declining business, persuaded by his assistant, Vincent Spaulding, to take advantage of membership of the Red-Headed League. 'Bore every mark of being an average commonplace British tradesman, obese, pompous and slow. There was nothing remarkable about the man save his blazing red head.' – Watson, *Red-Headed League*

WINDIBANK, JAMES. Claret importer's traveller. Stepfather of Mary Sutherland. 'He would get mad if I wanted so much as to join a Sunday-school treat.' – Mary Sutherland, *Case of Identity*

WINDIGATE. Landlord of the Alpha Inn, near the British Museum, where Henry Baker belonged to his goose club. 'Your beer should be excellent if it is as good as your geese.' – Holmes, *Blue Carbuncle*

WINTER, KITTY. Corrupted victim of Baron Gruner, enlisted by Shinwell Johnson to help Holmes influence Violet de Merville against him. 'I'm easy to find. Hell, London, gets me every time ... But, by cripes! there is another who ought to be down in a lower hell than we if there was any justice in the world!' – Kitty Winter, *Illustrious Client*

WOOD, HENRY. Former corporal in the Royal Mallows (or Munsters). Captured by Indian Mutineers and enslaved in North India. Lived as wandering conjurer. In his old age he returned to England, with his performing mongoose, Teddy. 'You see me now with my back like a camel and my ribs all awry, but there was a time when Corporal Henry Wood was the smartest man in the 117th Foot.' – Wood, *Creeping Man*

WOODLEY, JOHN ('ROARING JACK'). Associate of Bob Carruthers, whose family's music teacher, Violet Smith, he annoyed with his attentions. 'He made odious love to me, boasted of his wealth, said that if I married him I could have the finest diamonds in London, and finally, when I would have nothing to do with him, he seized me in his arms one day after dinner – he was hideously strong – and swore that he would not let me go until I had kissed him.' – Violet Smith, *Solitary Cyclist*

WRIGHT, THERESA. Lady Brackenstall's maid at the Abbey Grange, and her nurse from infancy. 'The kind of maid you don't pick up nowadays.' – Stanley Hopkins, *Abbey Grange*

15

Unchronicled Cases

Summing up his career, shortly before his last encounter with Moriarty at the Reichenbach Falls, Holmes spoke of having been engaged in over a thousand cases. There were many more to follow, after his resurrection; and, in relating the adventure of *The Second Stain*, Watson says that he has notes of many hundreds 'to which I have never alluded'.

Our regret at such heedlessness is deepened by his tantalizing passing references to several dozen of them, under titles which are apt to linger in the memory. Having myself known the frustration of trying to remember where exactly Watson refers to some of them, it seems worthwhile to keep a list. It is not an exhaustive one, tracking down every last allusion. I have included only those which ring bells in my own recollection, or which attracted underlining during this most recent re-reading. It omits also cases which are mere entries in Holmes's archives.

ABERGAVENNY murder. *Priory School*
ABERNETTY family. (Depth by which parsley had sunk into butter on a hot day alerted Holmes to dreadful business.) *Six Napoleons*
'ALICIA' cutter. (Sailed one spring morning into a small patch of mist from where she never again emerged.) *Thor Bridge*
ALUMINIUM crutch. *Musgrave Ritual*
AMATEUR MENDICANT society. (Luxurious club in furniture warehouse.) *Five Orange Pips*
ATKINSON brothers (at Trincomalee). *Scandal in Bohemia*
BOULEVARD assassin. See HURET. *Golden Pince-Nez*
CAMBERWELL poisoning case. (Holmes wound up victim's watch,

proving that it had been wound two hours before, thereby fixing approximate bedtime.) *Five Orange Pips*

CANARY-TRAINER. See WILSON. *Black Peter*

CLUB-FOOT. See RICOLETTI. *Musgrave Ritual.*

CONK-SINGLETON forgery case. *Six Napoleons*

COPTIC patriarchs. two. *Retired Colourman.*

CORMORANT. See POLITICIAN. *Veiled Lodger*

DUNDAS separation case. (Husband threw false teeth at wife after meals.) *Case of Identity*

FARINTOSH, Mrs. (Recommended Helen Stoner to Holmes, one of whose clients she had been.) *Speckled Band*

'FRIESLAND'. (Dutch steamship, in connection with which Holmes and Watson nearly lost their lives.) *Norwood Builder*

GRICE PATERSONS. (Singular adventures in island of Uffa.) *Five Orange Pips*

HARDEN John Vincent. (Peculiarly persecuted tobacco millionaire.) *Solitary Cyclist*

HOLLAND, reigning family of. (Holmes's service to them too delicate to confide, even to Watson.) *Case of Identity*

LEECH, red. (Repulsive case, involving death of Crosby, the banker.) *Golden Pince-Nez*

LIGHTHOUSE. See POLITICIAN. *Veiled Lodger*

'MATILDA BRIGGS'. Ship associated with giant rat of Sumatra: see SUMATRA. *Sussex Vampire*

MAUPERTUIS, Baron. (Most accomplished swindler in Europe, whose bringing down helped to exhaust Holmes.) *Reigate Squires*

MONTPENSIER, Mme. Frenchwoman defended by Holmes against murder charge.) *Hound of the Baskervilles*

NETHERLAND-SUMATRA company. (Involved in Baron Maupertuis's colossal swindles.) *Reigate Squires*

PARSLEY. See ABERNETTY. *Six Napoleons*

PERSANO, Isadora. (Well-known male journalist and duellist found mad, contemplating a remarkable worm, reputedly unknown to science, in a matchbox.) *Thor Bridge*

PHILLIMORE, James. (Stepped back into his house to get his umbrella, and never seen again.) *Thor Bridge*

POLITICIAN, LIGHTHOUSE, AND TRAINED CORMORANT. (Major scandal, whose particulars Watson threatened to reveal.) *Veiled Lodger*

RAT, giant. See SUMATRA. *Sussex Vampire*

RICOLETTI. (Subject of one of Holmes's earliest cases. Encumbered with a club-foot and an abominable wife.) *Musgrave Ritual*

'SOPHY ANDERSON', British bark. (Loss investigated by Holmes.) *Five Orange Pips*

STAMFORD, Archie. (Forger arrested by Holmes and Watson near Farnham, Surrey.) *Solitary Cyclist*

STAUNTON, Henry. (Holmes helped bring him to the gallows.) *Missing Three-Quarter*

SUMATRA, Giant rat of. (A story, in Watson's judgement, for which the world was not yet prepared.) *Sussex Vampire*

TANKERVILLE Club. (Holmes cleared a member, Maj Prendergast, of cheating at cards.) *Five Orange Pips*

TARLETON murders. (One of Holmes's earliest cases.) *Musgrave Ritual*

TIRED Captain. *Naval Treaty*

TOSCA, Cardinal. (Sudden death investigated by Holmes at the express desire of the Pope.) *Black Peter*. See also VATICAN. *Black Peter*

TREPOFF murder. (Investigated by Holmes at Odessa.) *Scandal in Bohemia*

UFFA, island of. See GRICE PATERSONS. *Five Orange Pips*

UMBRELLA. See PHILLIMORE. *Thor Bridge*

UPWOOD, Colonel. (Holmes exposed his atrocious conduct in a card scandal at the Nonpareil Club.) *Hound of the Baskervilles*

VAMBERRY. Wine merchant. (One of Holmes's earliest cases.) *Musgrave Ritual*

VATICAN cameos. (An investigation by Holmes on behalf of the Pope.) *Hound of the Baskervilles*. See also TOSCA. *Black Peter*

WARBURTON, Colonel. (The case of his madness, and that of *The Engineer's Thumb*, were the only two introduced to Holmes by Watson.) *Engineer's Thumb*

WIFE, abominable. See RICOLETTI. *Musgrave Ritual*

WILSON, notorious canary-trainer. (His arrest by Holmes removed a plague-spot from the East End of London.) *Black Peter*

WORM, remarkable. See PERSANO. *Thor Bridge*

16

The Writings of Sherlock Holmes

(Where first mentioned in the stories; not necessarily published or even completed.)

Practical Handbook of Bee Culture, with Some Observations upon the Segregation of the Queen – *His Last Bow*

Chaldean Roots in the Ancient Cornish Language – *Devil's Foot*

Early English Charters – *Three Students*

The Whole Art of Detection – *Abbey Grange*

Dating of Documents – *Hound of the Baskervilles*

Uses of Dogs in Detection – *Creeping Man*

The Human Ear – *Cardboard Box*

Tracing of Footsteps – *Sign of Four*

Polyphonic Motets of Lassus – *Bruce-Partington Plans*

The Book of Life (science of observation and deduction) – *Study in Scarlet*

Malingering – *Dying Detective*

Secret Writings – *Dancing Men*

Tattoo Marks – *Red-Headed League*

Distinction between the Ashes of Various Tobaccos – *Study in Scarlet*

Influence of a Trade upon the Form of a Hand – *Sign of Four*

Typewriter and its Relation to Crime – *Case of Identity*

Index of Quotations

For individual titles of stories see the General Index; the main fictional characters are listed in the 'Who's Who of Characters'

General Index